Jumping at Shadows

Also by SASHA ABRAMSKY

The House of Twenty Thousand Books (2016)

The American Way of Poverty (2013)

Breadline USA (2009)

Inside Obama's Brain (2009)

American Furies (2007)

Conned (2006)

Hard Time Blues (2002)

JUMPING *at* SHADOWS

THE TRIUMPH *of* FEAR *and* THE END *of* THE AMERICAN DREAM

SASHA ABRAMSKY

NATION
BOOKS
New York

Nation Books
116 East 16th Street, 8th Floor
New York, NY 10003
www.publicaffairsbooks.com/nation-books@NationBooks

Printed in the United States of America

First Edition: September 2017
Published by Nation Books, an imprint of Perseus Books, LLC, a subsidiary of Hachette Book Group, Inc.Nation Books is a co-publishing venture of the Nation Institute and Perseus Books.

The Hachette Speakers Bureau provides a wide range of authors for speaking events. To find out more, go to www.hachettespeakersbureau.com or call (866) 376-6591. The publisher is not responsible for websites (or their content) that are not owned by the publisher.

Print book interior design by Jack Lenzo.

Library of Congress Cataloging-in-Publication Data
Names: Abramsky, Sasha, author.
Title: Jumping at shadows : the triumph of fear and the end of the American dream / Sasha Abramsky.
Description: New York : Nation Books, 2017. | Includes bibliographical references and index.
Identifiers: LCCN 2017012751 (print) | LCCN 2017030056 (ebook) | ISBN 9781568585208 (ebook) | ISBN 9781568585192 (hardback)
Subjects: LCSH: Social perception—United States. | Risk—United States—Sociological aspects. | BISAC: SOCIAL SCIENCE / Violence in Society. | POLITICAL SCIENCE / Political Freedom & Security / General. | PSYCHOLOGY / Psychopathology / Anxieties & Phobias.
Classification: LCC HM1041 (ebook) | LCC HM1041 .A27 2017 (print) | DDC 302/.120973—dc23
LC record available at https://lccn.loc.gov/2017012751

LSC-C

10 9 8 7 6 5 4 3 2 1

To Eduardo Galeano (1940–2015),
a wonderful writer and tireless champion of the underdog,
whom, alas, I never got the chance to meet

Strained with gazing
Our eyes ached, and our ears as we slept
Kept their care for the crash that would turn
Our fears into fact.

—W. H. AUDEN, "The Age of Anxiety," 1947

He may be talking, but he'll talk faster with the torture.

—DONALD TRUMP, on CNN, March 22, 2016,
advocating an expansive use of torture
against terrorism suspects

Contents

Ciguatoxin

In early February 2015, two weeks after my family arrived in the atmospheric Chilean port city of Valparaíso to study Spanish for a month, I woke up in the middle of the night convinced I was about to die.

We were high up in the hills above the city center, in a compact neighborhood called *Cerro Mariposa*, staying in a small second-floor suite of rooms out back of our landlady Marisol's house. From our windows, the view of the Pacific in the distance, past the elegant center of the city, was similar to that which the poet Pablo Neruda, who had lived slightly farther up in the hills from our lodgings, so adored half a century earlier.

When I woke up that night, in our little bedroom opposite our even littler kitchen, I felt as if I were fading away. My blood pressure seemed to have disappeared; my heart was fluttering slowly, weakly. I stood up, and my legs took on a life of their own. They began walking frantically up and down the small apartment, back and forth, back and forth, faster and faster. They began running, as if they were seeking to help me to escape from my body. I tried to convince my legs to stop, but they

wouldn't. Back and forth, back and forth. They seemed to be
telling me to jump out of my skin.

I managed to wake my wife up. She started massaging my
back; my heart gradually, gradually started returning to its normal pattern. After a couple hours, I fell asleep, sitting upright in
an armchair—a forty-two-year-old man who suddenly felt like
a nonagenarian.

Of course, had I been thinking straight, I would have
woken up my landlady and her family to ask for help. For even
if an ambulance couldn't have navigated the twisting, turning
backstreets of our hillside *cerro* in the middle of the night, I'm
sure they could have found a taxi or a neighbor with a car who
would have gotten me down to the clinic. But I wasn't thinking
straight. Six thousand miles from home, I was more scared than
I had ever been, experiencing wobbles in my heart that I couldn't
imagine trying to explain in a language not my own. And so I
half-slept the rest of the night away and the next morning, on
nervous, uncertain legs, made my way down to our language
school. An hour later, Isabel, my Spanish teacher, horrified at
my condition, hurried me out of the school, bundled me onto
a *collectivo* minibus, and took me to the central clinic. There,
after an uncomfortable wait of a few hours—during which time
if I really had been having a heart attack I would almost certainly have died—I found myself spread-eagled on a hospital
bed, shirtless, the electrodes for an EKG attached to my chest
and arms and ankles, while Isabel laughingly told me that this
was the strangest lesson she had ever taught.

I wasn't having—and hadn't had—a heart attack, the doctors told me. Armed with a prescription for anti-inflammatories
and another for muscle relaxants, and feeling somewhat sheep-
ish at all the bother I had caused, I headed back to the language
school to resume my late-afternoon studies.

For a time, I seemed to be on the mend. True, my energy levels tanked, and there were days in the week following during which I spent twelve hours in bed; but when I wasn't resting up, there were also times I felt okay. Over the weeks that we had left in Valparaíso, our daily rituals resumed, albeit at a slower pace.

Assuming I was better, we traveled south, to the Lake District, a place of huge, shimmering blue lakes and towering volcanoes—many of them active. It was spectacular: the enormous alpine Lake Llanquihue set against the glacial peak of Osorno Volcano soaring heavenward. At lake level, it was fiercely hot. Up on the volcanoes, on the edge of the Andes, it was harsh winter. A glorious place, I hoped, to recuperate.

Two days in, however, my heart did the exact reverse of what it had done in Valparaíso. My blood pressure soared, and my heart started beating so hard and so fast I thought it was about to burst. We tried to go to a restaurant, but I had to leave immediately, feeling that I was about to pass out. Stumbling, I made it to the front desk of our hotel, told the young man on duty there that I thought I was having a heart attack, and asked him to take me to the nearest hospital. He and a colleague bundled me into a car, and we raced off.

Within an hour I was having the second EKG of my life. This time my heart had locked in at about 175 beats per minute. All I could hear was the awful beating of blood in my head. I have a vague memory of screaming at the nurses, irrationally ordering them to make my heart slow down before it exploded. I have a memory of concerned faces and another, which can't be accurate, of a small hospital room filled with the sound of my beating heart. But, again, the doctors and nurses told me I wasn't having a heart attack, and released me back out into the quiet midnight streets.

Twice in two weeks I had thought my heart was giving out—and both times the doctors had reassured me that it wasn't. My energy level was now just about nonexistent. And yet, since we were in one of the most beautiful spots on Earth, part of me was still desperate to enjoy the wonders of southern Chile.

Stubborn to a point, probably in denial as to the seriousness of my situation, we headed south again, flying over one thousand miles of ice fields to the city of Punta Arenas, on the Magellan Straits. There, in the little hostel we were staying in on the water's windswept edge, I felt my energy evaporate. For a couple days, I struggled even to get out of bed—though I also couldn't sleep properly, since it felt as if my internal clock had been turned off. I tried to nurse myself back to health, sitting in the common area of the hostel, overlooking the Magellan Straits, bundled up in my warm sweaters, drinking one herbal tea after the next and looking out for dolphins dancing in the waters just offshore; taking short walks along the windswept promenades during gaps in the rain; napping whenever I could; harvesting what little reserves I had.

To a degree, my strategy worked. After three days, I no longer felt as if I were about to die. Instead I simply felt very, very weak—an old man masquerading in a much younger man's body. And that was how it continued for the remainder of our time in Chile: okay for a few moments and then exhausted, seemingly on the mend and then floored by another bout of pain.

ONLY ONCE WE WERE ensconced in our California home again did I find out that my cousin in Los Angeles, with whom I had shared a farewell sushi meal two months previously, had, over the intervening weeks, experienced the exact same set of symptoms as I had: low blood pressure and low heartbeat, followed by high blood pressure and a heart rate high enough to ensure her a couple nights in a hospital, followed by calamitous exhaustion over a period of weeks.

Since the only point of overlap was the sushi meal, another cousin of ours, an infectious disease specialist, began reading up on fish toxins to see if we could have been poisoned. A few days later, while I was beginning a battery of medical tests at the UC Davis medical center, he phoned to tell me his conclusion. In all likelihood, we had eaten a fish tainted with something called ciguatoxin. It's a neurotoxin present mainly in tropical fish, the symptoms of which were first described by medical personnel on Captain Cook's South Pacific expedition in 1774, and it does terrible things to the body's systems controlled by electric impulses.

What makes it particularly unnerving is that there is no definitive test for the presence of ciguatoxin—a diagnosis is arrived at largely by process of elimination—and there is also no effective cure. When one has a set of symptoms that resemble ciguatoxin poisoning, all one can do is wait it out and avoid certain kinds of foods known to exacerbate its symptoms. The good news, my cousin told me, was that it usually wasn't fatal; the bad news was it could wreak havoc on one's health for more than a year.

And so began my months-long medical odyssey. I had gone from being the sort of customer health insurance companies love—someone who saw the doctor two or three times a year and took no medicines more serious than anti–hay fever pills—to being a money pit.

I DON'T KNOW FOR sure if I had ciguatoxin or some other, unknown ailment or food-borne poison. I'll likely never know, since there is no way to generate a foolproof diagnosis in situations like this. I don't know whether whatever made me so ill is still in my system or whether my body is gradually managing to eliminate it. I don't know for sure how much of what I experienced was purely physical and how much was a mental reaction to a feeling of physical decline, of losing control over my own destiny. And, above all, even though as I write this I sense that I am finally on the mend, and I feel healthy and well again, that well-being also seems appallingly fragile: I don't know if tomorrow will bring another round of sickness and pain, another crisis in yet another part of my battered body.

What I do know is that something as amorphous as a possible ciguatoxin diagnosis saps one of self-confidence. I know, in a way I never could before I became a medical mystery, that a chronic condition that every so often flares up into an acute episode affects one's psyche in unpredictable ways. It can make a person take unreasonable risks one day (like not flying back to California after the heart episodes) while leaving him or her awfully risk averse another day. It can make one live for the moment, and it can also make one irritable and unreasonable, apt to snap at the smallest provocation and desperate for sympathy and understanding.

I know in a way I never did before—at the most personal level—what fear of particular horrors and anxiety about unknown horrors lurking just out of sight feel like.

When you're battling an invisible, formless foe—a hard-to-define enemy against which there is no easy fix, an enemy with the power to upend daily certainties and to inflict chaos out of the blue—it changes how you live. It changes how you make choices, how you interact with the world. It alters your emotional state, making moroseness something of a default state and optimism appear more akin to naiveté. It is hard to stay upbeat if you always fear the worst.

SIX MONTHS BEFORE THE possible-ciguatoxin struck, I had been commissioned to write a book on the culture of fear. It was to be a book about fears of unknown assailants, overseas terrorists, hidden germs, pedophiles, violent kids, negligent parents, immigrants, inner cities, and a raft of other bugaboos. And it was to explore the political implications of this epidemic of fear.

I had been exploring these ideas in my reporting for decades, looking to understand what things and which people frighten us, and why, and exploring how we fathom risk: how our brains interpret risk and identify, rightly or wrongly, perceived threats, both at a neurological level and at a conscious one. Some of what we fear is innate. But much of it is the result of social conditions—in the economy, in how community is structured, and so on. Poverty and inequality are two themes that have continually drawn me in as a journalist. What happens when a wealthy country, such as the United States, makes political choices that result in tens of millions of people living deeply economically insecure lives? What happens to the democratic processes when a tiny group of people at the top of the economic pyramid exercise extraordinary economic, and by extension, political power? How do our stories, as individuals and as larger communities, our dreams and our fears, change in the face of this growing inequality?

While my reporting focus had long been on the United States, the story was, and is, in many ways, one playing out across the globe, affecting a growing number of countries, cultures, and legal systems in recent years. Indeed, as I write this introduction, more than two years after first starting work on this project, I am sitting in my parents' house in London shortly after voters in the United Kingdom chose "Brexit," an exit from the European Union largely driven by fear of immigrants—of the languages and cultural values and competition for jobs and social benefits that they bring with them. Meanwhile, on the European mainland, one polity after another has struggled to deal with the fears, resentments, and hostilities unleashed by the huge numbers of refugees fleeing wars and poverty in the Middle East and Africa, and seeking sanctuary in Europe. Over the past decade, in some African and Asian countries, vaccination workers have been attacked, and, as a result, attempts to eradicate diseases such as polio have been compromised.

Deeply authoritarian regimes, playing on the anxieties and insecurities of large numbers of voters, have, in recent years, been elected in Turkey, Russia, India, and many other countries. No one people or place has a monopoly on this fear-driven political rhetoric, or on its legal, educational, cultural, and even medical consequences. For whenever and wherever we divide people into "us" and "them," powerful political and psychological forces are unleashed.

What we fear and how we gauge risk is, all too often, a product of these other narratives: in America, for example, a poor person, or a black or brown person, is far more likely than a well-to-do white person to be viewed as inherently dangerous, as representing a fundamental threat to our well-being. Sometimes these views are conscious, but oftentimes, as shown in the groundbreaking research of psychologists Mahzarin Banaji, Anthony Greenwald, and their Project Implicit team, the biases exist deep below our conscious surface, influencing our behavior without the conscious "us" even being aware of their existence.

Of course, we also routinely miscalculate risks surrounding events that have nothing to do with the schisms of race and class in America. We overestimate, for example, the likelihood of being attacked by a shark while swimming in the ocean, and we underestimate the risk of dying of mosquito-borne diseases. We are more terrified of ick-factor diseases like ebola than of more mundane but infinitely greater killing machines like the flu or asthma. We fear flying more than driving, despite the latter being a massively more dangerous pastime.

What is the common thread? It is, I believe, that too often we calculate risk not by the probability of an event occurring but by the number of news items or talk radio minutes or Facebook postings or movie scenes devoted to a topic. As a result, we fear terrorism far more than run-of-the-mill, nonpolitical gunmen, despite the fact that by orders of magnitude it is the latter who, year in and year out, kill the most Americans. After all, a single large-scale terrorist attack is guaranteed to generate vastly more headlines, news stories, and follow-up feature articles on the victims than are the everyday murders-by-gun-violence or suicides-by-gun-violence that, over time, add up to tens of thousands of fatalities each year. An outbreak of ebola, similarly, is a *gimme* for the front pages, simply because it is such a nasty, ugly, stuff-of-nightmares way to die. But the flu, tuberculosis, and malaria, despite these three diseases having killed millions upon millions of people over the course of recent human history, are seen as yawns, unlikely to generate the sort of sensational coverage that the ebola outbreak produced in 2014.

Miscalculating risk comes with consequences. It influences the places we go and the medicines we take. It alters the way we parent our children and the interactions we have with our neighbors. It affects how we police our cities and how we think about our borders. And, of course, it skews our political preferences.

As I BATTLED MY own medical demons, and struggled to retain a sense of normalcy amid the chaos engulfing me, it struck me that in the book I was writing, I was exploring how, increasingly, large parts of our society behave as if under continual neurotoxin attack. I remembered those terrifying days after the 9/11 attacks, when it felt as if the pillars that hold our world in place were buckling. I remembered that feeling of nauseating horror when, weeks afterwards, envelopes filled with anthrax powder started turning up at random locations around the country— the sense that invisible forces, against which we, as individuals, had no real defense, were conspiring to destroy us. In the wake of the anthrax scare, one in twenty Americans—roughly fifteen million people—stocked up on powerful antibiotics, and about three million of them actually began taking the antibiotics as prophylactics, thus, paradoxically, massively increasing the likelihood of antibiotic-resistant strains of bacteria emerging.[1] I remember, too, the sense of disorientation when a few weeks later a sniper team began terrorizing residents of Washington, DC, shooting drivers and pedestrians seemingly at random. Nothing and nowhere appeared safe anymore. The DC police responded by urging pedestrians to walk in "rapid zigzag patterns," and to avoid open spaces. Reports soon emerged of drivers crouching down behind their cars while at gas stations filling up their tanks, and nearly half of locals polled said they were now avoiding outdoor activities.[2]

In a training manual produced in the wake of the September 11, 2001, attacks, the Federal Emergency Management

Agency (FEMA) noted that in cities such as Washington, DC, "ever increasing security became the norm, including disruptive street closures and military vehicles with mounted machine guns. . . . By the time the Snipers announced their presence on the morning of October 3 by killing four people, Washingtonians had already been pushed to the limits of their psychological stress tolerance."[3]

Less than one month after the 9/11 attacks, the Pew Research Center for the People and the Press polled Americans on their mental state. As subsequently reported by George Gray and David Ropeik of the Harvard Center for Risk Analysis, at the Harvard School of Public Health, the findings were bleak: "59 percent said they had experienced depression, 31 percent had difficulty concentrating, 23 percent suffered insomnia, and 87 percent felt angry."[4]

Perhaps those feelings wormed their way so deeply into the popular consciousness that they never truly left. In our post–9/11 collective imagination our community, our country, our culture, our civilization is always a toxic envelope or a hijacked plane away from unfathomable calamity.

In the wake of the 9/11 attacks, the Bush administration implemented a series of color-coded alerts. In the following years—often at politically expedient moments, when the government needed a jolt of popular support for, say, the invasion of Iraq—the color-coded alert system would be raised, always for nonspecific and thus all-encompassing threats. Because the actual nature and locale of the threat wasn't revealed—mostly, the government would issue an addendum to the warning saying something to the effect of "we have no specific information that a particular attack is imminent"—the impact was simply to sow anxiety. When, in February 2004, the House Select Committee on Homeland Security held hearings on the Homeland Security Advisory System, committee chair Christopher Cox warned of the dangers inherent in this. "We must," he told his colleagues, "strike an appropriate balance between providing meaningful warning where hard intelligence warrants it and causing a senseless, unfocused nationwide response to unspecified threat alerts."[5]

Cox's warnings weren't heeded. The color-coded alert system would remain in place for another seven years.

As the dial moved from yellow up to orange, and then hovered ominously close to red, so public angst would, on cue, increase. Hardware stores saw rushes on duct tape, bought by people terrified of chemical or biological attacks and wanting to seal their windows. In February 2003, as warnings of just such a biological or chemical attack were ramped up, one man in Connecticut reportedly wrapped his entire house in plastic.[6]

The media loved it. If, in the 1990s, the mantra was "If it bleeds, it leads," in the 2000s the equivalent might have been "If it scares, it blares." One network after another blared out the news: *Be afraid. Be very afraid.* On the cable news channels ticker tapes ran, nonstop, detailing the color of the latest alert.

Daniela Schiller, a neuroscientist who runs a brain imaging lab studying human emotions at the Icahn School of Medicine, at Mount Sinai in Manhattan, explains that our brains learn fear in three ways: through direct experience—we are personally exposed to something that makes us afraid; through observation—we see others exposed to scary events and people; and through instructed learning—we are told to be afraid of certain people or things or scenarios. And, Schiller says, the fear generated by each of these is etched into the brain in similar ways: "They capture the same basic process of rapid association, and then they are in the long-term memory."[7]

If television tells you, over and over again, to fear imminent terror attacks or rampaging criminal gangs, or people of a certain color or religion—people different from you, who can be considered members of an "out-group"—you will, in all likelihood, develop a deep and abiding set of fears, referred to by experts as "implicit biases" against particular groups or individuals. These fears are easily retriggered in the future and thus make you peculiarly vulnerable to the politics of demagoguery. "Under some circumstances, it's pretty easy for them [fears] to come back; for example, if you are stressed. It will bring fear memories back even if you thought they were extinguished," Schiller explains.

We are conditioned—by the way stridently ideological television and radio personalities cover events, by the manner in which ratings-conscious news executives prioritize stories, by the echo-chamber effects of social media, maybe even by an intuitive sense that the broad prosperity in which so many of us live our lives is deeply precarious—to fear unknown enemies. And, with this conditioning, our brains come to be flooded with an array of stress hormones that physically alter the neural networks in key parts of our brains, reshape how we act and how we think, make us more likely to inflate our sense of risk and less likely to respond rationally and in a proportionate measure to events and people we confront on a daily basis as we go about our lives.[8]

When the peanut-sized part of the brain called the amygdala is aroused, Schiller argues, it modulates "an array of responses in the brain, including perception, attention, and memory—influencing how you encode and what you retrieve; and decision making, making you more sensitive to risk and to ambiguity."

Our fears and anxieties, bubbling up in response to this increasingly toxic communications environment, are then treated as individual ailments by a medical system quick to diagnose anxiety disorders and phobias, and prone to hand out a growing array of pills to chemically tamp down our sentiments of woe. And to make matters worse, our political discourse is increasingly fueled by fear and defined by candidates playing to ever-more fearful political constituencies.

In stressful times, Schiller concludes, "our cognitive abilities narrow, and turning to someone charismatic might relate to that; because that person offers solutions. In a way, putting your trust in someone charismatic might reduce the stress and ambiguity associated with the situation. It's the nature of demagogy: it's easier to grasp; it's simple."[9] Voting for the demagogue during times of high anxiety might, in short, be the equivalent of binge drinking and drugging to avoid depression: it's the ultimate form of self-medicating.

Studies carried out by Yair Berson, a psychologist at Tel Aviv's Bar-Ilan University, suggest that in the presence of charismatic orators, be they self-help gurus in a business setting or politicians on the electoral stage, audience members' brains actually start synching; their reactions get more and more similar. MEG scans show, he reported that "across all bands of electric activity of the brain there is much more similarity across [test] subjects exposed to charismatic rather than non-charismatic messages. Charisma generates neuro-synchronicity."[10] It is, he believed, how group-think emerges. "When people are exposed to a very strong stimulant—like charisma or a really good movie—people are so focused that individual differences between people are erased. The masses start to behave like one. It leads to collective identity."

Some of Berson's other research, involving subjects who have been given additional oxytocin—a vital chemical the brain releases to establish bonds of trust, in particular between parents and infants—shows that they start imitating the behavior of putative "charismatic leaders" they are exposed to in lab settings far more than do those not given additional oxytocin. Berson hypothesized that, in real life, charismatic personalities might actually relate to audiences in a way that triggers a flood of oxytocin in their brains, resulting in what he calls a "charisma bond." As a result, audiences become more ready to trust these leaders, to follow them down any and all pathways, and, by extension, to bond with other enthused audience members.

A charismatic leader playing on widespread public fears thus has an extraordinary opportunity to build a movement based around their promise, however illusory, to make things better for their rattled followers. Primed to fear a long list of despised "others" by endless exposure to sensational cable television news reports, to social media, and to talk radio, a critical mass of voters in such an anxious age will throw their lot in with demagogic figures who pander to their anxieties.

"We call it 'neurocoupling,'" Princeton University psychologist and neuroscientist Uri Hasson explained. "Brain-to-brain coupling. The more you understand me, the more similar your brain becomes to mine." It is, Hasson believed, similar to the old adage that it takes two to tango. "It's like dancing." A charismatic speaker, standing on a podium in front of an angry or fearful audience primed to want to hear certain things, can connect extraordinarily well with that audience through successfully articulating their fears. "Sometimes," Hasson said, "the partners can really be coupled and dance together, and that's when it's an amazing thing."[11]

Hasson recalled an experiment that his team had conducted in which they recruited volunteers for a brain-imaging study, put the individuals into an fMRI scanner, and then read them a J. D. Salinger story. The narrative was about a husband who had lost track of his wife at a party, had returned home alone, and, anxious about her whereabouts, had phoned his best friend in the middle of the night. The best friend had listened to him but then, after a while, had told him that he was tired and needed to go to back to sleep. Half of the test participants were then told that the reason the best friend wanted to end the conversation was that the missing wife was having an affair with him, and, in fact, was with him in bed at that very moment. The other half was told that the best friend simply was exhausted and wanted to go to sleep.

In analyzing the data, Hasson's team found something remarkable. That simple one-sentence change created such distinct brain pattern responses among the test subjects that the psychologists studying the data could tell with 80 to 90 percent accuracy which story ending the participant had been told simply by looking at their brain's responses. Hasson's team had created two distinct brain-response communities through the manipulation and sharing of basic information.

The implications were stunning: in a country as politically and culturally and, in many instances, racially divided and polarized as the contemporary United States—where millions get one set of news feeds and political interpretations from Fox News and other conservative outlets, and millions of others get an entirely different set of news feeds from more liberal sources—a series of distinct brain-response communities were likely being created. "It's really brain wars," Hasson noted. "It's really sad to see it in action." For millions of Americans, he believed, it was the overriding fear of certain individuals and groups—people they had learned to hate or distrust not necessarily because of direct and personal negative experiences, but because of a constant drip, drip, drip of media coverage—that was generating many of their common brain-response patterns.

"When I think, I take things to the worst case possible," a thirty-six-year-old mother of a two-year-old boy told me at an expensive Montessori preschool in an affluent suburb just outside Salt Lake City—a school I was visiting in the winter of 2016 because it marketed itself as being particularly security-conscious and many parents chose the school more for that emphasis on security than for its educational philosophy. The $100,000-plus that the school's owners spent on security each year was, they believed, both necessary to make the institution safe and also a splendid advertising investment, drawing in dozens of additional families each year.

To get into the school, one had to put one's fingerprints into a computer recognition system before the door would open, and once inside the school every single classroom had webcams, allowing a bank of computer monitors in the foyer to show what was going on at any moment in any of the classrooms. Parents would routinely spend fifteen minutes, twenty minutes, half an hour of their day just staring at the screens, making sure that their children were being treated appropriately by the teachers and the other toddlers. Many wanted Internet access to the images—but the school had balked at that, fearing that online sexual predators would be able to hack into the stream of images. Inside each classroom, all the doors of which had state-of-the-art lockdown features, the teachers had access to long-distance bee spray, which, in the case of a genuine emergency, they were supposed to fire off at the eyes of intruders. The outside playground, looking out onto the majestic, snow-covered Wasatch mountains, was surrounded by a high fence—both to stop the kids making a mad dash for freedom and to prevent any potential predators from climbing in. The imposing front walls, facing out onto a busy road, across which was the parking lot for a gym, were similarly designed to stop any would-be molesters from looking into the school's classrooms.

"What is the worst possible outcome to the situation?" the mother, a finance manager at American Express, continued. "It's negative thinking. It's carried over into my personal life. I do not like going into extremely crowded places. I do not like a lot of people around me. I like to watch who I'm surrounded by. I don't like going to malls. Something as simple as going to a Wal-Mart: you see kids running around with no parents in sight. I get so fearful, so angry at the parents." As she talked, she knotted and unknotted her fingers; her pancake-powdered face, framed by long brown hair falling onto her shoulders, contorted with tension; and she looked, from one moment to the next, as if she would either cry in terror or scream in rage.

The woman had a concealed gun permit, and she and her husband kept at least ten guns around their home. She didn't worry about one of those guns being accidentally accessed and used by her child, or by someone else. Nor did she worry about driving her car to and from day care—despite the fact that far more children die in car accidents than die in school shootings. She didn't worry about dying of the flu, which kills tens of thousands of Americans annually, but she was utterly terrified of ebola—which killed a mere handful of Americans during the epidemic of 2014.

When I asked her why she was so scared of things that, in reality, posed a small risk to those she loved, while being largely disinterested in much more common killers, she explained that she took her fear cues from the media. "Because of the media, it's brought to our attention. Facebook. Twitter. You don't get those horrible stories if you don't have that. It's thrown in our face more. Makes us think about it more. Makes us more scared. When I was growing up, we didn't have computers; there was no Internet. The Internet has changed everything. I would like to feel more confident, just with society in general. But all you hear about is killings and beheadings all over the world. It's thrown in your face."

When I suggested that the crime rate when she was growing up was actually higher than it is today, she accepted that might, in fact, be true, but then explained that it didn't change her perception of fear. "I talk to my friends about it. It was different when we were growing up. Maybe it's the news. Everything we see on the news is all negative. That drives fear in us. I see kids riding bikes without their parents. It worries me. They could be snatched anytime. I see it on the news. It's scary." Her response was familiar to neuroscientists such as New York University's Joseph LeDoux. "In laboratory experiments, simply telling a subject that a CS [conditioned stimulus] is likely to be followed by a shock is sufficient for the subject to develop a conditioned response to the CS, even if the shock never occurs," LeDoux wrote in his 2015 book *Anxious: Using the Brain to Understand and Treat Fear and Anxiety*.[12]

The more exotic the sense of risk, the more it filled the American Express manager with panic. "No, I'm not as fearful of the flu—because it's so commonplace. We expect it. But these other diseases that could potentially kill you and aren't

as common here. If the Bubonic Plague came back, I'd be terrified, even if it killed [just] one person. Ebola. Anything that
randomly comes into this country. One person is infected.
They fly on an airline. It terrifies me. Our borders should be
shut." She was petrified of foreign germs being imported into
America, of "illegal" Mexican immigrants taking advantage of
lax border security, and of Muslim terrorists coming into the
country to kill her. When she found herself near someone who
she thought was Muslim, she said, she got very cautious, very
watchful, started scoping them out to make sure they weren't
doing anything untoward.

LeDoux had written about neurons within part of the
brain's amygdala being permanently altered by strong stimuli,
so that even subsequent related weak stimuli could trigger a
defensive response. The example he used was that of a person
being bitten by a dog and subsequently being afraid simply at
the sight of a dog.[13] For the woman, who had seen so many examples of Islamic terrorism on television and on her computer,
even the proximity of someone she perceived to be a Muslim
now filled her with dread.

Similar examples abound of people exposed repeatedly to
media stories about African American criminals and coming
to be afraid of any and all black men. In computer simulation
studies, originally created by University of North Carolina at
Chapel Hill psychologist Keith Payne, respondents looking at
images quickly flashed on the screens in front of them are far
more likely to recall that the black men they saw on the screen
were carrying guns—even when they weren't—than that the
white men were, even when it was the white men who were in
fact armed.[14] These results hold even when the respondents in
question are trained law enforcement officers. A study of Denver

police officers, for example, found that officers took longer to press the "don't shoot" response button when the images were of unarmed black men than when they were of unarmed white men; and they were quicker to press "shoot" when the image was of an armed black man than when it was of a white man with a gun.[15]

Another parent at the school outside of Salt Lake, a father in his mid-forties, bemoaned the fact that kids could no longer roam freely—walk to and from school alone, play unsupervised outdoors for hours with their friends—as he had done while growing up in California's Bay Area in the 1970s and 1980s. "Times are different now than they were then," he explained sadly, his arms, muscular from weight lifting, crossed against his chest. "There are more crazy people in the world now."

The man, who worked for a large plumbing and air-conditioning company, had a bachelor's degree in criminal justice studies. Intellectually he knew the statistics, knew that in fact violent crime rates were higher when he was growing up than they were in 2016. So I asked him if he was sure that the environment was less safe for his seven-year-old daughter than it had been for him. He paused—a long, long pause. "Probably not," he finally said. But he still couldn't shake the sense of dread. "It's hard. She is way too sheltered. I'd love to let her spread her wings a little bit more. But we do keep our thumbs on her. There's always the fear of a kidnap, a traffic accident. Turn on the news at night; we watch the news while we eat dinner. The media loves to create a sense of panic. They love bad news." On one level, he knew he was being sold a bill of goods. On another level, a gut level, however, he couldn't bring himself to turn away. And the more he watched, the more fearful he became of specific threats, and the more anxious he became about the likelihood of someone, somehow, inflicting catastrophic harm on his family. He had nightmares about mass shootings and kidnappings—his face got beet red with tension even in discussing it. Even though he had walked to school when he was in first grade, he couldn't imagine letting his daughter do the same before she reached eighth grade.

As a result of all of this fear and anxiety, our fundamental decisions around everything from parenting to gun ownership are, too often, made with worst-case scenarios as a psychic backdrop. Unable to fully identify the things and people we fear, we retreat into a state of chronic, omnipresent angst, waiting for the next enemy around the corner, behind the hill, beyond the horizon. Waiting for the next predator lurking in the shadows, ready and eager to take advantage of whatever weaknesses we make the mistake of showing.

"While fear and anxiety are perfectly normal experiences," Joseph LeDoux wrote in *Anxious*, "sometimes they become maladaptive—excessive in intensity, frequency or duration—causing the sufferer distress to the extent that his or her daily life is disrupted. When this happens, an anxiety disorder exists."

OVER THE LAST FEW decades, we have, as a culture, developed a serious case of collective anxiety disorder. And its impacts are now ricocheting through our educational systems, our political systems, our medical systems, and pretty much every other set of institutions that shape the way we live our lives.

How did tens of millions of Americans, in an election year in which unemployment was at 5 percent, the economy had been growing for six years, the country was an unrivalled military colossus, and the population had more accumulated wealth—however unevenly distributed—than any other society in human history, come to conclude that they lived in a bankrupt, weak, humiliated, militarily crippled, ripe for invasion, betrayed-by-fifth-columnists, failed state? How did tens of millions of voters, in electing Donald Trump to the presidency on November 8, 2016, buy into a political message in some ways redolent of the fears, paranoias, and extreme nationalism and chauvinism that swept the Nazis into power in the truly bankrupted, weak, and humiliated Germany of the early 1930s? Because fear sells—and fear *has sold* again and again and again in recent decades. Because, in the era of cable news and talk radio and social media, reality is frequently less important than perceptions.

"There's an old German proverb to the effect that 'fear makes the wolf bigger than he is,'" Donald Trump wrote in his 2009 book *Think Like a Champion: An Informal Education in Business and Life*. "And," he continued, "that is true."[16]

In 2016, running the most fear-focused presidential campaign in modern American electoral history, Donald Trump—whipping up fears of a "rigged election," attacking the media for conspiring to undermine American values, making one demagogic claim after another against one racial or religious group after another—became a very big wolf indeed.

In the days following Trump's Electoral College victory, one could see the fissures of fear playing out on America's streets: thousands of protestors, utterly terrified of Trump's agenda, and of his willingness to bring out the mob in support of his plans, marching in cities across the country. They feared mass deportations, clampdowns on dissent, dismantling of health care systems to cover impoverished Americans. They feared Trump's finger on the nuclear button and his cavalier hostility to any and all agreements on climate change. Meanwhile, Trump supporters showed their sets of fears too, in a far more visceral way: spraying walls with anti-black, anti-Mexican, anti-Muslim graffiti. In one locale after another, Muslims were attacked, women's headscarves ripped off, men beaten. In several schools, white kids taunted Latino students by telling them America would now build that damn wall. A friend of mine wrote from southern Arizona telling me that in the days immediately following the election, several Latino and Native American female friends of his had been threatened with rape and told to get out of the country. Trump's election was, without a doubt, a vast victory for the messengers of fear, a crushing proof that in an age of omnipresent angst, he who whips his crowd up most in opposition to distrusted strangers will in all likelihood prevail.

Chapter One

Cloud Cuckoo Clocks

O n September 15, 2015, parents of children at MacArthur High School, a large school in the suburban town of Irving, Texas, twelve miles northwest of Dallas received a letter. "Irving Police Department responded to a suspicious-looking item on campus yesterday. We are pleased to report that after the police department's assessment, the item discovered at school did not pose a threat to your child's safety. Our school is cooperating fully with the ongoing police investigation." The letter was sent out in both English and Spanish, and was signed by MacArthur's principal, Daniel Cummings.

What Cummings, who several months earlier had been appointed principal of the school—which had opened in 1963 and was named after General Douglas MacArthur—didn't tell parents was that the entire episode was an exercise in paranoia rather than a real threat to his institution and its students.

The day before, a fourteen-year-old boy named Ahmed Mohamed, one of six children of a local Sudanese immigrant family, had brought in his engineering project. It was a homemade clock housed in a pencil case and designed well enough to win the praise of Mohamed's engineering teacher. It was

25

also something that had wires, timing mechanisms, and large bits of metal, and was in the hands of a young Muslim male. While the engineering teacher was impressed, another educator, alerted to the device after it beeped during an English class, was less sanguine. It was, she feared, a bomb.

The English teacher promptly confiscated the clock, and then she alerted Cummings.

A few hours after bringing his timepiece to school, Mohamed, who had long been an electronics and robotics enthusiast, prone to showing off his inventions to his favorite teachers, found himself confronted by Principal Cummings, his deputy, and five local police officers, who had been called to the scene by panicked school officials. In a side room off of Cummings's office, the seven adults started interrogating Mohamed. *What was the clock for? Why had he brought it to school?* And so on. They didn't read him his rights, didn't let him contact his parents, didn't wait until an attorney was present.

At first, according to Ahmed Mohamed and Kelly Hollingsworth—a Plainview-based attorney later hired by the teenager's family to sue the city for damages—the police weren't quite sure what to do with him. It was clear to them that the contraption wasn't a working explosive device. And it didn't make much sense to accuse the boy of bringing in a hoax bomb, since he had spent the entire day telling teachers to look at the clock that he had constructed. Not once had he tried to insinuate, to teachers or to fellow students, that he was carrying a potentially lethal device around with him. Not once had he threatened the school or indicated that he was about to cause mayhem.

The officers decided to walk the decision up the chain of command. Finally, the assistant police chief made the call to bring the boy in for further questioning. Hollingsworth would later claim that Mohamed had managed to get on the wrong side of a conservative school district back in sixth grade, when he had been refused permission to say his prayers during the school day. He was, Hollingsworth argued, a boy prone to speaking his mind. When kids in middle school had mocked his Halal dietary restrictions by calling him "Bacon Boy," "Bin Laden Boy," and "Sausage Boy," he had protested. And when a white kid had followed him in the school hallway one day and put a chokehold on him, Ahmed, along with his attacker, had both received an equal punishment—a suspension for getting into a fight on school property. Mohamed's family, who were on friendly terms with the head of the local NAACP chapter, had gotten the organization to represent them in meetings with school officials, and the suspension had been overturned. But the saga had left them feeling intensely vulnerable.

For the NAACP, it was just one more example of disproportionate punishments handed out by school officials in Texas to black and brown kids. Anthony Bond, who headed the local Irving chapter, had had an ongoing dispute with the school district about this. "Man, I tell you what," Bond said. "I've been out here since 1994. I've been on all thirty-nine campuses in the school district, answering allegations of racism in the school district."[1] He had eventually succeeded in getting the district to sign a memorandum of understanding putting a corrective action plan into place. And the board had, as a part of this agreement, commissioned a report, *The Skin They're In*, written by Sam Houston State University professor Mack Hines, to study the problem. Hines concluded that racial disparities were commonplace within local schools and that in some schools black and Latino students were involved in what he described as a "race war."[2] Data from the Texas Education Agency showed

that black students in the district were nearly twice as likely
to be suspended or expelled as were their white and Latino
counterparts—data that would subsequently comprise part of
the backdrop to a US Department of Justice investigation into
the district regarding allegations that students were harassed
and/or disciplined for racial and religious reasons.[3] Statewide,
the disparity was even worse: across Texas as a whole, black students were nearly five times as likely to be suspended.[4]

Hollingsworth believed that, in a school district long bedeviled by prejudice, in calling the police on Mohamed the principal had seen "an opportunity to scare the hell out of the kid."
The school's mission statement stresses diversity: "Our mission
at MacArthur High School is to meet the needs of culturally
diverse students who will be equipped to become productive
citizens and critical thinkers in a global society. We will accomplish this by providing a safe and positive learning environment
that promotes school-wide success." Nevertheless, the NAACP
and other local racial justice groups had long been concerned by
the treatment of minority students in the district. More generally, the Southern Poverty Law Center, which investigates right-
wing hate groups, had found Irving to be the headquarters for
at least two such groups. Both the city council and the local
school board were controlled by extreme conservatives—men
and women deeply uncomfortable with the rapid growth of the
local Muslim population over the previous few years.

And so, as the school day wound down, five of Irving's
finest, working in a suburban city west of Dallas that had recently garnered national attention after the ultra-conservative
mayor, Beth Van Duyne, declared that a local Muslim group
was attempting to establish Sharia law, handcuffed and arrested
Mohamed—exactly for what remained unclear, since they had

found no indication that the clock contained any sort of explosive device. They took him to the local station, where he was fingerprinted and photographed, and then they carted him off to a juvenile detention center.

Better safe than sorry, the police probably reasoned, despite the lack of any evidence that Ahmed Mohamed had intended to harm anyone with his clock. After all, Mayor Van Duyne had on display in her office a picture of a tattered Stars and Stripes flag embroidered with the dates of al-Qaeda attacks. And she had recently been touring the country, speaking with Tea Party groups about the threats posed by Sharia law, and demanding that Texan legislators pass an "American Laws for American Courts" bill. No matter that the Sharia law controversy in her town was actually little more than a local group attempting to use religious ethics to mediate local disputes, as was done all the time by churches in communities around the country. It was, wrote journalist Avi Selk in the *Dallas Morning News*, "unusual only because they were Muslim imams instead of Catholics or Jews."[5]

Even after experts confirmed that Mohamed's invention was, indeed, nothing more than a clock, and even after a slew of national figures, from President Obama to Facebook founder Mark Zuckerberg, expressed their support for the teenager, the school still refused to back down. Released from the detention center, Ahmed Mohamed was promptly suspended for three days for bringing forbidden items to MacArthur High, and the school principal treated the whole incident as if the town had narrowly averted its own version of a Pearl Harbor sneak attack. Local news outlets reported that Cummings announced ominously over the school PA system, "We have a very different version of what happened than what you are seeing from the

media."[6] What that version was, he never got around to saying—and, once the lawsuit against the school district was announced, he, along with other school and district officials, also
stopped answering requests for interviews.

Shortly afterward, local political leaders—who had been
warned by the city's legal officers that they were likely facing a
serious lawsuit—began circling the wagons. Mayor Van Duyne
went onto Fox News to talk about the case, and did not contra-
dict host Glenn Beck when Beck told his viewers that there was
more to the case than met the eye and that Mohamed's clock
was actually a "hoax bomb."[7] Beck's other guest, Jim Hansen,
offered that the bizarre episode was part of a "civilization jihad"
being waged against America. Van Duyne, striking looking,
with long blond hair, photogenic and charismatic, knew how
to play to her audiences, whether Fox News viewers or crowds
at the raucous Tea Party events at which time and again she
had denounced local Muslim groups. She repeatedly made out-
landish assertions, and she did so with enough confidence and
panache to come off as simply telling it like it is, of being a
straight shooter, or, as Donald Trump would put it in his stump
speeches during the 2016 election campaign, of not being afraid
to stand up to "politically correct" etiquette.

Neither Beck nor Mayor Van Duyne—whose office declined repeated requests over the course of a year for comment
from the mayor—provided any additional evidence to back up
the claim that the skinny, bespectacled boy with the clock was
actually a masterful terrorist propagandist. In fact it was, said
Hollingsworth, laughing, a patently absurd notion. There was
no way anyone could have known in advance that so many authority figures in Irving would have responded disproportionately to a nerdy ninth grader bringing a clock to school.

By then, Hollingsworth and his colleagues had also experienced some of the venom directed Ahmed Mohamed's way. When his law firm took on Mohamed's case and, on November 23, 2015, announced that they would be suing Irving officials, the firm's phone lines and email accounts were inundated. "Is Laney and Bollinger a part of the attempt of Muslim takeover of the United States? Is there no shame?" one correspondent asked. Another wrote, "I just read your shakedown, uh, I mean, Notice of Claims and Demand. $15m? That's what you think is fair compensation for someone mistaking a clock (that looked like a bomb) for a bomb. $15m? How do you say that with a straight face?" "Shame on you for taking this case," another emailer announced. "If anyone should be represented in multi-million dollar lawsuits, it's the families of those who have been beheaded, burned or murdered by ISIS. Since law firms are not obligated to take any case that walks in your door, your choosing to do this unmasks you as anti-American." "You make me sick," averred another writer. "No wonder people think attorneys are scumbags."[8]

The law firm started getting six calls a minute that first day. People would phone up from around the country, even from overseas, to accuse them of being in league with terrorists, of being un-American. Some said they hoped the office was bombed. Others announced their intent to come in person and vandalize the building. "The ladies [at the front desk reception] would pick up the phone," Hollingsworth recalled, "and they'd just explode. We had to send one of the ladies home. She couldn't take it anymore." Marya went to her grandparents' house, put her cat Dummy—whom she had had since she was in third grade—on her lap, sat on the couch, and watched TV to calm down. She petted Dummy, stroking his fur back and forth, back and forth, the repetitive motion calming her frayed nerves. And then she decided that her work was important, that she didn't want to be intimidated—and she returned to the office to field more calls and read more bilious emails.

Marya—fresh out of high school, soft-spoken, church-going—was simply bemused by the amount of bile being directed her way. "We got so many phone calls, it was not even funny," she recalled a few months later. "We were all taking calls. We had to record all of them into our database and record what people said. I'd answer the phone, and people would just start hating on us, dogging on us. 'I hope someone walks into your office and detonates a bomb.' I was scared, honestly. How do you react to bomb threats? I've never been threatened like that before. I'm eighteen. It was so scary. I talked to the other ladies up here. We got together and prayed over it; over our building, our attorneys, ourselves. Prayed nothing would happen and God would protect us."

The phone callers, few of whom gave their names, didn't shy away from foul language. Marya and the other women in the office were called scumbags, filthy animals, un-American. They were told to go back to high school to learn right from wrong. From all over the country, the hate calls came in: from New York, Washington, North Carolina, the Dakotas. But none, they remember proudly, came from their local area code. "Our community has supported us," said Marya, the relief in her voice palpable. "One of our doctors in Plainview called and praised us for a good ten minutes. An older veteran came in and shook my hand and said, 'I appreciate what you are doing.'"

TWO MONTHS AFTER AHMED Mohamed's misadventure, gun- and flag-toting vigilantes, calling themselves the Bureau of

American-Islamic Relations (BAIR) moved their protests from the mosque in Irving identified by Mayor Van Duyne as promoting Sharia law to the town of Richardson, accusing the Islamic Association of North Texas of "a documented history of funding terrorism." Local media had already investigated these claims and found no evidence that the mosque was involved in funding terrorist activities.[9] That the claim couldn't be substantiated, however, didn't stop the armed group from journeying to the mosque to state their case. Some carried the Stars and Stripes in addition to long-barrel rifles. Others hoisted "Three Percenter" flags; in the top left corner, instead of the fifty stars, were thirteen stars in a circle, surrounding the Roman numeral III. This was the flag flown in recent years by radical militias. It was a call to arms, and a declaration that the existing political system was no longer considered legitimate. The Three Percenters, whose flag signified the original thirteen colonies, and who advocated a second American revolution, had their own motto, part of which was, "You cannot intimidate us. You can try to kill us, if you think you can. But remember, we'll shoot back."[10]

Mayor Van Duyne wasn't necessarily a Three Percenter. But her words and her actions played well on the nativist and conspiracy circuits. She addressed Tea Party gatherings as well as meetings organized by the Center for Security Policy, which peddled the notion that President Obama was a closeted Muslim. And she repeatedly warned of the dangers of a fifth column working to destroy the United States "from within."[11]

Over the following months, the armed protests at mosques began spreading beyond Van Duyne's hometown. On April 2, 2016, a group of masked, flag-waving, camouflage-wearing BAIR vigilantes descended on a Nation of Islam mosque in South Dallas, accusing it of being part of a coalition of groups with "the goal of destroying our Country and killing innocent people to gain Dominance through fear!" They were met by hundreds of counterprotestors, some of them also armed, and, wrote Sarah Mervosh, in an article posted on the *Dallas Morning News* website that afternoon, "racial tension in South Dallas almost exploded."[12]

As 2015 bled into 2016, among parts of the population a pogrom mind-set had begun to take root, whipped up at the local level by the rhetoric of figures such as Van Duyne, and at the federal level by Donald Trump. Violence and intimidation directed against one particular religious group had become a default response, its practitioners reveling in the sorts of acts made notorious by the anti-Jewish mobs, the SA, of Nazi Germany eighty-plus years earlier.

Mosques were firebombed in Houston, as well as in several California cities.[13] The Council on American-Islamic Relations (CAIR) office in Washington, DC, was evacuated after receiving an envelope with unidentified powder, along with the message "Die, Muslims, Die."

In the five weeks following the ISIS attacks in Paris, on November 13, 2015, in which more than one hundred Parisians were brutally killed, thirty-eight anti-Muslim hate crimes were reported in the United States.[14]

In Queens, New York, a Muslim shopkeeper was beaten by a customer who shouted anti-Muslim statements as he assaulted his victim. Later that year, an imam in the borough was killed. Schoolgirls wearing the hijab were harassed in many neighborhoods. In Salt Lake City, an Iraqi man came to work one morning to discover a swastika had been painted on his pastry shop front.[15] In Michigan, a man of Indian descent was shot in the face in the store he worked at by an attacker who thought he was

Muslim. In North Dakota, a restaurant owned by Muslim So-
mali refugees was firebombed.[16] In Pittsburgh, on Thanksgiving
Day, a Muslim cab driver was shot and wounded by a passenger
who asked where he was from, talked to him about ISIS, and
then tried to kill him.[17] In Northern California, a state corrections worker was arrested after throwing a cup of hot coffee at a
Muslim man.[18] And in Tulsa, Oklahoma, a Lebanese Christian
man, mistaken for being a Muslim by his neighbor, was killed
by that neighbor after years of harassment and physical threats.[19]

Around the country, several Sikh men, mistaken for Muslims on account of their turbans, were also physically assaulted
and in some cases killed—reflecting a pattern that had begun immediately after the 9/11 attacks—and Sikh temples vandalized.[20]

"I DO THINK IT's a real microcosm of what's going on all around
the country," attorney Hollingsworth later explained, regarding
the events in Irving, Texas.[21] "There's a percentage of people out
there, some in leadership, promoting an attitude of scapegoating and bias and prejudice. There's a lot of retrenchment going
on now."

Anthony Bond, founder of the Irving chapter of the
NAACP, agreed with the lawyer. "A little boy just tried to show
something to his teacher and he ended up handcuffed. Five or
six officers interrogated him without even the presence of his father or mom. Ahmed is a victim of a racist system and a victim
of a perfect storm. He's a brown boy, a Muslim and the victim
of Islamophobia, whipped up by the mayor and the Tea Party."[22]

In Irving, Ahmed's uncle, Aldean, also concurred. What
happened to his nephew, he believed, was "part of ignorance and
radicalism. They have hate. Whether it be the teachers or the

police or the mayor . . . " He trailed off, pondering the ugliness of what had happened to his young relative. "What happened to Ahmed? The mayor has been going around the country ginning up Islamophobia. Out of fear, [Ahmed's family] left the country. They're in Qatar. He says, 'I'm not going to be the same Ahmed I was before.' When a little kid tells you that, that is something. He had the American Dream. 'I can be an inventor. I can be somebody.'"[23]

THE ARMED PROTESTORS WHO congregated outside the Islamic Center of Irving, the large local mosque that Mayor Van Duyne had labeled a hotbed of Sharia law, were, explained a member of the local police force who spoke on condition of anonymity, simply exercising their Second Amendment rights in a state that had embraced open-carry gun laws in recent years. As such, they weren't doing anything illegal. He did not remember anyone calling the police to complain about the armed group. And, in a state with one of the highest arrest and incarceration rates in the country, and with a long history of police brutality and use of excessive force—in the first six months of 2015, the Mapping Police Violence project estimated that law enforcement officers in Texas shot dead sixty-four people[24]— the local officers saw no call to get involved just because one group of heavily armed Texans was surrounding the worship site of another group of Texans. In fact, that day the police were, according to a department spokesman,[25] simply concerned with making sure that the protestors' First Amendment right to free speech and Second Amendment right to bear arms were not infringed upon.

He did not see this as part of a broader culture of intimidation and fear, one that might help to explain why an adolescent boy was arrested for making a clock. The two events had nothing to do with each other, he explained, despite the best attempts of "the traditional media" to link the two.

Attorney Hollingsworth, not surprisingly, saw things differently. When a city official essentially encouraged an armed mob to protest outside a mosque, it established a climate of intimidation. When a fourteen-year-old Muslim boy was then arrested on a ludicrously flimsy charge after working on a science project, it further corroded the culture of tolerance. And even though the police had subsequently released Mohamed, for the many men and women who called Hollingsworth's office to protest his decision to represent the boy, forevermore Ahmed Mohamed's name would be associated with bomb making and terrorism.

Mohamed's family, in the wake of the furor, had left Texas for Doha, Qatar. But they were lonely there and wanted one day to return. Texas was, after all, the family's home, and suburban Irving was the only world the children were truly familiar with. But, worried Hollingsworth, if they returned, they would have to be protected by a personal security detail, and even then, he worried, they would always be looking over their shoulders, always having to look out for "that springing crazy. In a gun-toting country it don't but take one of them."

Chapter Two

They All Want to Kill Us

A year before Mohamed's misadventures in Irving, in September 2014, Jan Morgan, a glamorous, dressed-to-the-nines, gun-range owner in Hot Springs, Arkansas, had announced that her indoor firing range, Gun Cave, was "Muslim-free." Why, she argued, would she help Muslims train in the use of firearms when they wanted to kill her?

Not surprisingly, Morgan—whose Gun Cave was advertised on Facebook with a photo of the bottom half of a couple; the man in a tuxedo and black pants, a gun hanging loosely from his right hand, backed up against a woman in a black skirt, slit up the leg to the waist, with a silver gun held to her upper thigh by a black garter, sporting black stilettos—promptly became the subject of a federal investigation and a series of lawsuits. She also became a go-to analyst for Fox News and an Internet sensation. Her website—its homepage showing a camouflage-outfitted Morgan, in glasses and ear protectors, her long hair cascading over her shoulders, a semiautomatic in her hands as she turns her head to smile coquettishly at the camera—was visited by huge numbers of supporters; her Facebook page attracted over 166,000 followers.

As she explained in a long essay on her website, she did not want any Muslims on her range because "The Koran (which I have read and studied thoroughly and which muslims align themselves with), contains 109 verses commanding hate, murder and terror against all human beings who refuse to submit or convert to Islam. . . . I hold adults accountable for the 'religion'/ ideology they align themselves with. I have to assume that if you are a muslim, you have read the quran and agree with those 109 verses. So . . . Why would I hand a loaded gun to a muslim and allow him to shoot lethal weapons next to people his koran commands him to kill?"[1]

Morgan told her audience that she had been informed by the FBI that she was on an ISIS hit list, and also stated that there were thirty-five Islamist terror training camps operating on US soil. The latter was an old claim, one usually traced back to a variety of conspiracist websites and frequently debunked by investigative reporters and law enforcement agencies.[2]

"Since I have no way of discerning which muslims will or will not kill in the name of their religion and the commands in their koran," Morgan wrote, "I choose to err on the side of caution for the safety of my patrons, just as I would anyone else who aligns himself with an organization that commands him to commit crimes against innocent people."

Morgan was convinced that Muslims, as a group, were engaged in a vast, international, terrorist conspiracy, and that the media, law enforcement, and political leadership of the country were involved in their own conspiracy of silence on this issue. She claimed, as a result, to be afraid of the consequences of teaching Muslims to use deadly weapons. "The last two Islamic terror attacks on US soil were committed by Muslims who trained at gun ranges near where they live," she told me in a phone conversation in October 2016. "I'm not going to allow my facility to be used by people who train for murder." And then she repeated what she had announced on her website: "I have read and studied the Koran for twelve years. There are 109 verses that dictate hate, murder and terror against non-Muslims. I'm not going to hand a loaded gun to a person who aligns themselves to an ideology that is a theocracy. I don't think people should be able to practice Islam in America—because it is a theocracy. Mohammed was a very vile mass murderer and pedophile. What kind of civilized human being wants to align themselves with that kind of prophet? Their prophet is a problem." Morgan had concluded that no more Muslims should be admitted into America, and that Muslims already in the United States who refused to renounce the 109 chapters of the Koran that she had identified as preaching violence against nonbelievers should be deported. In the meantime, they certainly weren't going to have access to her gun range.[3]

MORGAN WASN'T ALONE. A gun range owner in Inverness, Florida, who posed for photos with a Confederate flag and who urged people to put bumper stickers on their cars declaring their vehicles to be "Muslim Free Zones," had also barred Muslims from the property—or at least had put up signs saying his business was a "Muslim Free Zone." When the owner, Andy Halinan, was sued, the American Freedom Law Center, a conservative legal group, with two staff attorneys, based out of Ann Arbor, Michigan, represented him, arguing that the signs Halinan had put up were simply an example of his exercising his right to free speech. "The gun range owners don't want to train the next Chattanooga shooter, San Bernardino shooter, Fort Hood shooter," AFLC attorney Robert Muise explained. "They don't want blood on their hands. If you haven't noticed, we have an issue now with Islamic terrorists." Furthermore, he averred, in America one had the right to put up whatever sign one wanted. "Whether it says it's an Islamic terrorist free zone or a Muslim free zone, they're both protected by the First Amendment."[4]

The courts agreed with the free speech argument, and the lawsuit was thrown out.

A FEW MONTHS LATER, in the tiny rural community of Oktaha, Oklahoma, a fifteen-minute drive from the larger town of Muskogee, yet another controversy erupted. This time, a mom-and-pop range named Save Yourself Survival and Tactical Gear, the office of which was a one-story affair down the end of a long rural road, and which catered to the local Doomsday Prepping crowd, became "Muslim Free" over the summer of 2015.

Not surprisingly, this gun range, too, immediately attracted national attention. As criticisms mounted, supporters of the owners, Chad and Nicole Neal, organized via a Facebook campaign and came out to the range fully armed with assault rifles to patrol the grounds against potential jihadist attackers.

On October 23, a few months after the Neals, who lived in a trailer out back of the office, put their signs up, Raja'ee Fatihah, an army reservist who lived in Tulsa, decided to put their policy to the test. He had heard about the range months earlier and had reached out to the Oklahoma chapters of the ACLU and CAIR to seek advice from them on how to test the ban. Fatihah is African American and a Muslim. He is also an avid gun enthusiast and had visited many ranges, both indoor and outdoor, in the Tulsa area over the previous years.

It was a gloomy, cloudy day, with rain in the air. Fatihah, twenty-nine years old at the time, was wearing blue jeans, a

T-shirt, and a black jacket with camo patches and a US Army emblem—a star inside of a yellow square. He packed his gear—though he forgot to include his eye and ear protections—and got into his vehicle. Later, when he tried to recall whether it was his black F150 pickup truck or his wife's gray Honda minivan, he drew a blank. Either way, he did recall plugging in his phone and putting on music for the forty-minute drive.[5]

When he arrived at the gun range, with, he recalled, his rifle in a case strapped over his shoulder, Nicole Neal was staffing the desk. She greeted him in a friendly way, and they engaged in small talk while he started to fill in the legal waiver form required for all gun range users. He mentioned he had forgotten his ear protectors and goggles, and said he'd have to purchase some new ones from the range. And then he got his debit card out and handed it over to Nicole so that she could charge it the small fee for access to the outdoor range.

At that point, since she hadn't yet asked him whether he was Muslim, Fatihah decided to broach the issue. As she was getting ready to process his card, he mentioned to her that he was a Muslim. Right away, her attitude changed, he remembered. She called her husband, Chad, from around back, shouting out that there was a Muslim in their range. And Chad came running—with a pistol on his belt. "I don't know if you're here for some kind of jihad," Fatihah remembered Chad saying. "Or something like that."

When Fatihah talked about the event later on, he was struck by how surreal it all sounded. He had tried to explain that all he wanted was to shoot at the range that day like any other paying customer, but, he alleged, Chad's response was to keep telling him what the Koran mandated believers do to unbelievers, and kept insisting that Fatihah was a follower of

Sharia law and must be there to hurt the Neals. Later on, the Neals and their attorneys from the AFLC would allege that Fatihah had entered the range with a loaded AK-47 in hand. "I've never had an AK-47," Chad countered. "It's interesting they said I had an AK-47—which is the iconic terrorist weapon."

The Neals made it clear they weren't going to let Fatihah shoot. First they said that they would both have to accompany him onto the range. Then they said that they would have to process his application and would get back to him to let him know if he could shoot at a later date. Finally, to end the conversation, they simply told him, "You're not shooting today."

Fatihah drove home and wrote up his experience for the ACLU and CAIR. The groups decided they would sue the gun range for violations of protections codified by the federal Civil Rights Act and seek an injunction preventing the Neals from banning Muslims from their business in the future. Over the following months, the battle lines would be drawn. Fatihah would blog about his experiences in Oktaha, and the ACLU and CAIR would file legal papers. Meanwhile, supporters of the gun range would launch their own social media offensive. On February 18, Scott Osborn, one of these supporters, posted on Facebook: "Can you go over to Save Yourself Survival and Tactical Gear and give those folks some kind reviews. They own a gun range that is under attack right now by liberals and muslims because they refused to allow a SHARIA ADHERENT, CAIR board member muslim the right to shoot at their facility." Pamela Geller, a staffer at the American Freedom Law Center (AFLC), accused CAIR of having set the gun range up in a "jihad sting." And attorney Robert Muise wrote that CAIR was waging "civilization jihad against America and our freedoms."

Months later, as I neared completion of this book, the lawsuit was still wending its way through the legal system. It was just one more flash point in an increasingly acrimonious national conversation about the rights of Muslims in America during an era of widespread jihadist-inspired terror attacks in countries around the globe.

THE OKTAHA EVENTS HADN'T bubbled up out of the blue. For years, politicians and fundamentalist preachers in Oklahoma had made hay out of venomously anti-Islamic politicking. The state—which has a grand total of between thirty thousand and forty thousand Muslim residents—was the first in the country to pass a constitutional amendment banning Sharia law, an extraordinary example of attacking a straw man or, as Adam Soltani, executive director of the Oklahoma chapter of the Council on American-Islamic Relations put it, of a "solution in search of a problem."[6]

Several of Oklahoma's elected representatives had built up reputations on the conservative speaking circuit for their uncompromising Islamophobia. State Representative John Bennett argued that Christians ought to be "wary" of Muslims, because the Koran "makes it obligatory to commit violence against non-Muslims,"[7] and told groups that there was "no difference between moderate Islam and extreme Islam," and that Muslims "need Jesus."[8] In one extraordinary tirade, in the late summer of 2014, he reportedly told an audience that Islam was a "cancer that must be cut out of the American society."[9] Meanwhile, Bennett's colleague, State Representative Sally Kern, was busy making a name for herself with a string of venomous comments against a range of minority groups. Blacks, she stated, "don't work as hard" as whites, homosexuality was a "cancer," and, by extension, gay people posed a threat to the nation "even more so than terrorism or Islam."[10]

Out of this toxic brew a culture of violence had percolated. Mosques in the state had been shot at, both with bullets and paintballs, and their walls daubed with hate messages. Several Muslims had been beaten while their attackers screamed racial and religious slurs at them. In one particularly strange incident, a Christian Arab woman was assaulted, and during the attack her assailant screamed that she was a "Muslim bitch." Some mosques had been vandalized by attackers who left bacon and pig entrails strewn on the front steps, over the door handles, and in the parking lots.

Soltani's group routinely received grossly violent emails and voice-mail messages—the senders spewing out a fantastic, and pornographic, litany of insults and threats.

The calls usually came in late at night. "Fuck the camel. Fuck Mohammed. You're not going to take our country, you Muslim piece of shit," one caller screamed. "We're going to destroy you first." Another, delivered at 10:08 one night, calmly and precisely intoned, almost as if the man were reading off a script in a tryout for a ghastly theatrical production, "You are not wanted here. Get out of our country. We are tired of you people trying to take over the world. You are not a faith or a religion of peace. You are violent and we do not like you. LEAVE!"[11]

In October 2014, the CAIR office received the following two messages: "Why are you in our country? Bunch of pigs released on you. We will rule through Jesus Christ. Eat pig shit." "The difference between my God and your God is my God is what has a big dick and watches football, while your God is brown and smelly and has a small dick. Fuck you fucking assholes." A few months later came this note: "We will kill this nigger Muslim President and take back our country."

Politicians in Texas, Florida, Georgia, Tennessee, and several other states had similarly whipped up anti-Muslim sentiments. In the summer of 2015, news outlets reported that Texas agricultural commissioner Sid Miller had put up a Facebook post apparently advocating using nuclear weapons against the Muslim world.[12] The post had been deleted by the time other news organizations tried to follow up on the story. During his ill-fated run for the Republican presidential nomination in 2016, US Senator Ted Cruz advocated only letting non-Muslim refugees from Syria into the United States and called for "patrolling" Muslim neighborhoods within America. In Tennessee, State Representative Susan Lynn distributed a virulently anti-Muslim DVD to her colleagues entitled *America's Mosques Exposed!*[13] During Republican Party presidential debates during the winter and spring of 2016, proposals were floated that included making American Muslims carry a special ID card delineating their religious affiliation.[14]

This was a Pandora's box, and politicians like John Bennett were taking a crowbar to its lid. Open up such a box, spread its ghastly contents around the country, and it wouldn't take long for a demagogue with a national platform to reap the benefits.

After all, as Daniela Schiller at Manhattan's Mount Sinai explained, no matter how much of an effort we make as individuals and as a society to overcome biases and fears developed over decades, those fears remain etched into our brains, ready to be set loose again by hyperbolic politicians or ratings-hungry media: "There are a lot of studies where they kept images of black and white faces and associated images with electric shocks. And you can reduce the fear gradually by presenting the image without the shock. But if you're a white person and seeing black images [originally] associated with the shock, it takes longer to reduce the fear."[15]

We have evolved to remember fear fast and to forget it only slowly and with numerous caveats. And when we fear groups, we tend to do so without nuance, fearing all rather than some; We are, therefore, primed to respond to the sorts of generalizations bandied about by Bennett. "If you hear an expression like 'a crowd of Muslims,'" said Schiller, "This will echo in your mind. You're planting a seed. It's an out-group. You have less information on them. That negative bias will have a lot of effect. This is automatic. It's not explicit. It's just the way we operate on many levels."

In December 2015, a Reuters/Ipsos poll found that nearly 15 percent of Americans were "generally fearful" of Muslims.[16] That's nowhere close to a majority, of course, but those millions of fearful people *were* a large enough demographic to play a major role in an electoral cycle in which Donald Trump, in particular, was carving out a political niche through Muslim bashing, the spreading of conspiratorial theories about Muslim fifth columns and mass rejoicings among Muslim Americans when the World Trade Centers were destroyed, and a promise to register and track the country's Muslim population. A September 2015 poll found that fully two-thirds of Trump's supporters believed that President Obama was a closet Muslim, and in Iowa, the state that holds the first caucus of the presidential election season and thus plays an outsized role in shaping campaign discourse, nearly one-third of Republican voters believed Islam should be outlawed in the United States and another 20 percent hadn't yet made up their mind on the matter but were open to the idea.[17] In December 2015, *Vox.com* ran an extraordinary article detailing incidents of anti-Muslim actions around the country that included an advocate for an Islamic center in Spotsylvania, Virginia, being attacked at a meeting on zoning permits for representing "an evil cult," and an armed militia showing up at the Islamic center in Irving, Texas, to stop the "Islamicization of America."[18]

Since September 2001, when planes hijacked by Al-Qaeda flew into the World Trade Center, the Pentagon, and a field in Pennsylvania, destroying thousands of lives, fear of a particular set of fundamentalist beliefs, and of the small minority of Muslims who adhered to the ideology of terror, had for millions of Americans morphed into something much more generic, something easier to grasp but impossible to intellectually justify.

Boil all of these fears down, and they came out somewhat as Jan Morgan formulated it: *they* all want to kill *us*. It's hard to think or to act calmly when you have a gut feeling that you are under siege, that you are somebody's prey, and that you are always on the verge of becoming a violent crime statistic. It's easy, in such circumstances, to throw your lot in with the demagogue who shouts the loudest about safety and security, who makes the most noise about ruthlessly dealing with the country's enemies, and who is most shameless in rhetorically dividing the world into an "us" and a "them."

ON FEBRUARY 23, 2016, I met many people who had embarked down just such a road. The setting was a fairly nondescript Baptist church in Sparks, Nevada. The church was a caucus site for seven precincts casting ballots in the Republican Party's presidential nominating process. And as was the case throughout Nevada that evening, turnout was high, and a solid plurality of those voting were Donald Trump supporters.

As the evening progressed, I sat and talked with many of the Trumpites, asking them, in particular, what they thought about Muslims. Their answers were bloodcurdling; there's no other way to put it. Psychologically, they had made the leap that the *genocidaires* in Rwanda had made twenty-two years earlier, or that the Nazis had made three-quarters of a century before. They no longer thought of their religious and/or ethnic opponents as fully human. They were a nuisance, a danger, a menace, and therefore had to be removed.

There was the retired supervisor at a sugar factory who felt that Muslims would "be happier in their own country where they can pray the way they want. They're not here in America to do any good. They're here to do evil." If they didn't leave voluntarily, he said, he would give them a choice, "a trench on one side or a ticket out of here." When I asked for clarification, asked whether he was talking about execution, he answered without hesitation: "Absolutely. That's what they do to us in their countries. I'd give 'em a choice: get out of here or else." A lady sitting nearby and listening to our conversation gave a thumbs-up and murmured her agreement.

There was the retired carpenter who believed that "they ought to register all Muslims. The Muslims, or ISIS, or whatever you want to call them, they should be screened." I asked him whether Trump's comments about executing terrorists by shooting them with bullets dipped in pigs' blood bothered him. They didn't: "Not really. What are they doing over there? No difference. He's giving them mercy. Shooting them, not cutting their heads off, not killing women and children. You fight fire with fire. The Bible says if they don't want to conform to what society is like, get rid of them. What did God tell Joshua? 'Get rid of every man, woman, child and beast.' If the Lord says it's ok, he has the final say so."

The carpenter's wife felt that Trump was just trying to defend flag and country: "I like what he stands for. I want to bring our country back," she explained. "I want us to honor and respect our country. I want us to love our country and be proud of it. I want to bring God back into our country. He loves our country so much. He loves our country."

Then there was the fifty-five-year-old man with a gray beard, in a cap, jeans, and a long, untucked, blue flannel shirt, who owned a moving company and was attending a caucus for the first time. He didn't think Trump had anything against the Muslim religion—he just wanted to control "people from that country. Eastern countries."

A young elementary school teacher didn't believe that Muslims should be killed, but nor was she particularly bothered that so many of her fellow caucus-goers did. It was, for her, simply a matter of personal preference, as morally inconsequential as, say, one's choice of breakfast cereal in the morning. "Everyone is entitled to their own opinion. A lot of people are very angry with Muslims right now. That's what it boils down to."

TWENTY YEARS BEFORE THAT caucus, I had covered the US Taxpayers' Party convention, in San Diego, held concurrently with the GOP convention that was then nominating Bob Dole as the Republican Party's presidential candidate. I was a young journalist attracted to fringe stories, and there was nothing more fringe than the Taxpayers' Party, founded by Howard Phillips, a far-right ideologue who had worked with the GOP for twenty years before breaking with the party in 1974 to form the Conservative Caucus. Phillips believed in a theocratic government run according to strictly biblical principles, in an America unbound by any international treaties; he opposed legislation on hate crimes, supported armed militias, and opposed any role for Muslims in American public life. I checked into a local youth hostel not too far from the Taxpayers' event and made my way each day into the maelstrom. At that convention, one could find adherents to every conspiracy theory under the sun; one could hobnob with racial bigots and shoot the breeze with religious extremists. I still remember the bemusement I felt as I tried to navigate the byzantine web of conspiracy theories and white supremacist argot peddled by the attendees. It was one of my first journalistic Alice-Down-the-Rabbit-Hole moments, when all that was normal was suddenly inverted, when the bizarre was espoused as the holy, patriotic truth and the rational was denounced as some sort of "mainstream" treasonous plot.

Two decades on, those views and, quite possibly, many of those same people, were capturing the GOP from the inside. This was the bile now surging up out of the Grand Old Party's base, drawn to a candidate who, with his venomous statements on Muslims, Mexicans, demonstrators who spoke out against him, and anyone else who disagreed with him, gave a nod and a wink to their assorted bigotries. This was the *reductio ad absurdum* end point of the party's endless pandering to Tea Party fanatics, to birthers, to gun-toting militias, and other zealots.

In December 2015, researchers at the University of Massachusetts, Amherst, had sampled 1,800 voters about their political preferences. They found that the more a person defined themselves as authoritarian and the more fearful they were of terrorism were the two best predictors as to whom they would vote for. Forty-three percent of Republicans, they found, considered themselves to be strongly authoritarian in inclination. Those men and women were more likely to be Trump supporters. Fear of terrorism also pushed people who didn't always consider themselves as authoritarians down that road as well. "Take activated authoritarians from across the partisan spectrum and the growing cadre of threatened non-authoritarians, then add them to the base of Republican general election voters, and the potential electoral path to a Trump presidency becomes clearer," the study's architect, Matthew MacWilliams, wrote in *Politico.*[19] "From pledging to 'make America great again' by building a wall on the border to promising to close mosques and ban Muslims from visiting the United States, Trump is playing directly to authoritarian inclinations."

When the businessman-cum-politician crossed one moral Rubicon after another, when he called for the summary execution of terrorists using bullets dipped in pigs' blood, when he announced that he wanted to punch a protestor in the face, or when he told Southern audiences that he longed for the good old days when you could send a heckler out on a stretcher, he spoke to this audience directly. They loved him not *despite* his over-the-top rhetoric but *because* of it.

"ISIS IS ALREADY HERE. Arm yourselves. Learn to shoot firearms. Protect your family. ISIS is already here," screamed a middle-aged man, stocky, hair cut short, in a red "Make America Great Again" baseball cap, as he waded into a crowd, several thousand strong, of anti-Trump protestors outside New York's Grand Hyatt Hotel, next to Grand Central Station, on East Forty-Second Street, on April 14, 2016. It was a cold, clear, early spring evening. The protestors had arrived early, many picketing and chanting from four in the afternoon onwards. Inside, the New York State Republicans were holding their annual gala, and Trump, Senator Ted Cruz, and Ohio governor John Kasich—the last three Republican presidential candidates still standing in April—were being hosted. Trump had arrived by helicopter in time for the start of the gala, at seven o'clock, having earlier that afternoon addressed a large crowd in Long Island, near the site of the killing of an Ecuadorian immigrant a few years before.

This choice of location for his anti-immigrant, nativist stump speech was particularly crass and deliberately inflammatory.

All along Forty-Second Street, from Park Avenue to Lexington, on the south side of the street from Grand Central station and the adjacent Grand Hyatt, protestors were holding up signs accusing Trump of fascist sympathies. Meanwhile, on the north side of the street, a smaller crowd of Trumpists were making their views heard too. "ISIS is already here," the man shouted. Again and again, his voice raw with urgency. "Arm yourselves. Protect your families. ISIS is already here." Eventually, a phalanx of police escorted him back across the thoroughfare to those more sympathetic to his message.

Down the street a few yards to the west, on the southwest corner of Pershing Square, just off to the side of the green-painted ironwork supporting the overpass along which the limos carrying gala attendees were driving, another Trump supporter had set up shop with a large sign saying simply, "Build the Wall." How tall should it be, I asked him? He answered without hesitation, as if he had been waiting for a considerable time for someone to ask him just this particular question: "Twenty feet should do it. With barbed wire on the top."

It was a suitably precise answer to the endlessly complex issue of securing the largest border on earth between the First World and the Developing World. The sort of precise answer that Trump routinely threw out to his enthused crowds. The sort of precise answer that was easy to turn into a sound bite and thus to achieve cyber immortality. The sort of precise answer that actually made no sense and would do nothing to solve the crisis of undocumented immigration north by poor and desperate Mexicans and Central Americans.

Chapter Three

Laws for the Limbic System

In addition to being venomously anti-Muslim, pandering to much of the public's increasingly shrill anti-Islamic mood, Trump's campaign was absolutely rigid in its interpretation of the Second Amendment, with the candidate arguing time and again that any restrictions on gun ownership were un-American. Guns, lots of them, he told his audiences, were the best defense against terrorists—except when it came to gun ownership by Muslims, who were, as a group, viewed with suspicion by Trump's people. It was but a short hop from the National Rifle Association's argument that homeowners should all keep weapons on hand against putative home invaders to the notion that in a war of the civilized against the barbarian, it was the obligation of all who cared for the "civilized" side to take down their enemies with massive firepower. Had Parisians not been prevented by their country's antigun laws from carrying weapons with them, the presidential hopeful announced shortly after terrorists in Paris had slaughtered roughly 130 people on November 13, 2015, they would have been able to prevent the carnage by taking out the shooters at the start of their rampage. No matter that the French ambassador to the United States promptly retorted that the presidential hopeful was "a vulture" for taking advantage of the massacre to push his political agenda, Trump refused to back down.

Had the dozens of doomed clubbers in Orlando been armed when Omar Mateen stormed the Pulse nightclub the following June and sprayed the partygoers with bullets, one of them might have shot him between the eyes—and that, Trump told America shortly after the massacre, in the same speech in which he accused President Obama of being in league with ISIS, would have been "a beautiful thing."[1] That bullet entering soft brain tissue wouldn't have been a necessary evil; no, in the Trumpian universe, it would have been a truly beautiful, glorious event. There was a cartoon quality to this imagery, but it was a cartoon being conjured up as reality by a man running for the most powerful position on earth.

Trump's sadistic lingering on the supposed virtues of a death-torture regime played into ISIS's hands in more ways than one. Not only did it have the potential to drive young Muslims toward extremism, but it also served to suck oxygen out of the broader political debate, focusing the public and the media's attention on a small set of ghastly proposals at the expense of the much broader, and in many ways more important, conversation, and thus, in the process, weakening the American polity.

In the Trumpist milieu, other very real problems and dangers get subsumed when a panic sets in about one particular type of violence or of risk. In focusing so selectively on the dangers of Islamist terrorism, for example, Americans have, in recent years, failed miserably in tackling another growing danger: the militarization of civil society. Gun purchases surged after 9/11 and surged again during the Obama presidency, when

Americans purchased between 1 million and 1.5 million guns per month, month in and month out throughout the eight years he was in office.[2] Not surprisingly, over the decades there has been a normalization of levels of gun violence that are seen in no other Western democracy.

For many Trump supporters, euphemistically labeled as "raucous" by media outlets such as the *New York Times*, guns weren't just hunting tools, or self-defense weapons, they were also—and this was where Trump's legions beat a path distinct from that trodden by most other pro-gun advocates within the two major political parties—instruments of political expression. As the primary and caucus season grew ever uglier, many Trumpites took to the Internet to suggest that they carry weapons to the voting booth with them. "If it's legal in your area. CCW [concealed carry weapons] permit holders may want to bring their guns when they vote for Trump on Tuesday," read one tweet, tagged #MakeAmericaGreatAgain and sent on March 12, 2016.

During this same period, as protests around Trump's speeches escalated, a vigilante group named the Lion Guard formed online as a sort of praetorian guard to protect the candidate and prevent protestors from disrupting his speeches. Online, they railed against "afro-chauvanist" (*sic*) groups, "rabid Marxists," "neo-bolsheviks," "rootless barbarians," and "Trotskyte terrorists."[3] Bikers identifying with the Lion Guard organized to protect Trump's rallies in Arizona. Another group set up shop in New Hampshire. The group was, wrote a Lion Guard recruiter on June 26, "a call to organize resistance against the Red Terror that hates Mr. Trump and his supporters and a proposed a plan [*sic*] on how to stand up to these bolshevik goons."

Through the spring of 2016, with the delegate math still, at that point, indicating the likelihood of a contested convention in Cleveland that summer, many of Trump's supporters also suggested that they attend the GOP convention armed to the hilt, ostensibly to defend themselves against protestors—a proposal looked on with disfavor by the Secret Service, which announced that the convention floor would have to be gun-free.

That probably wasn't a bad idea. After all, during the ferocious GOP primary season, large numbers of these angry men and women phoned in death threats, many delivered anonymously and from locales far away, to regional party leaders in states where behind-the-scenes deals had led to anti-Trump delegates being selected. In Colorado, the party's chairperson, Steve House, told the media that he had received more than three thousand threatening phone calls. "Death threats over running a caucus instead of a primary because it is the law here and over the fact that one candidate had a better strategy and a much bigger team on the field. Shame on the people who think somehow that it is right to threaten me and my family over not liking the outcome of an election," House wrote on Facebook, in a comment widely covered by the media in mid-April 2016.[4]

Meanwhile, prominent Republicans who decided that they couldn't stomach Trump's candidacy and endorsed Hillary Clinton were subject to a barrage of ferociously threatening emails and twitter responses. One correspondent, emailing Sacramento-based Doug Elmets, a one-time staffer in the Reagan White House who spoke at the Democrats' convention in Cleveland against Trump and in favor of Clinton, told Elmets that he hoped his wife and daughters were raped and killed. Others accused him of treason. Still another wrote that he was ex-Special Forces and strongly implied that, if given the opportunity, he would physically harm Elmets. A woman wrote, succinctly, "You FUCKING progressive PRICK!!!" A man emailed Elmets to tell him he was an ASSHOLE for "going to vote for the most lying, corrupt, and lesbian bitch on the planet named hillary [*sic*]." A woman slammed him for not supporting a "Great Patriot" after "eight years of a Communist Muslim." "You and your ilk are shit," wrote still another furious Trumpite. "Your stench reaches all strata of society. You know what shit is. You are shit. If history is any lesson, you and all of your kind will prolly be among the first to have your heads lopped off by your 'friends' the islamo fascisti. . . . Repent and live you ignoramus."

This wasn't the rough and tumble of ordinary democratic debate; it was another beast entirely. A beast feeding on fear and convinced that disagreement equated to treason. Trump had, Elmets felt, given voice to "the underbelly of America." His candidacy was "the embodiment of the worst that America has to offer."[5] And it was backed by millions of heavily armed people who increasingly viewed their arsenals as the core component of their social and political identity.

FOR MANY OF THESE men and women, gun rights and antipathy to Muslims danced an uneasy dance. Many had come to agree with Morgan's stance, essentially saying, "guns are great for you and me, but represent a menace in the hands of this one particular group."

Now one can certainly argue—and many, myself included, do—that *nobody* outside of law enforcement and the military ought to be allowed anywhere near automatic or semiautomatic weaponry; that such finely tuned killing machines, designed to maim and kill large numbers of humans at speed and in combat, rather than as hunting props, have no legitimate role in civilian life. Especially given that time and again, in an era in which there is a mass shooting on US soil almost every day,[6] the consequences of having such weapons widely and easily available have, in recent years, been brought home in the worst ways possible. But that's very different from selectively banning certain people from access to weapons, not because of their actions but simply because of their religious background.

One could argue, too, that courts should be able to issue restraining orders, ordering individuals whom family and friends deem to be unstable, to hand over their guns or face criminal prosecution. That's the position taken, for example, by leading gun control expert Garen Wintemute, who has produced a wealth of data in recent years showing who most of the perpetrators of gun violence in the United States are: a disproportionate number of gun homicides, he finds, are carried out by young black men; but an equally disproportionate number of gun suicides are carried out by old white men. And since there are so many more older white men in America than there are younger, black men, Wintemute argues that sensible gun control policies have to focus on who's most at risk of inflicting and being the victim of gun violence rather than simply playing to stereotypes. If it turns out that more whites use guns to kill people than do blacks, then we have to ask ourselves a question: What is it, in our culture, in our history, that makes it so easy for us to dismiss the significance of violence carried out by whites, but to seize on any evidence of violence carried out by blacks as somehow emblematic of African American culture as a whole?

Passing concealed carry laws, Stand Your Ground laws, and the raft of other laws that make it easier for "law-abiding" Americans to own guns—and that tend to win support in conservative white suburbs—may give the illusion of security,

Wintemute explained, while in fact making the country, especially for those at risk of suicide and for their family members, a
far more dangerous place. From the age of thirty-five onwards,
he continued, far more whites die of gunshot wounds than do
blacks, because of sky-high suicide rates among the middle-aged
and elderly white population. White men age eighty-five and
older were, he estimated, five times more likely than similarly
aged African American men to intentionally shoot themselves.
In 2010, Wintemute and several of colleagues reported in an
article in the *Annual Review of Public Health* that the total cost
to America of gunshot injuries—in work hours lost, medical
bills, funeral costs, police investigations, and so on—totaled a
staggering $174.1 billion.[7]

"Laws for the limbic system are what Stand Your Ground
laws and the like are," Wintemute argues, his lean, wiry body
wound like a spring, his eyes lit up with the intensity of argument. "They go straight to the emotional, nonrational—
certainty and correctness are completely uncoupled—parts
of the brain." In other words, laws passed in haste to counter
perceived threats (home invasion, carjacking, inner-city gangs,
drug cartels, illegal immigrants rampaging through the countryside, terrorists and random mass shooters holding crowds
hostage, and so on) may in fact end up doing far more harm
than good, as measured by the body count and the cost to the
medical system at the end of the day. In an era where tens of
millions of Americans believe their only pathway to safety is
carrying weapons wherever they go—either openly, in states
that allow open carry, or hidden on the person somewhere, in
the growing number of states that allow concealed carry—and
stockpiling ever more weapons, with ever higher firepower in
their homes, it's not surprising that gun deaths inflict such a

vast toll on the country each year. Nor is it surprising that the likelihood of any one individual being shot by a nonterrorist is exponentially higher, year in and year out, than is the likelihood of that person being murdered by someone motivated by political or religious extremism; and that even within the subcategory of "terrorist" killings, in most years more Americans who die at the hands of terrorists are killed by white supremacists than by Islamists. Far more Americans are killed by people they hold dear to their hearts—relatives, close friends—than by fanatical jihadists sent from overseas to cause American mayhem.

For despite all of the ink spilled on terrorism in these years, and all the hundreds of billions of dollars spent on wars and security systems designed to thwart terrorists, Americans were more than one hundred times more likely, in those years, to have been killed by a gunshot fired by a run-of-the-mill criminal or to have killed themselves in a fit of suicidal despair than to have died at the hands of terrorists.

In fact, of the several hundred fatal mass shootings that occurred in the United States in the years leading up to the 2016 presidential election, only three—the Orlando slaughter, of June 12, 2016; the massacre of December 2, 2015, in San Bernardino, California; and the November 2009 shooting at Fort Hood—were carried out by Islamist terrorists. The others were executed by a motley crew of homegrown right-wing zealots (Dylann Roof in South Carolina), anti-abortion extremists (Robert Dear in Colorado Springs), the mentally ill, angry colleagues, spouses, children, parents. A seemingly endless body count, which elicited prayers from anti–gun control politicians but never effective legislation to reduce access to high-powered weapons. And yet, when Syed Farook and Tashfeen Malik used legally purchased automatic weaponry to kill fourteen people and injure dozens more at a party for social workers in a county building in Southern California, suddenly anti–gun control advocates rushed to declare that the country was at war. A few hours after the attack, Jan Morgan posted on her Facebook page, "MUSLIMS prove that I was right all along in declaring my range a muslim free zone a year ago. . . . I will not train the next jihadist." The next day, after a night to think it over, the gun-range owner returned to the fray. "Let me make clear what the media is stumbling all over themselves to not say," she wrote in a new Facebook posting. "Two Muslims ambushed innocent co-workers and murdered/injured them in a pre-planned attack at a CHRISTMAS party."[8]

It was a very different response from what she had had after other recent large-scale killings. On November 27, the day of another mass shooting in America, this one at a Planned Parenthood clinic in Colorado Springs, Colorado—the perpetrator an upper-middle-aged white male, Christian, from North Carolina—Morgan's Facebook page made no mention of the deaths. In fact, the only posting that day was about Muslims: "Since I declared my gun range 'A Muslim Free Zone' over a year ago, Gun ranges and gun stores in SIX STATES have followed my lead. I'm happy to announce today that one of them, sued by CAIR had a major legal victory! The judge said that declaring his range a muslim free zone was free speech protected by the 1st Amendment." On June 17, 2015, when a young white supremacist killed nine African Americans in a South Carolina church, Jan Morgan's response was even more succinct: that day, she didn't write anything at all on her Facebook page.

Across the anti–gun control community, the response to the events in San Bernardino was orders of magnitude different from the responses to the hundreds of other mass shootings that had destroyed lives and shattered communities over the previous years. As the *New York Times* scathingly noted two days after the ISIS-inspired horror, in a rare front-page editorial, "motives do not matter to the dead in California, nor did they in Colorado, Oregon, South Carolina, Virginia, Connecticut and far too many other places. The attention and anger of Americans should also be directed at the elected leaders whose job is to keep us safe but who place a higher premium on the money and political power of an industry dedicated to profiting from the unfettered spread of ever more powerful firearms."[9]

WE OUGHT NOT TO have the moral luxury of being able to ignore the huge, and utterly pointless, body counts that accumulate yearly across the land. Yet too often we do. In early 2016, the BBC calculated that in the first eleven months of 2015 the United States had experienced 353 mass shootings, all but one of them, the San Bernardino shootings, unconnected to Islamic terrorism.[10] Fourteen years earlier, when analyzing responses to the Washington, DC, sniper killings, researchers for the Federal Emergency Management Agency had reached a similar conclusion: "In the three weeks that the Sniper terrorized over five million people, shooting thirteen and killing ten, 'routine' crime continued unnoticed." During that period, the authors found, 239 people were assaulted by assailants carrying deadly weapons, 32 people were shot, and 22 people were murdered. "None of these crimes merited front page coverage."[11]

Even in June 2016, after Omar Mateen carried out the largest mass shooting in modern American history, killing 49 people in a few minutes of absolute carnage, terrorism still killed far fewer Americans than did nonpolitical gun murders. In fact, according to research by the Gun Violence Archive, in the single week following the massacre, more than 500 Americans were shot, 228 of them fatally.[12] The vast majority of these shootings went largely unnoticed, generating only local news-in-brief stories, unleashing heartbreak among the families and friends of the victims but hardly a ripple in the broader culture. Their victims remained silhouettes, shadows in the dark alleyways off to the side of the American Dream.

Preoccupied by one form of violence, we neglect other far more common carnage. Between 2001, when Al-Qaeda brought down the World Trade Centers and attacked the Pentagon, killing 2,996 people and setting off a series of global conflicts that continue to play out a decade and a half later, and 2013, more than 406,000 Americans were killed by gunshots deemed by law enforcement not to be motivated by terrorist ideology.[13] Sixty percent of these deaths were suicides,[14] but that still left well over 150,000 dead victims of others' gunplay—many of them victims of mass shootings that, by and large, were carried out by young white men. During those same years, 350 Americans were killed in overseas terror attacks, and another 3,030 were killed in terrorist incidents in the United States—all but thirty-four of them on September 11, 2001.[15]

None of that is to say that Al-Qaeda, ISIS, and other jihadi groups aren't a serious threat to national security and to global peace. They clearly are. Their ideology is utterly destructive and their belief systems heinous. They thrive on the shedding of blood and the theater, the spectacle, of unfathomable violence. Their beheadings, crucifixions, mass shootings, bombings, and so on are designed to inflict maximum carnage and create maximum fear and political instability from one country to the next. And they use these events as recruitment tools around the world, each one serving as a calling card for young, disaffected, angry people to flock to their call for an apocalyptic jihad.

Yet no matter how ghastly such groups are, we deal with them best when we put them in perspective, when we refuse to give them what they want by magnifying their significance and by turning them into larger-than-life bogeymen. Too often, that lesson is ignored in our dealings with those deemed to be our enemies, most of whom are in fact far from the sophisticated, lethally resourceful killers of Hollywood's imagination: captured terrorism suspects were, the Bush administration averred, so dangerous that they would use their teeth to gnaw through hydraulic lines on airplanes transporting them to Guantanamo Bay were they not blindfolded and chained to their seats.[16] We deal with them worst when we allow them to dictate the terms of our policy discourse, permitting them to assume such outsized significance in our collective psyches that we stampede away from the open, pluralist society in our efforts to root such groups out. That's what happened when lawyers such as John Yoo crafted detailed legal justifications for "enhanced interrogation techniques," thus putting the imprimatur of the US government behind what rapidly grew into a web of torture chambers—in Iraq, in Afghanistan, at Guantanamo Bay, and in CIA "black sites" in several other countries. In legitimizing waterboarding, sleep deprivation, the holding of suspects in stress positions for hours at a time, in threatening them with dogs and poisonous insects, in enacting mock executions, and even enclosing them for days on end in coffin-like boxes, the infamous "torture memos" set American democracy down a terrible path toward the normalization of torture and creative brutality against people deemed to be cold-blooded killers existing utterly outside of the social compact.[17]

THE PHRASE "ASYMMETRIC WARFARE" is often bandied about. It's the idea that groups like Al-Qaeda and ISIS, knowing they cannot take on the military might of NATO directly, turn to forms of hit-and-run attacks that are particularly hard to guard against: massacres at soft-target sites, cyber attacks intended to sow chaos, the disruption of trade routes, assaults on countries' tourism infrastructures, and so on. As much as any of these, the manipulation of fear, the ability to amplify one's terroristic actions through the echo chambers of social media, to inculcate the idea that anyone and everyone is a potential enemy, is an asymmetric weapon. A society riven by fear, by misunderstood perceptions of risk and by all of the suspicions that arise in a period in which one no longer trusts one's neighbor, and in which civilians build up arsenals to deal with putative risks surrounding them on all sides, rapidly turns in on itself. It becomes the perfect feeding ground for demagogues. "An armed society," argued Wintemute, a highly trained emergency room doctor and public health advocate, sitting in his small office on a side street off of the huge UC Davis medical complex in Sacramento, California, "will certainly be a vigilant, on-edge society; which has implications for the sense of community we have, and so on."

Firearms trainers, some sponsored by the NRA, others by smaller organizations that host weekend-long exercises around the country, talk to their clients of always remaining in "condition yellow." This is a state of omnipresent alert, when you, as an individual, are always on the lookout for bad guys you assume are always present, always scouting for weaknesses, always looking to do harm to you and your loved ones. In condition yellow, everyone is a potential enemy. And in condition yellow you are measured for worth by your willingness to engage in violence quickly, lethally, without much of a second thought, at the slightest indication that your environment is under threat.

The culture of democracy becomes a soft-target victim when the dogs of fear are unleashed, when religious and/or national groups are pitted against each other by extremists, and when electorates embrace autocratic strongmen, with visions of state-inflicted violence or vigilante behaviors dancing before their eyes, in response to the actions of terrorist organizations or criminal individuals.

Which is exactly what started to unfold during the 2016 election cycle, as Donald Trump began riding a vast wave of fear in the most demagogic political journey in modern American history.

In speech after speech on the campaign trail, Trump embraced the expansive use of torture against America's enemies. He said he would "bring back a hell of a lot worse than waterboarding." He advocated the mass shooting of terrorism suspects—using bullets dipped in pigs' blood. And, at various times, he stated that he would order the American military to kill the families of terrorism suspects. When the ex-head of the CIA, Michael Hayden, argued that the army would refuse to obey such orders, Trump's response, in a *Fox News* interview, was: "They won't refuse. They're not gonna refuse me. Believe me."

On the stump, in front of huge crowds, Trump repeatedly declared that he wanted to smash in the faces of protestors—and the crowds, far from lapsing into a stunned silence at this brutishness, roared their approval.

In his 2000 credo, *The America We Deserve*, the businessman wrote of the punishment for murderers: "My only complaint is that lethal injection is too comfortable a way to go." Indeed, as far back as 1989, during the infamous Central Park jogger rape case, Trump took out a newspaper advert calling for the suspects—a group of African American teenagers, between the ages of fourteen and sixteen—to be executed; or, rather, in practice to be lynched, since they had not yet been convicted of the crimes of which they were accused. (Those young men spent years in prison before ultimately being exonerated. Despite this, during the presidential election, Trump once again asserted they were guilty and deserved to die.) Time after time, he has said that the police need to take their gloves off and get truly tough against criminals and dissenters.

Why did Trump fetishize the iron fist? And why did he urge the public, and the institutions of state—from the army to the courts, from local police forces to the border patrol—to join in this violence? Because, I believe, he wanted as many people and as many institutions as possible to be complicit in it.

After all, if he genuinely believed that torture was a vile but occasionally necessary tool of the state, he could advocate a position similar to that of the Bush-Cheney administration, or even to that of the Israeli government. He could say that he would play hardball and, quite simply, leave it at that. What then went on in the darkest shadows would remain largely an unknown, something ghastly that went unsaid. The depredations of Abu Ghraib, of Guantanamo, and of the CIA's black sites were utterly appalling, but if there was any saving grace in that vastly criminal web of torture, it was that the government of the day didn't go out of its way to flaunt its embrace of wholesale torture. Yes, government officials crafted legal justifications for the morally unjustifiable, but they also expressed a degree of embarrassment when the scale of the torture was revealed. Bush did not address huge crowds urging ever more torture on ever more people. He did not publicly enfold himself in the Inquisitor's garb and declare torture to be a cleansing, purifying social force in and of itself.

In drawing back the curtain on the state and its dirty practices, in glorying in the torture that he promised he would unleash, Trump was essentially inviting all of his supporters into the torture chamber. In publicly, and repeatedly, lauding the virtues of torture, not to extract intelligence (however nebulous the idea that torture yields useful intelligence actually is) but simply to punish America's enemies, he was inviting a mass moral complicity in crimes. And the more people who supported him in this, the more he would be able to reinvent the state in his own sadistic, twisted, image. Bush, in rationalizing torture in extraordinary circumstances, may have started America down this road. Trump now threatened to take the country to a point of no return.

The more Trump urged wholesale deportations of millions of people, or the barring of entire religious groups from entry into the country, or the registering of Muslim residents already in the country, or the iron fist against protestors, against suspected criminals and terrorists, the more he fueled a pogrom atmosphere.

This is a project that would be all too familiar to earlier totalitarians, be they named Stalin or Franco, Mussolini or Hitler. A complicit population, a population that has, at the urging of a charismatic leader, crossed one moral Rubicon after another, is one that has ceased to *think* in a democratic and tolerant manner.

Hannah Arendt understood the power of this sadistic imagination all too well: if a charismatic leader publicly urges institutions and individuals into criminal violence, all too many individuals will go along, not necessarily because they too are sadists but because it is much easier to say yes than to stand up to one's neighbors and friends and political leaders. It is easier to be a part of a crowd, or a mob, to go along with atrocities committed by fearful, insecure people against purportedly threatening groups, than to react as a morally autonomous individual.

"The trouble with Eichmann was precisely that so many were like him, and that the many were neither perverted nor sadistic, that they were, and still are, terribly and terrifyingly normal," Arendt wrote. "From the viewpoint of our legal institutions and of our moral standards of judgment, this normality was much more terrifying than all the atrocities put together." Fear can serve as the solvent binding individuals to vastly criminal political projects. Fear can convince a person to follow orders unthinkingly, until so many Rubicons have been crossed that the person has no way to return to a more decent moral space.

In 1961, a mere sixteen years after the end of the Second World War, a Yale University social psychologist named Stanley Milgram conducted a series of experiments in which he put test subjects into a room with people who were supposedly taking a battery of exams. The exam takers (who, unbeknownst to the subjects, were actors) were hooked up to a machine that the subjects were told generated electric shocks. Whenever they answered a question wrong, a lab official, in a white coat—and thus seen to be an authority figure—would order the subjects to give an electric shock. Each time the exam takers gave a wrong answer, the subjects were told to increase the voltage that they administered.

The actors very convincingly responded as if they were in excruciating pain (they weren't, as in reality the machines weren't giving out jolts of electricity). After a while, they began begging for the subjects to stop hurting them, sometimes even claiming that they felt as if they were about to die. Yet, so long as the authority figure kept telling them to administer the shocks, a majority of the participants did so. They did so because they feared the consequences of disobeying authority, and they did so, too, because they feared that without those pillars of authority, anarchy would run riot.

The results, wrote Milgram in an article he published in the 1970s, titled "The Perils of Obedience," were devastating. "Stark authority was pitted against the subjects' strongest moral imperatives against hurting others, and, with the subjects' ears ringing with the screams of the victims, authority won more often than not." If figures of authority and in positions of power tell a populace to act sadistically, the default is that they will.

I don't know if Trump ever read about the Milgram experiments—frankly, he's never struck me as one who reads much of anything. But if he did, he surely took the lesson to heart. Once the state, having whipped up a frenzy of fear among the populace, sanctions purely vindictive, punitive violence on an everyday basis, it's a pretty good bet that much of the populace will go along. And once the populace does so, it becomes so morally compromised that it rapidly loses its ability to resist further encroachments of violence and coercion. That violence-born-of-fear, the detestation of the foreigner and the outsider, becomes the glue holding the totalitarian project together.

THE SELECTIVE NATURES OF our fears and furies are, frequently, easily apparent. Had Jan Morgan, a self-proclaimed Second Amendment expert and Tea Party aficionado, had a road-to-Damascus moment after yet another massacre and come out against the sale of, and training with, powerful weaponry capable of killings scores of people in a handful of seconds, then perhaps she would have done something noble. But to shut down her range only to Muslims, using the flimsy rationale that Muslims as a whole adhered to a death-cult agenda, was disingenuous at best. To argue, as did she, and as did the National Rifle Association and its supporters in Congress and in statehouses around the United States, that automatic weaponry's easy availability made the country safer—except when it came to Muslims (in November 2015, one Texas legislator, who was an outspoken supporter of the NRA, argued that Texas couldn't accept Syrian refugees because it was so easy to buy guns there)—was to ignore the horrifying scale of American gun violence.

It has never been so easy to own guns in America, or to own such powerful guns, as it is in the early twenty-first century. There has never been another time where so much political effort has gone into creating a permanently armed citizenry. And there has never been a period in US history where mass shootings have been more common. Total up all the gun deaths—from mass shootings, attacks on individuals, suicides, and accidents—and you find that every couple years roughly as many Americans are shot dead as the number of Japanese who died in the atomic bombing of Hiroshima.

Since 9/11, no community in Jan Morgan's home state of Arkansas had been the victim of a gun rampage carried out by Muslim extremists. Meanwhile, the state, with a population of just under three million, *had* had a huge number of shootings in the years since 2001: in the first decade of the century, the state saw more than four thousand gun deaths, and a homicide-by-gun rate 50 percent higher than the national average. In 2011, the Brady Campaign to Prevent Gun Violence scored Arkansas at 4 out of 100 points in the implementation of sensible measures aimed at reducing gun violence, and guns were exported from Arkansas and used in crimes elsewhere in the country at a far higher rate than was the case for guns bought in most other states.[18]

Arkansas also had the thirteenth-highest rate of gun deaths among children.[19] Not that the problem of children being killed by guns was limited to that state: in 2014, the research group Gun War News reported that nationally for every American soldier killed in Afghanistan over the previous eleven years, thirteen American kids had died as a result of being shot.[20]

Chapter Four

Egosyntonia

In 2013, I spent a considerable period of time interviewing so-called Doomsday Preppers in northern California. These were men and women convinced that a combination of economic collapse, ecological disasters, and a growing tide of both homegrown and externally inspired violence would, at some point in the not too distant future, kick out the pillars that prop up Western civilization. And they were determined to buck the trend, to survive the coming apocalypse through careful stockpiling of food, weapons, water, and medicines. For many of them, that quest had become all-consuming, influencing every decision they made and every dollar they spent. Their present realities were, to an extraordinary degree, shaped by fears they had about how the future would unfold.

Economists generally believe that humans, sometimes subconsciously, sometimes quite deliberately, place a discount on the value of future events. They are less likely to modify their behavior to attain desirable outcomes that will only come into play many years or generations down the road.

Nobody wants, for example, the waters of a warming planet to submerge great coastal cities, but so long as those epic floods are thought of as being something that will affect people long in the future, long after this current generation has died off, on a daily basis we don't tend to change our behaviors very much. The convenience cost of driving less today, or eating less beef, or traveling less far for our vacations is seen as outweighing the potential benefits to a future generation of limiting climate change. We empathize less with those not yet born and not likely to be born during our lifetimes, or, alternatively, we think that the space between today and an undefined distant future will be filled by technological advances that will neutralize the problem of accumulating greenhouse gas emissions.

And so we postpone necessary lifestyle changes that, rationally, we ought to embark upon now so as to avoid far larger dislocations for us and our descendants later on. The closer that undefined future becomes to today, however, the more we respond forcefully to perceived disaster. When climate change ceases to be abstract, when we see in increased intensity hurricanes and typhoons, droughts and urban floods the early warning signs of chaos, when we realize that we, or certainly our children, will be directly affected by such events, then that discount rate declines. In other words, we start to value the near future almost as much as we do the present. And only then, at the eleventh hour, does our collective behavior gradually start to change. By that point, of course, the cost of reversing course is far higher than it would have been had we, as a community, gotten our act together to tackle this problem earlier.

In July 2014, the Executive Office of the President of the United States released a report exploring the costs of delaying action on climate change. Its experts concluded that if international action could not be implemented in time to limit human-made climate change to a global temperature increase of 2 degrees Fahrenheit the costs would be enormous, and ongoing. If temperatures were stabilized at a 3-degree increase, it would lead to annual costs that equaled 0.9 percent of global output, a cost to the United States alone of $150 billion per year. In an era of budget woes and a growing national deficit, that's a huge amount of cash, a sum that is not far off one quarter of the entire annual Medicare budget. And the prognosis only got worse from there on in: "The next degree increase," the authors wrote, "from 3° to 4° would incur *additional* annual costs of approximately 1.2 percent of global output. These costs are not one-time: they are incurred year after year because of the permanent damage caused by additional climate change resulting from the delay."[1] Ignore climate change of that magnitude, and we set ourselves up for possible civilizational catastrophe.

THAT WE TEND TO procrastinate when it comes to tackling big-picture risks that necessitate significant lifestyle and policy changes is a bad thing—since it prevents us, as a community, from taking concrete steps, far in advance, to avert massive, and extremely expensive, problems down the road. And it also limits our abilities to focus on well-documented, confirmed risks instead of manufactured, phony crises.

But, the opposite, Doomsday Prepping, embraced by increasing numbers of Americans, is also a bad thing. For the Prepping culture acknowledges, indeed exaggerates, future risks, yet it responds not with programmatic policy suggestions but instead by molding current behavior in ways not likely to prevent those problems from becoming a reality in the future. It encourages people to turn in on themselves, to isolate themselves and their small group of family and friends from the

broader community, to save themselves even as the rest of the
world goes to hell in a handbasket. To find high ground as a
heated earth raises sea levels; to stock up on canned goods as
climate-change-induced droughts threaten the food supply.

It is commonplace to say that one can only truly understand a person if one knows that person's past. With the
Preppers, however, something else holds. One can only truly
understand them if one can grab a glimpse of the future they
believe awaits them. For the Preppers, something approximat-
ing an inversion of discount-rate psychology occurs. Obsessed
by potential, often undefined disasters on the road ahead, they
modify their current behavior more than can be rationally justi-
fied. They discount the present, and frequently either ignore or
inflate data about current risks, so as to mollify the gods of fate
standing guard over our collective tomorrows.

When people are afraid of imminent scarcity, or of rapid
and unpredictable change, Yaacov Trope, an expert on social
psychology at New York University, believed, "they get into a
fear mode. They become more competitive and cling to their
own kind. More and more, in the last decade or two, there is
this sense that resources are scarce, that there's not enough for
everybody—there's a sense of 'I may lose stuff.' That produces a
sense of the present and not being open to the future. Scarcity
narrows your perspective. It creates a sense of being defensive.
Fear specializes in proximity. Fear is the way we orient to now.
It masks the future. It blinds us to the future. So we are easily
tilted away from our agenda by fear."[2]

I MET MY FIRST group of local Preppers, the Sacramento Emergency Preparedness Group, in the back room of a Raley's

supermarket in Roseville, its door adjacent to a display case of kids' stuffed animals. It seemed an unlikely stamping ground for a group of Sacramentans convinced that the end-of-all-things-familiar was nigh.

In a small room with rows of Formica tables, a white board, a Stars and Stripes flag resting at a 45-degree angle, and a small JVC television screwed into the top left corner, just over a dozen local survivalists convened to share anecdotes and tips about how to survive economic collapse, ecological catastrophe, asteroid hits, polar shifts, terrorism strikes, and government ineptitude.

They brought with them books such as *The Survival Handbook* and recommended YouTube links for everything from how to build a bunker to how to can one's own foods, from how to judge the speed with which a radioactive cloud will approach your town and inundate it with fallout to how to decontaminate a flooded building rendered lethal by the presence of mold spores.

Some of the self-described Preppers were ex-military; one was a retired postal worker; one a carpenter and dirt bike enthusiast; another a Mormon who explained to his fellow attendees about his religion's requirement to always keep a year's supply of food on hand. Edgy about being followed, put under surveillance, or monitored by agencies they do not trust, they asked that their last names not be used.

Who they were, however, was at least partially subsumed by who they were *not*. Unlike the survivalists I had interviewed in northern Michigan in the 1990s, shortly after the Oklahoma City bombing, these men and women were not militia. They weren't right-wing fanatics convinced that everything started going wrong when paper money replaced gold. That Social Security is an illegitimate Ponzi scheme. That a one-world government is busily enslaving them. They weren't arming themselves for a Waco-styled confrontation with the feds; nor were they interested in totally absenting themselves from the goings-on of the broader society. If bunkers entered their imagination, more often it was when they critiqued the architecture of the underground citadels built by reality TV survivalists than when they were building their own fortified caves. On the occasions when antigovernment ideologues, looking to fan the flames of violent insurrection, had tried to attend their meetings, the group members quietly dissuaded them from future visits. They told them, plain and simple, that they were trying to join a club that wasn't particularly interested in having them as members.

In fact, the core of the group was surprisingly ordinary. John M. was a millwright, a machinist, and his wife, Pat, to whom he had been married for twenty-four years, worked in a grocery store and fed stray neighborhood cats. Jeff was a carpenter-cum-handyman who dreamed of being dropped off in the High Sierra with a backpack and a tool kit for a week of man-against-nature adventures. And Rick was a retired army nurse. They were quintessentially suburban, but with a twist. Each, for their own reasons and in their own way, had come to believe that there was a not-insignificant chance that in the next few years there would be serious interruptions in the infrastructure that make possible our comfortable, technology-reliant daily lives. And each of them had decided to take their futures into their own hands as far as was humanly possible. For some, the catalyst toward this behavioral shift had come after witnessing the inadequate government agency responses to natural disasters—the Loma Prieta earthquake, Hurricanes Katrina and Sandy—and after seeing TV news footage of the chaos a large city faces when attacked by terrorists or bombarded by the forces of nature. For others it had come after witnessing the disruption caused by the 2008 financial collapse. Some, perhaps, had simply watched one reality show too many. After all, National Geographic's *Doomsday Preppers*, which first aired in September 2011, was a favorite in this crowd, as it was with Preppers around the country. In fact, it was the most-watched show in the channel's history.

The intent of the Sacramento Preppers who congregated at the Roseville supermarket wasn't to entirely absent themselves from society in the here and now, but rather to equip themselves with the skills and tools needed to survive should that society go temporarily offline. They wanted to be able to drink safe water should water-cleaning systems fail; to have food on hand should supermarkets shut; to have cell phones and laptops that work should power outages or massive power surges bring down grids or fry electronic circuit boards across a wide area. (Most of them had read national threat scenarios about how electronic gadgets across thousands of square miles would be fried should a nuclear bomb be exploded at high altitude over the country.) They wanted to be able to safely stay put in their homes, with barterable possessions on hand—rare coins, cigarettes, liquor, and so on—to exchange for vital commodities. Or, should the emergency be either more localized or more intense, should Sacramento become temporarily uninhabitable, to be able to "bug out" to a safe house somewhere in the countryside. To that end, John and his wife had bought some land up near Klamath Falls, Oregon.

"Observe, orient yourself to your surroundings. Where can you get help? Where are your supplies?" John M. asked his audience, as he took them through a military survival guide detailing seven priorities for navigating one's way safely through a crisis. "Food is the lowest of the seven priorities. Your need to eat is mostly mental. You can go a long time without food; healthy people can go without food for a week or more, so long as you're hydrated."

He had a clipped style, somewhere between that of a military officer—he spent years as an Air Force mechanic (a "maintenance technician," in the argot)—and a boy scout troop leader. Using definitive language rather than conditional verb tenses—talking about hypothetical events as if they had already happened or would definitely occur—he talked his audience through a range of scenarios that, progressively, ginned them up into a collective unease. When, for example, North Korea launches a nuke at San Francisco, the resulting radioactive cloud is going to be heading east and will take six hours to reach Sacramento. Head north or south to avoid it, he told his note-taking audience.

"The well-prepared may be threatened by those who weren't," John explained. "There is strength in numbers. People who are going to overpower you and take what you have are going to be very put off by those who look strong. Like all predators in nature, before you attack prey, you evaluate the risk to yourself." John referenced national threat scenarios; he talked about the economy, climate change, the fragility of infrastructure. His audience looked at him, rapt. For those few minutes, John M. was the biggest fish in the pond.

His was a story not of political extremism but of fear; not of fanaticism but of Boy-Scout-ism, perhaps back-to-the-land romanticism, writ large. Preparing for end-times is a sport that goes back thousands of years. Preparing for high-tech collapse, and using high-tech methods—fuel-efficient cars to maximize the distance one can flee, keeping laptops in antistatic bags to protect them from the pulses generated by nuclear detonations—to survive that collapse . . . well, that's more a product of our modern times.

"What are we really preparing for?" John asked. "If we're preparing for the end of the world, is it worth surviving? Are we preparing for the zombie apocalypse? Or are we preparing for a temporary situation? We're not extreme Preppers. We're not the local militia."

Many of the Preppers spent hours each day online researching survival techniques, looking at YouTube videos to learn how to can food and purify water. They looked up places to buy solar-operated phone chargers and hand-cranked vegetable-peeling machines, in case the electric grid goes down, pet stores from which they could secure supplies of antibiotics without prescriptions, methods of field dressing deer they had recently killed for food.

Some viewed prepping as a social enterprise, a way of securing a small community of friends in the event of disaster; others were, by temperament, more solitary in their prepping rituals. Jeff B., for example, had the survival ethos of the lone wolf. Fifty years old, with a buzz cut of red hair and a long goatee trimmed to a point, a green tattoo of a dagger cutting through a snake on his left forearm, and thin, plastic-framed spectacles over his eyes, Jeff cut an imposing figure. "I've always been a Prepper, since Boy Scouts," he explained. "I've always loved camping, hiking. When my kids got cars, we prepared survival bags for them. When I was in the army, in Alaska, we always had survival bags in our cars." Come summer, he took groups of fellow survival aficionados on backcountry camping expeditions.

Perhaps as a legacy from his Alaska days, traversing the vast wilderness with only the bare necessities for survival, Jeff liked to travel light. "If people want to learn how to fortify their house, pack ten thousand pounds of food, build a bomb shelter, we can teach them that. But I'm more into gardening, solar kitchen, solar ovens. It pushes away less people if we don't show up with M-16s, camos, preparing for the doomsday."

If crunch time came, however, Jeff was ready to bug out fast, to head out into the Nevada desert, to the little town of Silver Springs, with his food supplies and water purification systems. "'Bug out' is pack your bags, change your lifestyle the way it is, and move to somewhere totally different. The place we want to move has 2,500 people, one stop sign." He paused, and shifted a gear. He became, in that shift, a lapsarian, a quester for lost innocence. "I keep telling my wife, 'I'm closer to Burning Man.' When I was young, I was that rebel type, curly hair, long beard, earring. Then we had kids, and I had to be civilized. Now all the kids are gone."

And so, as he started to age, Jeff was using his doomsday prepping fantasies to recalibrate his life. "I'm raising worms for composting. I eat my own apples. They're my babies." He stopped, then resumed in a sarcastic dialogue with himself. "'You're turning into a hippie.' Maybe I'm just turning into the person I was before."

SIXTY-SIX-YEAR-OLD RICK T. AND his wife lived deep in West Sacramento suburbia. They had three kids and seven grandchildren. They had a pet dog. Their home was heavily carpeted, their kitchen spotless. Look inside, and one saw serenity. But scratch beneath the surface, and one encountered a worldview bedeviled by anxiety.

In the early 1990s, Rick retired from his job as an Air Force nurse. Several years later one of his daughters gave him a book titled *How to Survive the End of the World as We Know It*. It "scared the tar" out of him. He began reading more, became convinced that there was a strong possibility of the government temporarily ceasing to function at some point, and started hoarding food and water. He commenced buying thousands of dollars worth of military MREs—ready-to-eat, vacuum-sealed meals—water purification systems, tools, knives, axes, tents, and guns. He kept "bug-out" bags for himself and his wife packed and ready to go.

Rick also bought two enormous Liberty safes, with heavy metal lock mechanisms that had to be spun to the right numbers to open—one to safely store his weapons, the other for his ammo, which he stockpiled because he feared that in the event of an economic collapse there wouldn't be stores in which to buy bullets for his guns. He convinced his wife to start target practice sessions at a local shooting range. The lungs, heart, head are "definite kill" areas, he explained with something more than a touch of bravado, a slight lisp accentuating his words. There was a "bring-it-on" quality to his language when he talked about his guns. *Just you try to steal my food*, was the subtext. *Make my day.*

After a while, one of the spare rooms in Rick's home became filled, carpeted floor to ceiling, with his emergency preparation supplies and gear. Out of self-interest (there is safety in numbers), he concluded that his best bet of surviving the apocalypse was to have enough food on hand to feed much of his cul-de-sac for a year. In exchange for food, his neighbors would pull guard duty, pump water, do whatever needed to be done for their community to make it through the chaos intact. And so he searched the Internet, looking for the best vacuum-packed food bargains. He bought vast amounts of canned goods as well, carefully labeled them with the date of purchase, stored them with the methodical sense of order that makes for a good librarian, and, every few months, when the end didn't come, as the use-by date approached he rotated the old food out, gave the cans to local food banks, and bought more food to update his cache.

"I prep for *possibilities*," Rick explained. "And I live for *probabilities*. I prep on everything—the possibility of an EMP [electro magnetic pulse] taking out the whole country. Two or three taking out all the electronics. There's no transportation, electricity, water pumps. It puts you back to the early 1800s. Wagon trains, what you see in Westerns. Then I go to probabilities—the most likely thing to happen is a flood. We have levies all the way around." He compared his behavior to that of a person buying a lottery ticket—knowing the probability of winning is small, but recognizing the possibility is always there. We don't buy lottery tickets because we expect to win, but because there's a small chance we might—and we'd feel awfully silly if that dollar saved ended up costing us tens of millions of dollars in lost winnings. It's the same with prepping. Rick didn't wake up each morning expecting the onset of the apocalypse, but he believed that there was enough of a chance of disaster upending the comforts of his life to make preparation a rational, relatively pain-free lifestyle choice.

In retirement, Rick spent much of his time reading about complexity theory, trying to understand the interplay between all the events that, cumulatively, make up our lives. How would failure in one part of this system affect basic services in another part? How would an attack or ecological disaster in one region ricochet outward in its impact? How would institutional collapse in, say, the financial sector, affect food availability or water safety or the ability to police communities?

One could go insane endlessly studying the potential for catastrophe. But Rick seemed, instead, to find it empowering. "I don't have nightmares as far as what ifs," he said. "[With] both my military training and my prepping, I should be able to get by."

AT THE END OF the day, the Doomsday Preppers were trying to find their own community, to make themselves feel indispensable. "I would not let anybody go hungry," explained John's wife, Pat, as she discussed what she'd do post-catastrophe. "I can't. I'm a feeder." It's a quintessentially human, existential yearning. The Preppers were readying themselves for situations so scary to most of us that we tend to discount the possibility of their occurring, and they were doing so, at least in part, to make themselves matter. "I just want to be one they would choose," a short, aging woman with salt-and-pepper hair, said, explaining her desire to be useful to others in the event of an emergency. "'I want that nurse, that fireman, that wood-chop guy. And I want *her*.'"

We buy life insurance and fire insurance; in our trunks we carry spare tires for our cars, explained Jeff B. So why not also keep on hand "a survival bag, a blanket, flashlight, gallon of water in the car? A lot of people are Preppers. They just don't realize it."

It was a strange philosophy, a disconcerting stew of deep pessimism—*the world is about to go to hell in a handbasket*—and naïve optimism—*but I'll be able to survive when it does*. Somehow, it fit perfectly with the aging of the Baby Boomers, a generation that had spent the previous half century carving out its own identity, searching for its own meaning in life, using technology evermore creatively to make itself stand out from the crowd.

Every so often, Jeff watched *Doomsday Preppers* on his TV. The men and women on the show scared him a little. "One person on there had a missile silo; he wanted someone to share it with. This desperate weirdo looking for someone to climb into the silo with him." One can download Doomsday Prepper apps onto mobile phones, the purpose of which is to play a game with other users, a competition to see who can design the best bunkers and equip them in the most survivor-friendly way possible. Jeff's wasn't there yet. "Maybe five years from now I could get there," he said, laughing, as he drank an iced coffee concoction in the courtyard of a downtown Sacramento Starbucks. In the meanwhile, he'd rather grow his own food and spend a week in the mountains once in a while testing his own limits. If he ever got to the point of building a bomb shelter, it would be more a way to carve out his own territory than to protect himself from the North Koreans. "I think it'd be cool to have a bomb shelter. It's a big man-cave, a big hole in the ground."

THERE IS, I BELIEVE, a little bit of the Doomsday Prepper in all of us. We don't have to be right-wing zealots to fear that the walls that hold up our reality will one day come tumbling down, even without really agreeing on what will cause that cataclysm.

Take, for example, parents who read rumors on the Internet that vaccines might be linked to autism and thus refuse to have their children inoculated for diseases such as measles, diphtheria, and pertussis (more commonly known as whooping cough).

Since the inception of mass-vaccination campaigns in the nineteenth century, every so often a public panic has set in against one or another vaccine program. Early advocates of the smallpox vaccine were ridiculed and attacked by skeptics.

Some believed that diseases were sent by God as punishment for human sins, and that any attempt to inoculate against them was an affront against divine authority. Others feared the vaccines would hurt young children. Still others resisted compulsory vaccination programs for political reasons, fearing the intrusion of the state into intimate family decision making. In England, in the nineteenth century, thousands of families were fined for resisting the smallpox vaccine. In the United States, from 1879 onward, antivaccine campaigners coalesced into the Anti-Vaccination Society of America and also, a few years later, the Anti-Compulsory Vaccination League.

In our era, the panic was triggered by Andrew Wakefield, a British gastroenterologist who in 1998 published a research paper in the prestigious *Lancet* journal claiming to have found a link between the measles, mumps, and rubella (MMR) vaccine and the sudden emergence of autism and bowel disease in previously healthy children. On both sides of the Atlantic, Wakefield's work set off a storm of hostility to vaccinations. The only problem? It turned out that the good doctor had fabricated much of his data. Wakefield was ultimately barred from practicing medicine, and the *Lancet* retracted the article, with the editor in chief denouncing Wakefield's work as "utterly false."[3] Between 2003 and 2015, the Centers for Disease Control funded nine large-scale studies investigating the purported vaccine-autism link. No such link was found.

Yet the suspicions Wakefield unleashed have proven harder to contain. When I contacted a group called Vaccination Liberation, hoping to line up an interview on antivaccination theories, I received back a list of questionnaires and reports that represented a smorgasbord of conspiracy thinking. "Are you dangerously stuck in the matrix?" was the title of one of the group's

questionnaires, which came complete with a set of "true" answers. Ostensibly designed to contextualize the antivaccine ideology, it argued that the fluoride put into drinking water was
"toxic waste"; that the US Constitution ceased to be the law of
the land in 1933, when "Federal Reserve bankers bankrupted the
'federal government'"; that "the media in America was captured
by the Robber Barons back in 1917 via the Council of Foreign
Relations"; and that the visible trails of heated air created behind jet planes are, in fact, "part of a covert geoengineering/
weather control program."⁴ All of this might be funny—clichéd
conspiracism—were it not for the fact that the VacLib woman
who emailed me this from her headquarters in rural Idaho also
emailed me a set of questions that she wanted me to answer
before talking to me, all of them clearly intended to steer participants toward a conspiracy-based understanding of vaccines.
"Do you believe that injections of pus from cowpox pustules led
to the eradication of smallpox?" "Do you believe that polio has
been eradicated due to vaccines?" And so on. In case correspon-
dents weren't sure which way to answer these questions, under
her email signature was the slogan "Free Your Mind . . . From
the Vaccine Paradigm."

Less than 1 percent of children are unvaccinated for the
common, and preventable, childhood diseases in the United
States, but those children tend to live in clusters, their families either responding to religious sentiments against vaccines
in the communities in which they reside or to political and cultural discomfort with vaccinations. Like-minded people often
group with each other. And so, rather than a random distribution of nonvaccinated children nationally, they are found in
particularly large numbers in certain regions of California, Oregon, Washington, New Hampshire, New York, Pennsylvania,

Minnesota, and a few other states, making those communities particularly vulnerable to disease outbreaks. In some states, at the height of the antivaccine craze as many as 5 percent of children weren't being inoculated.

"It's risk perception combined with the fear factor. A real gut fear, your body being invaded by a needle. It's personal," argued Catherine Martin of the California Immunization Coalition, as she sipped an iced tea at an outdoor café across from the California Capitol building in Sacramento. A year earlier, the Coalition, along with the California Medical Association, the American Academy of Pediatrics, and other scientific groups, had gone to bat on behalf of SB277, a state bill to require all families to vaccinate their children unless those children had a medical condition that made it unsafe for them to receive vaccines. If parents refused to vaccinate, the kids would no longer be allowed into public or private schools in the state. The bill, which eventually passed and was signed into law by Governor Brown, had been very controversial, and Martin, suntanned, wearing a short polka-dot dress in the California sun, her long, wavy brown hair falling over her shoulders, still recalled the huge numbers of opponents who came into town to argue their point in the halls and offices and hearing rooms of the Capitol. The antivaccine movement had, after a while, begun to grate on Martin. "It's a lot of conspiracy. 'Make it up and say it.'" She distrusted the anecdote-driven pseudo-science behind the movement and also the "parental choice" arguments. After all, she said, laughing, we don't give drivers a choice as to whether or not to obey the speed limit, because we know that if people can drive at a hundred miles an hour down a residential street, there will at some point be casualties. The same held, she believed, for choosing to leave one's children exposed to potentially lethal diseases.[5]

Unvaccinated children, argued Amy Pisani, the long-time executive director of the pro-vaccine organization Every Child By Two (ECBT), are thirty times more likely to come down with measles during an outbreak than are vaccinated kids.[6] If they are not protected against pertussis, the risk factor for whooping cough increases eightfold. These are potentially deadly diseases, spread quickly both within families and into the broader community. When outbreaks occur—as one did with measles in 2015, after an infected child visited Disneyland in California and spread the germs to other visitors; soon afterwards dozens of measles cases were reported in several states around the country—unvaccinated children are peculiarly vulnerable. Just as importantly, when a critical number of children in a given area aren't vaccinated, what doctors term "herd immunity"— the general resilience within a community to a disease, based on the overwhelming numbers of immunized individuals acting as a firewall against its spread—begins to break down, and the risk of epidemic increases. With a highly contagious disease such as measles, you need upwards of 96 percent of the population vaccinated to ensure this herd immunity. Once you head much south of that number, you risk large outbreaks of the potentially deadly virus.

The World Health Organization estimates that each year, around the world, up to 3 million children avoid death from diseases such as diphtheria, tetanus, whooping cough, and measles simply because they have been vaccinated. Yet another 1.5 million children, unvaccinated, still die from these diseases.[7] Most of these kids are in poor countries with dilapidated public health systems. Their parents, one can only assume, would give pretty much anything to have had access to medical services that would have helped protect their children from the diseases that ended up killing them. Yet some are from wealthy countries, such as the United States and the United Kingdom, with massive vaccination efforts in place. They die not because of shortages of vaccine sera, or trained nurses who can deliver the vaccination, but because their parents have bought into Wakefield's antivaccine narratives that argue, without providing scientific proof, the sera are linked to children developing autism.

Misunderstanding risk comes with societal consequences. If I read a debunked report about the extreme dangers of immunizing my children, and I don't realize that the science is faulty, I might jump to the erroneous conclusion that inoculating my children is as dangerous as playing chicken with them on the highway. And so I refuse to have them immunized. As long as all the other kids in my neighborhood are still vaccinated, it's fairly likely my kids will be okay; they will be free riders in an overwhelmingly immunized society. But if I don't vaccinate my children, and if my neighbors, on my advice, also don't vaccinate theirs, and if clusters of unvaccinated kids start to show up all around town, at some point, as happened with the unvaccinated children who visited Disneyland, there will be a measles, or polio, or whooping cough, or diphtheria outbreak, and there's a pretty good chance that a lot of kids will end up very sick, and some of those kids will die.

The same holds for the recently perfected vaccine against Human Papillomavirus (HPV). HPV is an extremely common sexually transmitted disease, and it is known to trigger cervical cancer, which kills upwards of a quarter million women globally each year, as well as penis cancer and several other cancers. It's not that every woman who is infected with HPV will subsequently develop cervical cancer; in fact, most won't. Rather, it's that without having been infected with HPV a person will not develop cervical cancer. It's a necessary precursor to the more serious disease, and thus preventing its transmission is, from a public health standpoint, a very good idea.

Since most everyone has sex at some point in their lives, it ought to be a no-brainer that as children approach adolescence they are given this potentially life-saving vaccine. But, as with most things sex-related, an awful lot of parents get awfully squeamish and kick up all kinds of fuss about having their kids vaccinated. Some argue, despite the lack of research evidence backing up the claim, that simply having children vaccinated against HPV will make them more likely to engage in promiscuous sexual activity. Others cherry-pick information from the Internet, much of it bizarre in the extreme, to bolster their reluctance to vaccinate. "We have a cancer vaccine, and they're delaying it for their children," Pisani said, her voice conveying bemusement more than anger. "Why? Because of these crazy notions they get on the Internet. One report said a woman got the HPV vaccine and could only walk backwards afterwards.[8] She was a famous cheerleader, so it went all over. Another story said a woman could only talk French afterwards. It's so irrational."

WE ALL HAVE OUR particular set of irrational fears, be they of exotic diseases or of everyday vaccines—and usually we can find ample examples online, on TV, on the radio, or in the newspapers to add fuel to the fire of our specific terrors. So, too, many of us experience, at one time or another, a pervasive, nonspecific sense of dread, a sensation of everything going off of the rails. Through a selective reading of the world around us—a substitution of anecdote for big-picture data—and an evermore pervasive and sensationalist mass media that feeds off of our fears and our anxieties, we can create echo chambers within which our nightmares reverberate.

I'm far more scared of air turbulence when I fly than I am of slippery roads when I drive, despite the fact that road travel is, by an order of magnitude, a more risky proposition than is flight. In the ten years leading up to the writing of this sentence, more than 400,000 vehicular passengers and drivers died in crashes on US roads,[9] and roughly another 45,000 pedestrians were killed.[10] Meanwhile from 1945 through 2013, the total number of civil aviation fatalities in the United States, spread over 760 accidents, was 10,505.[11] In 2015, after seven consecutive years in which the number of road fatalities declined, car crash deaths in America increased by more than 8 percent compared to the previous year,[12] as more and more drivers engaged in "distracting" behavior such as texting. Thirty-eight thousand Americans died that year on the road, nearly four times more than the total number of Americans killed in plane crashes in the *seventy years* following the end of the Second World War.

In other countries the discrepancy is even greater: in China, according to the Bloomberg Global Road Safety Program, 230,000 people die on the roads each year; in India close to 200,000; in Brazil 35,000; in Egypt 31,000.[13] Taken as a whole, globally 1.3 million people die annually in road accidents. That's more than nine Hiroshimas each year. By contrast, according to data compiled by the Aviation Safety Network, in the entire history of civil aviation the most number of people to have died in plane crashes in any single year is 2,373. And that's a global total, not the tally from any one country.[14] In many years, air fatalities add up to a mere fraction of that number.

And yet, despite the unambiguous nature of these numbers, far more people are terrified of flying than of driving, and thriving businesses have emerged in recent years specifically to treat people for their aviophobias and to provide them with mental tools that allow them to at least temporarily circumvent their terror so as to board aircraft. The National Institute for Mental Health estimated, in 2013, that fully 6.5 percent of Americans exhibit signs of this particular phobia. Other reports have found as many as one in four Americans are at least somewhat scared of flying.[15] Phobic fliers pop Ativan, Valium, and Xanax before flights. Frequent fliers with phobias take beta-blockers on a regular basis. Some pay top dollar for cognitive behavior therapy to reduce their fears. There are exposure therapy courses in which patients do everything from drawing pictures of airplanes to walking near planes, all to gradually modify their fears. Ultimately, when they are ready to handle it, they are taken on air trips to put their anxieties to rest. These days, there are even virtual reality therapy sessions involving simulated flights.

By contrast, the blandly named "vehophobia," or fear of driving, ranks only twenty-eighth on global fear lists, nine spots behind aphenphosmphobia—the fear of being loved or touched; thirteen behind ornithophobia—the fear of birds; and a whopping eighteen places behind trypophobia—the fear of holes.[16]

Despite all the focus on aviophobia, however, in fact on any given day a person flying has a far greater likelihood of being killed or maimed in a car crash on the way to or from an airport than of dying during the flight itself.

Post-9/11, when millions of Americans temporarily stopped flying and took to the roads instead, road fatalities spiked sharply upwards—for the somewhat obvious reason that, faced with events that were so extraordinary they overwhelmed our normal risk-calculating apparatus, people shifted from a form of transport that, historically, had actually been pretty safe to a method of getting from one place to another that, over the past century, has proven year in, year out to be notoriously risky. In the year following September 11, 2001, according to the calculations of Gerd Gigerenzer, a psychologist at Berlin's Max Planck Institute, 1,595 more Americans died in car crashes than would have been the case had there not been a stampede away from air travel and onto the roads.[17]

Air travel isn't the only thing where my intellect and my emotions aren't in synch when it comes to calculating risk. Thunderstorms fill me with a sense of impending doom, even though I don't know anyone who has ever been hit by lightning—though I read that, for meteorological reasons that remain obscure to me, there *are* actually fairly large numbers of people killed by lightening each year in India and in Bangladesh, two countries that I do not live anywhere near. But swimming pools, in which people who live in the sort of neighborhood in which I reside *do* frequently drown—the CDC estimates that on average more than 3,500 Americans drown each year, and that drowning accounts for more toddler deaths than anything other than birth defects[18]—have never generated that sort of sensation in me. During the ebola outbreak of 2014, I read every news article on the disease obsessively, fearfully, though one small part of my brain was well aware that I was more likely to die of a mundane condition such as the flu or pneumonia—the Centers for Disease Control and Prevention reports that more than 56,000 Americans died of the flu in 2013[19]—and certainly more likely to die of a heart attack or of cancer than of an exotic B-movie horror show of a virus like ebola.

When a crowded rush-hour underground train, with standing commuters jammed together like sardines, stops for longer than normal in a tunnel, I have to control my racing heart, to stamp out the urge to panic. But when a more empty train sits in that same tunnel for the same amount of time, I just relax deeper into my seat and continue reading my book, unflustered and serene. The objective risk of asphyxiation or being buried alive or being left stranded far from light is the same—but for some reason my calibration of fear and risk doesn't produce the same results each time around.

I can't imagine living in Tornado Alley, yet I quite happily park myself in California, a state atop some of the most active earthquake fault lines on earth. And, on a daily basis, that threat of the earth shaking and my surroundings crumbling doesn't preoccupy me. Take me on a drive through Oklahoma or Nebraska in the spring or early summer, however, and every thunderhead sets my nerves jangling.

It's possible that I am simply particularly prone to fear manipulation, but on balance I don't think that's the case. In fact, given the amount of data I have access to through my journalism work, and given my awareness of the issue, in all likelihood I am *less* prone to exaggerate certain forms of fear than are most people who don't spend their days working on books such as this one. I have my fears, but I also have enough information to know when I need to rein those fears in.

Yes, I was terrified of ebola during the panic of the fall of 2014. But I wasn't as scared as the 5 percent of respondents who told a Fox News poll that they had changed their travel plans because of the hemorrhagic fever outbreak.[20] Since it's more than a stretch that 5 percent of American travelers that year were planning to go anywhere near Liberia, Sierra Leone, or Guinea, the three countries at the center of the medical calamity, presumably most of these people were canceling trips to places nowhere near the hot zone. Nor was I as petrified of the disease as the 5 percent of respondents who told Gallup, in October 2014, that ebola was now the single most important problem facing America.[21] At the time, you could count on one hand the number of ebola patients in the United States. By contrast, only 3 percent of those polled listed poverty/hunger/homelessness as the country's most urgent problem—despite the fact that roughly one in six Americans were living below the poverty line and on any given days tens of millions of families were struggling just to feed, clothe, and house themselves.

I also wasn't as caught up in the hysteria as the parent of a kindergartner at my local elementary school, who demanded that a Sudanese child be withdrawn from the school simply because he was African and had recently visited Sudan—apparently not realizing that Sudan was about as far from the epicenter of the ebola epidemic as, say, London. And I certainly wasn't as scared as the people who argued that Western public health workers who came down with ebola while working with patients in Liberia and other epicenters of the killer disease ought not to be allowed back into their home countries for treatment. "The U.S. cannot allow EBOLA infected people back. People that go to far away places to help out are great—but must suffer the consequences!" Donald Trump tweeted on August 1, 2014. It was a brutal proposal that, if implemented, would surely have guaranteed that fewer doctors, nurses, and health educators would have ventured into the eye of the storm, and that the epidemic would have raged out of control for far longer. Ultimately, if those with expertise were scared off of traveling into the ebola zone, the likelihood of the epidemic acquiring such momentum that it could no longer be geographically contained would, paradoxically, have greatly increased.

And it goes without saying that, being a child of the *Jaws* era, I get a slight frisson whenever I swim in the ocean. I can hear the soundtrack, the drumbeat of approaching horror, and

I can imagine that awful fin poking up out of the swell and the grotesque creature with the deadly teeth under the surface. But, unlike the nearly 40 percent of Americans who report being scared to swim in oceans because of sharks,[22] I have never thought it more likely that I would actually be chomped on by a Great White than, say, felled by a melanoma—which, in recent years, has been killing somewhere in the region of nine thousand Americans annually[23]—as a consequence of spending too much of my beach time sunbathing. And yet I can understand all too well the feelings behind the comment that a friend of mine made when we started talking about perceptions of risk over lunch one day. "As a child growing up, I would not swim in lakes if I could not see the bottom: I was scared of sharks. But I'd ride my bike all over town without a helmet. And I loved riding in the back of a pickup truck. And I went hiking all the time where there were rattlesnakes and mountain lions." (I did not point out to her that almost all sharks live in salt water, not in lakes.)

Intellectually, I know when my internal risk sensors are off, when I am becoming too fearful about things that, in reality, ought not to be my biggest, most immediate concerns. Yet, emotionally, however much knowledge I bring to the table, at the end of the day it's often hard to separate out real, pervasive threats from more illusory ones. In terms of our emotions, like it or not, sharks and airplanes and hemorrhagic fevers will always trump flu bugs, cars, swimming pools, and disease-carrying ticks.

IT TURNS OUT THAT pretty bizarre understandings of risk and fear are the norm rather than the exception. It takes a continuous effort to even remotely calibrate scales of risk correctly. And this has huge effects on how we live, how we allocate resources, and how we interact with others. For if we can't work out ways to contain our internal Doomsday Prepping impulses, if we let our fears run amok, be they of particular diseases or particular groups of people, the end results can be utterly destructive of civic society. As with the unvaccinated children and the spread of measles, if critical numbers of people fall prey to certain fears we can end up with the cultural equivalent of an epidemic. Panics around school safety, say; or about the risk posed to civic peace by immigrants; or about the dangers bubbling up out of the inner city. When we compete with each other as to which of our fears is more worthy of attention and of resources, we spiral into a black hole, into a place of crushing anxieties. It's hard to think about creating a better future if you're being pushed down onto your knees by the burdens of a present that you perceive to be filled with miscellaneous terrors.

What psychologists term "the experiential system" of risk assessment is, wrote risk expert Paul Slovic and three of his colleagues in their 2004 essay "Risk as Analysis and Risk as Feelings," "intuitive, fast, mostly automatic, and not very accessible to conscious awareness."[24] Our neural networks are wired to recognize perceived dangers at extraordinary speed, and to set off bodily responses that channel blood, oxygen, and fear-response chemicals into different parts of the body almost instantaneously. When our internal alarm bells start ringing, we send out emergency response teams, decked out in glucose, cortisol, and other powerful chemical concoctions, without waiting around to work out exactly what the contours of the problem are first.

The evolutionary benefits of such a process of constructing understandings of, and responses to, risk, are obvious: taking

shortcuts allows us to act very fast and with great certainty, saving for later the hemming and hawing that accompanies rational,
analytical, thought. It allows us to gauge danger in a broad-
brush kind of way. There's nothing particularly subtle about such
a measure of risk, but over the eons it has been a remarkably
important tool for survival within the animal world. And it allows children to develop a sense of independence, to be at least
partially able to navigate a world through acquiring some basic
notions of what, in their surroundings, is good and what is bad.

"It relies on images and associations, linked by experience
to emotion and affect (a feeling that something is good or bad),"
the authors continued. "This system represents risk as a feeling
that tells us whether it is safe to walk down this dark street or
drink this strange-smelling water."

What we fear grows out of these simple presentiments of
risk—learned early on in life and so hardwired in that they become essentially nonconscious reactions to certain stimuli. We
share this in common with every other animal species. It's akin
to muscle memory, allowing species to learn to flee, or to hide
from, particular predators, to avoid certain toxins, to beware of
particular smells and noises, and so on. We see what we think to
be a snake in the path ahead of us, and having learned through
experience and the warnings of others to be scared of snakes,
we immediately jump away from it without having to think
through our response. We do so, in many instances, without
even being at all consciously aware of what we are doing or why.
Even when, a split second later, we realize it was only a stick,
that sense of panic remains for a while, the adrenalin coursing
through our bodies, our heart beating faster, pumping oxygen
and blood to our muscles—so that they harden like protective
body armor—our every instinct primed for danger.

For more than a century, psychologists and neuroscientists have posited a range of theories as to how emotions such as fear are generated in humans. In the 1890s, William James and Carl Lange hypothesized that emotions are the result of, rather than the cause of, physiological responses: we know that if we see a large wild animal approaching us there's a good chance it's hungry and that we are its prey. And so we run. And in running, our bodies create the conditions that our brains interpret as "fear."

A century later, with brain imaging equipment now available to chart which parts of the brain are involved in different events, the neuroscientist Antonio Damasio came up with a more complex explanation. Called the Somatic Marker Hypothesis, this explored how a complex feedback system linked experience to emotions to decision making. We see, hear, feel, smell, or touch something that, when run through our brain's data processing centers, sets off warning systems. Those warnings then get processed through parts of the brain that are skilled at conjuring up, at speed, associations—this particular smell usually is linked to this particular toxin; the toxin generally results in this kind of pain or organ failure; and all of the pain produces emotions of fear, discomfort, helplessness, and so on—which, from experience, we can say don't feel good. Those associations, in turn, help us make decisions about what to do when confronted by a particular set of sensory data: if we want to avoid those bad feelings, we need to respond in a way likely to neutralize the threat represented by whatever it is that we initially perceived. In the blink of an eye, several distinct parts of the brain, including the ventromedial prefrontal cortex, somatosensory cortices, the insula, and the basal ganglia, all kick into gear to help us decide how to respond to a given situation.

If Damasio's ideas are correct, our emotional response systems are biologically indispensable to us as decision-making beings; take down, through injury or disease, the parts of the brain that process emotions, and you don't end up with a coldly calculating rational machine; instead you end up with a person often unable to make the most basic choices about how to respond to a given situation.[25]

In recent years, some neurologists have also detailed what they call the Polyvagal Theory. Although it's by no means universally accepted in the field, it does offer up interesting ideas about how fear affects bodily systems, exploring how impulses surge from the brain to the far corners of the body and then back to the brain again, via an extraordinarily complex neural circuitry centered around the vagus nerve. This nerve, the longest of the cranial nerves, stretches from the brain stem to the abdomen, via the heart, the lungs, the esophagus, and other critical parts of the body. The vagus nerve, according to the theory's proponents, creates a circuitry that links facial expression with the body's fight-flight-or-freeze response systems, creating an autonomic mechanism that integrates emotional and physical responses to certain stimuli. See a face that, when you lock eyes with it, looks dangerous, and without any conscious awareness of the process your body starts readying itself for battle. "Our nervous system gets biased towards negativity when we're in states of defense," explained Indiana University at Bloomington distinguished scientist Stephen Porges, the leading proponent of Polyvagal Theory. "If you make people scared, they will see negative when there's neutral there."[26]

But here's the thing: even though the extraordinarily rapid processes necessary for girding ourselves in response to threats are largely unconscious—that's something neuroscientists, no matter which particular theory they champion, generally agree on—they are still heavily influenced by broader cultural patterns. If you live in a calm environment, where you are part of a broader community, where you are nurtured by others and have a social support network to help you through the down times, the chances are that you will be calmer than if your environment is continually sending you danger signals: you'll breathe slower and digest your food better, and your body won't prep for conflict at the smallest provocation. There's a reason that meditative, contemplative communities, monasteries for example, promote calm environments—places of quiet, where people walk instead of run, whisper instead of shout, where distractions (be they electronic games or noisy washing machines) are discouraged. A community at peace with itself is far more likely to foster calm among the individuals who make up that community. And those calmer individuals will, in all likelihood, feel physically better than their ever-stressed peers in the communities existing outside of the monastic walls.

By contrast, if you grow up in troubled times, and enter adulthood in a tense, stressful, socially atomized environment, you're far more likely to experience an array of bodily woes that accompany an out-of-whack nervous system: you're more likely to suffer digestive problems, irritable bowel syndrome, high blood pressure, headaches, depression, and so on.

And it's not only a matter of being more predisposed to these physical ailments. It's also about the ability to think clearly, to navigate the thickets of complex social situations. As it turns out, we don't tend to do that terribly well when we are in a state of terror: activate our danger-response systems, and more blood than usual flows to muscles, at the expense of the gut and skin—which is why our intestines can spasm during moments of intense fright. Our pupils dilate, we salivate less, but our heartbeat increases—so as to send more blood more quickly to essential parts of the body's fear-response system. We tool up for war. Our bronchial passages dilate. Our rectums contract. And so on. None of which bodes well for our ability to calmly analyze events. Everything about our physical state in that instant becomes simply about survival.

In humans, the thinking species, our conscious minds respond to these feelings, but, at least as importantly, our bodies, as with those of other animals, primed by the brain's responses respond chemically. A part of the brain called the thalamus sends out first impressions to the amygdala, which runs the images through a database of stored memories of traumatic, fear-inducing situations to see if they match, then almost instantly forwards the message to other nonconscious parts of the brain, including the hippocampus. Our bodies start responding before the contemplative, conscious part of the brain—the neocortex, within which patterns produced out of sensory data are analyzed to allow us to create a sophisticated representation of the external world—is even aware that something unusual is unfolding. "We detect danger before we interpret data," Joseph LeDoux explained.[27] The brain has automatic responses to threat "because of what's going on under the hood—in the amygdala." A stress hormone called norepinephrine is unleashed, working in tandem with the neurotransmitter glutamate, which is a vital part of the brain's learning and memory-imprinting process. This combination etches fearful events into the memory folders of the hippocampus so that in future such events will automatically trigger the body's threat responses, which then in turn create conscious sensations of fear. The nonconscious danger alerts combined with the sensation of fear lead to the release of a surge of glucose, which gives the brain a shot of energy, and also vast amounts of cortisol, an adrenal steroid that regulates blood pressure, metabolism, immune, and anti-inflammatory responses, heart tone, and the functioning of the central nervous system. It also tamps down the production of oxytocin, a chemical that helps us build trust within a group, lowers anxiety levels, and facilitates calm interactions with others.

These days, scientists can slide test subjects into huge Magnetom MRI machines, or wire them for Transcranial Magnetic Stimulation, or use EEG technology to chart the electric impulses that signify active areas of the brain, and conduct experiments by showing them a series of images designed to stimulate certain responses. On their computer screens the researchers can watch, in real time, as cross-sectional images of the brain flash up. They can map out the different regions of the brain that are activated, that show increased flow of oxygenated blood, in response to different stimuli: the parts of the brain that kick in for different kinds of pattern recognition, or in response to different sorts of sensory cues, in response to images or words that represent happiness, in response to love, and in response to fear. In presentations, neuroscientists now talk, like early maritime explorers, of atlases of the brain, and even atlases of individual areas within the brain. They can look at what goes on in brains where specific regions, including the amygdala, have been damaged by injury or disease—what emotions or memory-recall functions or physical responses go AWOL minus, say, a functioning amygdala or hippocampus. The computers can, at speed, analyze oxygenated blood flow into different regions in the presence of different stimuli and identify which parts of the brain are being utilized in response to a variety of images and problem-solving tasks.

To a layperson, there's something miraculous about seeing these images, the coils and whorls, the delicate, almost floral or coral, arrangement of different parts of the brain. There, inside those few pounds of pink brain tissue, inside its beautiful, delicate structures, are the mysteries of the human experience. In those incredibly intricate neural networks are the structures that make possible all human emotion, all human culture, all human aspiration, all art, religion, music, language, math. Inside those coils are systems for calculating risk and measuring character at extraordinary speed—experiments have shown, time and again, that we can get a pretty good bead on a person's likability, intelligence, trustworthiness, and so on after seeing them in action and hearing them speak for less than the time it took you to read this sentence. There are systems in place for categorizing experiences and individuals, groups and places, sights, smells, tactile sensations, and myriad other variables. Inside those coils are stored references to things we have, as a species, learned over millennia: things to welcome and things to shy away from. Inside those coils are the instructions that keep our bodies functioning—from our heart beating to our lungs breathing, from the creations of enzymes and proteins through to the generation of vast numbers of chemicals needed to keep the organism alive and flourishing.

When I met Damian Stanley, he was running a series of brain imaging experiments in the basement labs of the Broad Center for Biological Sciences at Cal Tech, in the southern California town of Pasadena. Computational neuroscientists like him see the brain as an extraordinarily powerful computing machine—an organic supercomputer that is continually running probability estimates of events occurring or not occurring based on a continuously updated database of inputs. You might think you can't do the simplest math equation, but that's just the conscious you; look behind the scenes, and it turns out that even the most mathematically challenged of us are piggybacking off of unconscious mathematical powerhouses.[28]

Should we be scared of, say, a given person or smell or sound? Well, that depends on what inputs we have: on what past experiences we have of similar people or sights or smells, of what media images we store of these people or sights or smells, of how often bad things have followed on from their presence, or good things, or neutral things. Of what sorts of reactions our peers, or our political leaders, have to these stimuli. Will the cup of coffee we are sipping from burn us? Again, our ability to gauge risk in large part depends on our accessing past experiences: Have we been burned by coffee in the past? Were we burned by coffee sold us by this particular café that our current cup comes from? Was the lid sealed properly? And so on. We won't always get these calculations right, but, behind the scenes, the unconscious part of our brain is continually making probability estimates on the vast array of experiences we encounter daily. And it is continually updating those calculations based on new information, new data input, newly identified patterns. It is continually making new neural connections, new associative links, based on experience. Without these estimates, explained Stanley, a slightly rumpled, balding figure, with a trim beard, a dress code that runs to jeans and striped shirts, and a pair of small earring hoops in his left ear, we simply wouldn't be able to survive. At every turn, we'd have to stop and slowly, lugubriously ponder the myriad of possible options confronting us.

Much of the time, our brains work exactly as they are intended to, matching fear with real risk and giving us a vital chance to sidestep danger. But every so often the high-speed computations break down and produce what we might think of as "false positives." Taking shortcuts, we get things wrong. And if the thing we get wrong is an estimation of danger—perhaps in the aftermath of a massive shock to the system such as a highly visible terrorist attack, amplified by 24/7 media coverage, which, in introducing an utterly novel element into the mix, essentially scrambles the brain's ability to compute risk—the effects can be devastating. In such a situation, Stanley explained, it's likely that the brain decides, for survival purposes, to err massively on the side of caution, hugely overinflating the sense of risk until it can get an accurate bead on what's going on. Shock, said Stanley, "obliterates our expectations and increases the rate of uncertainty. If I don't know what's going to happen, then I really need to protect myself. [We] go into a very conservative, or preservative, mode."

Within milliseconds of the brain recognizing danger, without our being consciously aware of what is happening, it sends out a raft of signals essentially ordering the various parts of the body into action. Then, if that danger continues over minutes and hours, a secondary fear-response mechanism also kicks in: the pituitary gland triggers the brain to release waves of cortisol, which, over time, produces a sensation that we know as "stress."

In the short-term, stress helps an organism adapt to conditions of danger. In the long-term, however, if the conditions don't ease up, all of that cortisol starts affecting our memory, our energy levels, and, ultimately, even our immune responses. It becomes counterproductive: it makes us feel bad. And it adversely affects our decision-making process. It leads, Stephen Porges believed, to an "inability to feel other people's presence. Political movements of fearful people are very capable of hurting others if they don't see them as themselves. The inability to connect to other people results in the capacity of being able to kill someone else."[29]

When researchers at the University of Chicago deliberately raised test subjects' stress levels by immersing their arms in icy cold water for several minutes—a technique known to significantly raise a person's cortisol levels—before asking them questions, they found that as stress levels increased the ability to analyze a situation carefully by taking context into account diminished.[30]

Increasingly, recalled Jeni Kubota, who runs the Social Justice Neuroscience and Psychology Lab at the University of Chicago, the test subjects made what psychologists call a "fundamental attribution error."[31] Sitting in her office, wearing purple jeans and a horizontally striped black and white shirt, her hair braided back from her forehead, she explained how, essentially, they came to judge others' motives differently from how they judged their own. The classic example of such an error is how we judge ourselves and others differently regarding aggressive driving. *Why did I cut that person off?* Because I'm in a hurry, I have a legitimate need to get somewhere fast. *Why did that person I don't know just cut someone off?* Because he's a jerk. That the "jerk" could be trying to race a seriously ill person to the nearest emergency room doesn't cross our minds.

Kubota's researchers created a scenario in which test subjects encountered a situation involving a man with a crying baby in his arms who quickly leaves a restaurant without tipping the waitress. As stress levels increased, they found that their subjects' ability to fully contextualize a situation, to make the imaginative leap that the man might have been simply too harried because of his crying kid to remember to leave a tip, declined; instead, they took the easy option: he didn't leave a tip because he was an unpleasant human being. "Stress increased their negative evaluation of people," Kubota concluded. "If you stress people out, people are even more likely to ignore the context. The attribution error goes up under stress."

In a society permanently subject to stress-inducing imagery and rhetoric, the implications are huge. The images and the language physiologically affect us and in all likelihood render us as a society peculiarly vulnerable to political snake oil salesmen pitching easy us-against-them answers to complex problems.[32]

Sit in front of the television for hours at a stretch watching violent movies or catching the latest sensational local news stories, or continually check your smartphone or tablet for the latest doom-and-gloom headlines, and you'll not only start to feel like you're continually under threat, but likely as not your body will start responding as if it is really, really stressed. You are changing your physiology, creating long-term chemical and nervous conditions that evolved to help your ancestors flee hungry predators or avoid surging floodwaters but that don't necessarily work well in response to 24/7 if-it-bleeds-it-leads news cycles.

What's even more concerning is that you are not only altering your own chemical balance, but there's a growing body of evidence that suggests your elevated stress levels may actually pass down the generations. That how a person's genes express themselves can actually be affected, at speed, by environment was long dismissed as science fiction. Now, however, a growing number of epigeneticists argue just this point.

At the Icahn School of Medicine, at Mount Sinai Hospital in New York, Rachel Yehuda studied Holocaust survivors as well as their descendants. She found that the survivors themselves had low levels of an enzyme that breaks down cortisol. More cortisol in their bodies would have been a good thing in

an environment in which food was scarce and threats were omnipresent; as reported by journalist Tori Rodriguez in *Scientific
American*, it would have allowed "the liver and kidneys to maximize stores of glucose and metabolic fuels." The younger these
survivors were, the lower the levels of the enzyme they produced
later on in their adults lives and the higher their cortisol levels.[33]
Their descendants, by contrast, had lower levels of cortisol than
others in their community—and, since cortisol helps the body
return to a normal state after experiencing trauma, that then
likely predisposed them to anxiety disorders, up to and including post-traumatic stress disorder (PTSD). It also made them
more likely to become obese and to develop hypertension and
an array of other ailments.

Yehuda's team ultimately concluded that the low cortisol
levels in children of Holocaust survivors are due to the fact that
the pregnant mothers, lacking adequate supplies of the cortisol-
controlling enzyme, weren't sending enough enzyme to the
placenta to protect the fetus from the mother's cortisol. As a
protection response, the fetuses were then generating additional
supplies of their own enzyme. That worked well in utero, but
after birth it meant, Yehuda theorized, that the children now
had too much of the enzyme and, as a result, too little of their
own cortisol. What made sense as a bodily response to the extreme conditions experienced by one generation became counterproductive for the next generation.

Yehuda isn't alone in her findings. Other epigenetic research suggests that children born to survivors of the "hunger
winter" in the Netherlands during the last year of the Second
World War were more likely to develop diabetes, heart disease,
and other sicknesses than were their peers.[34] There is considerable evidence that people become more vulnerable to certain

respiratory diseases if they are exposed to an array of physically challenging environments early in life.[35] Scientists at Emory University in Atlanta, Georgia, have devised experiments that suggest that when mice are trained to fear certain smells—by associating those smells with electric shocks—they pass along that fear to their offspring.[36]

At the University of Notre Dame, psychology professor Darcia Narvaez has been exploring what happens to kids when they are exposed to increasingly stressful environments in infancy and early childhood—in, say, an environment where the parents are permanently on edge because of broad fears of terrorism or random violence, or so stressed about work and earning enough to put food on the table that they don't have time left over to engage with their children in nurturing play and other activities. "We create a brain that's very stress reactive," she concluded, explaining that human babies are born in a far more physically immature state than is the case for many other mammals, meaning that much of their critical brain development actually occurs *outside* of the womb. In an environment where the parents aren't able to properly nurture their kids, "the systems get off kilter, and stress responses kick in and shut off higher level thinking. We create personalities that almost have PTSD from very early in life. We learn to use rage to get our way, tantruming—the kind of thing that Donald Trump does."[37]

While cortisol is, Narvaez continued, a vital "mobilizing hormone," kicking into high gear emergency response systems that allow us to navigate danger and find ways to survive challenging circumstances, too much of it—like too much of anything else—is a bad thing. It becomes, she argued, "toxically stressful. It melts synapses that are supposed to be growing."

Fear, and the ways it interferes with the nurturing, creative environment that young children need, also has a direct impact on how brains grow into maturity. Keep a kid indoors all the time, say, using the iPad or television as a long-term babysitter, because you're scared that if you let them play outside with other kids, unsupervised by adults, they'll be kidnapped, and you may undermine the development of neural connections that help people think empathically and be able to view the world through other people's eyes.

In Narvaez's understanding, feedback loops of fear and coercive parenting styles end up stunting the development of young, plastic brains. If we all have something of a battle for supremacy going on inside of our heads between the tendency to regimented, detail-oriented, linear thought process and more free-flowing, artistic, creative processes, those feedback loops may help tip the balance toward the former. We become more rules-oriented and less willing to think outside the box. We might crave more discipline and view with suspicion the slightest sign of chaos.

"Stress reactivity," Narvaez argued, "shuts down open mindedness. When you are open-minded, open-hearted, you are able to understand there are multiple perspectives in any situation. When that capacity is not grown or emphasized, you think your way is the only way, and anything that looks threatening to your belief system you try to shut it down." In an environment where the default condition is stress, Narvaez had concluded, one tends to stick with one's own, and to view outsiders as an inherent threat. "If you've grown up to think you're superior, as an American over anyone else, a white over a black, a man over a woman, that sense of superiority gives you a sense of comfort and alleviates your fear. If someone steps up and challenges that worldview, you're going to want to slap him down, because your ego identity is very fragile."

It becomes a vicious cycle, fear in adults begetting fear in kids, who then grow up into adults more predisposed to knee-jerk responses, which tend to generate conditions that beget more fear.

In studies conducted on rats, anxiety-controlling genes in young rodents raised in nurturing environments are turned on to a far greater extent than are those for rodents raised in more stressful situations.[38] It is reasonable to assume that similar variations occur in humans too. Turn off the anxiety-controlling genes, explained Narvaez, and one might well need medications to substitute for the function of the genes. Or, and this is where the political implications become clear, one might have a greater tendency to gravitate toward ideologies that scrub ambiguity from one's life, that negate the need to navigate a maze of anxiety-producing explanations to complex questions by instead offering clear and simple "solutions." In recent years, researchers at the University of Quebec, in Canada, have developed a measure they call "intolerance of uncertainty." They have concluded that there are strong correlations between an inability to tolerate ambiguity and anxiety disorders. The inability to deal with uncertainty causes anxiety and worry, but it seems also to be a consequence of that anxiety.[39] Unable to tolerate complexity, it's entirely possible that deeply anxious people are more likely to throw their lot in with political movements that promise a return to a simpler, more homogenous time. "You can feel safe again," through a black-and-white ideology, Narvaez hypothesized. "You're part of the in-group. You feel safe."

WHEN THREATS TO OUR well-being are detected, our bodies undergo incredibly rapid changes that affect how fast our heart beats, how much oxygen we intake as our breathing rhythms shift, how focused we are on the immediate risk at the expense of tuning out the broader environment. As a result, over time, as we are subjected to prolonged stress and threat, our brain states shift. We feel intense sensations of goodness or badness in the presence of things that either trigger safety sensations or deep warning sensations that things aren't right. Risk expert Paul Slovic calls these feelings "the affect heuristic."

"If you bombard a body with chronic stress, eventually you will have an effect on production of cortisol and growth hormone," explained Dr. Sally Winston, codirector of the Anxiety and Stress Disorders Institute of Maryland.[40] "You'll get reduced levels of cortisol. But then, if you stimulate them, it's excessive." In a culture in which, increasingly, we are all primed to fear, our brain chemistry ping-pongs between extremes, from lows of cortisol one moment, which can lead to the feeling that one's brain is in a fog, or lead to exhaustion, inflammation, and other ills, to excessive highs the next—which can raise one's blood pressure, interfere with one's immune system responses, lead to nervous agitation, and so on.

Jeni Kubota put it this way: "In a threat mode, you don't have a lot left in you to do other important tasks. Your focus is more on survival." As a result, kids who feel surrounded by threats tend to do poorly in school; adults, subjected to nonstop media images and political rhetoric that hype the risks we all face on a daily basis, tend to find it harder to concentrate, to perform to their maximum potential at work, and so on.[41] The database of danger signals, stored in our amygdalas and ready to set off fear responses at a moment's notice, gets larger by the day. For once in the amygdala, those triggers remain there. And thus, as we find more and more things to be fearful of, we rejig our brain chemistry so that those things frighten us evermore effectively. It's a vicious cycle. And it's one that, according to Rachel Yehuda and others, can be transmitted from one generation to the next, with our environments (including the chemical environments we experience in our mothers' wombs) serving as epigenetic switches that turn on or off various genes and thus alter the production of an array of chemicals influencing how we behave and how we understand external stimuli as we go through life. We may, quite literally, be in the middle of an unprecedented social experiment, amping up our anxiety levels so profoundly that we change ourselves at a genetic level and, in so doing, massively alter the way we interpret, and interact with, our environment and our community.

"Our modern world does not require us to run from people who look different," said Mahzarin Banaji, a Harvard psychologist who, in 1988, cofounded Project Implicit, a large-scale experiment intended to measure people's implicit, unconscious biases. But, she continued, "the brain is an old, old machine; it's out of sync with the demands made on it in the modern world."[42]

As we get more anxious, Sally Winston felt, our ability to calculate risk precipitously declines. "Normally, when we have a sense of risk, we have a combination of stakes and odds— how likely would it be and how bad would it be if it did happen. But if you're already anxious, the odds completely drop out of the calculus, and people respond only to the stakes." Never mind that the chance of you being struck by lightning is only one in several million; if you happen to be fixating on lightning, all you can think about is how lethal such a strike would be. The same with terrorism or school shootings or being randomly murdered by a stranger on the street. "The sense of danger comes only from that," Winston continued. "Their risk assessment monitoring system is broken. They're not figuring in the odds; they're only looking at the stakes."

It's a sensation that Trisha Allen-Gibby, whose child was among those attending the Montessori preschool we encountered earlier, could relate to. Five years before I met her in a Utah suburb just east of Salt Lake City,[43] Allen-Gibby, a tall woman with long, dyed-black hair, was obsessively watching the news, tuning in to one or another television station at least five times a day to find out what was happening in the world. And every time she turned on the news—especially her local Fox channel—she was bombarded with horror stories. She became depressed and had to go onto antidepressants; she became irritable with her wife and their children; and she started drinking to excess. She felt that if she could establish total control over her environment things would become safer, but, she soon found out, establishing total control over an environment is all but impossible. And the less in control she felt, the angrier she got: "I was unable to cope with all of it. There were some nights I felt freaked out. I was putting the fear in the kids. 'You can't do this—because this and this and this might happen.' I felt like I was this paranoid, scared person."

And then, shortly after the Aurora, Colorado, movie theater mass shooting, on July 20, 2012, when James Holmes killed twelve audience members during a screening of *The Dark Knight Rises*, Trisha decided she wanted to go see that movie. She asked several of her friends if they would join her, but all refused. They were, she remembered, all petrified that a copycat killer would target another screening of the film. And it was at that point that she had an epiphany: she decided to unplug. After all, she reasoned, there were so many movie theaters in the United States that the chance of anything happening in the particular theater she wanted to go to was miniscule.

Trisha had hit upon a calculus of risk that allowed her to function again as a whole person. She began thinking about probabilities instead of simply going with her gut.

"If you limit yourself by every bad thing you hear on the news, then you pretty much stay home. And even that gets scary, because you hear about home robberies. It's an endless cycle of fear." She went to the movie, decided to stop watching the television news so compulsively, and noticed that she was beginning to feel healthier. "It's easier for me to do things that I might not have done before. I don't feel there's always somebody watching. I let things go. With my kids, I'm at that happy medium: there are some things I need to care about, some things I don't. I feel like I'm out from under a dark cloud." While for many parents the school's security systems were its top selling point, Trisha liked it for its educational philosophy, for the way the teachers interacted with their young students.

Many of the other parents at the school in which I talked with Allen-Gibby, however, were still very much under that cloud of constant worry. "Security was the number one factor for me choosing a school," explained one mother, a quality control expert at a dietary supplement company, who vividly remembered the jolt of horror unleashed in her by the Columbine massacre in 1999. "I fear a gunman walking into my child's school and gunning up the place. And I fear someone walking onto the playground and swiping a kid. And I fear an employee of the school damaging my child. These things happen more commonly than people expect. I don't want to be sitting at work one day and get a call there's something going on in my kid's school."

She and her husband had decided that they wouldn't let their eight-year-old daughter go anywhere by herself, except to the house right next door—but even then they watched her until she was safely inside. They felt angry and scared when they saw other children playing unattended. The parents of those children, she had decided, must be "scatterbrained."

"Sometimes when we go to a trampoline park we can relax a little," the woman, her mouse brown hair shoulder-length, her face padded with pancake makeup, said softly. But for the most part, she worried, her daughter felt too "invincible," too safe in the world, to be allowed to go out on her own. Until her daughter really understood fear, she said, she wouldn't let her spend even a few seconds by herself.

Making these fear spirals worse, anxiety produces what Dr. Winston terms "sticky" thoughts. People start obsessing on particular things, and as they obsess they further lose all sense of perspective. You get "the fuzzing of all of danger into peak danger," and you cease to be able to analyze your fears rationally. We know that trauma begets trauma. Researchers who have studied soldiers with PTSD believe that those who suffered traumas earlier in life are more likely to come down with PTSD as a result of what they experience on the battlefield than are their fellow soldiers who haven't had trauma in their past.[44] Hence a society as collectively traumatized as was America in the wake of the 9/11 terrorist attacks is a fertile breeding ground for such obsessively sticky thoughts.

In such circumstances, argued psychologist Sonia Bishop, a British-born researcher now based at the University of California, Berkeley, we cease thinking long-term and averaging out risks of events happening based on accumulated data from months or years, and instead we only pay attention to the immediate past. *A plane crashes due to mechanical failure?* Statistically, explained Bishop, sitting in her small third-floor office in a modernist building on the western edge of campus, because of the rarity of such an event, that one plane crash today shouldn't radically alter one's calculus about the danger of flying tomorrow. Yet, with saturation media coverage of the accident, people's anxiety levels spike, and their unwillingness to get on an airplane dramatically increases.

"We rely on what people tell us to interpret events that we are not directly involved in, or personally impacted by," Bishop continued. And much of the time, it's an anecdote-driven media that does the telling, creating narratives that hook audiences emotionally but aren't necessarily accurate as gauges of overall risk. "The media has a huge influence on how we think about risks that have not personally impacted us yet."[45]

And, in an anxious environment, that influence goes up. Already predisposed to worry, we glom onto any and every image or story that justifies and rationalizes our concerns. As our anxiety levels rise, researchers have found that our ability to correctly calculate risk declines. We begin underusing our prefrontal cortex, which means our ability to make complex, nuanced decisions goes down, and we start overestimating the likelihood that bad events will occur. Even in broadly stable conditions, we start assuming that anomalous events are the norm. And when conditions aren't stable, in rapidly changing environments we begin to leap to worst-case conclusions. "If people are anxious," Bishop concluded, sitting forward on her cream-colored office couch, "they are very bad at using information of prior outcomes to inform their decisions."

IF ENOUGH PEOPLE IN a community start obsessing on the same fears, then something starts to happen that has extraordinary political implications. For when a lone person obsesses on a fear, usually they recognize that at least in part the fear is psychological, that it is inside their head. It is what psychologists term an "egodystonic" fear. But when everybody starts to panic, increasingly it becomes "egosyntonic," the fear validated not by the likelihood of particular events actually coming to pass but simply by dint of volume. If enough people fear some event or some individual or some group of individuals, then, argued Winston, "those individuals don't think of themselves as having an anxiety problem. It's supported by everybody they know, so it becomes the right way to think." If large numbers of people become absolutely terrified, say, of young black men, then no longer is it seen as a psychological problem; instead it becomes a political problem demanding solutions. "Do something to make me safer." That, said Winston, is when people start arming themselves, start tolerating high levels of police brutality. "The facts go out the window."

Chemically, we amplify our own rapid-fire judgments about people and events, creating our own echo chambers through a complex interplay of stereotyping—the particulars of which will change from one culture to another, as well as over time within a given place—and brain chemistry. If, for example, a policeman in the United States, with its long and sorry history of racial exploitation, tension, and inequalities, has concluded that most black men in poor neighborhoods are dangerous, then the mere sight of a black man at night in a high crime area may set off a cascading series of fear responses. And those can, as we have seen time and again in the horrors captured on cell phone and dash cam cameras, lead to devastating responses. If, by contrast, we trust a group of people or an individual, our brains produce more oxytocin, which leads to a cooling off in our reactions.

A policeman who beats or shoots a black suspect may well be consciously racist, but he doesn't necessarily have to be. He also may be amped up on a vast number of fear-produced chemicals, exacerbated by repeated exposure to negative stereotypes about African American males, in particular, that work to skew his judgment and set off fight-flight-or-freeze responses. "You can intend well, and yet your actions can be misaligned. To anyone who cares about social justice, this should be a problem," argued Mahzarin Banaji.[46]

On the Project Implicit website are several IATs: timed computer tests intended to measure implicit biases around race, age, gender, and ethnic identity. The tests pair categories: black Americans and bad, for example, white Americans and good. They then ask the test subjects to push a given computer key with their left hand if a word that flashes up on the screen is either associated with blackness or badness ("Martin Luther King," say, or "evil") and to push a computer key with their right hand if the word is either associated with whiteness or goodness ("Jimmy Stewart," for example, or "gentle"). After a while, the parameters are reversed. Push with the left hand if the word that flashes up is either associated with blackness or goodness; push with the right if it is associated with white or badness. Time and again, the researchers have found that most test takers measurably slow down when they are confronted with the second set of associations. Most people, it turns out, no matter how nonprejudiced they believe themselves to be, unconsciously make certain associations around race. The same holds for gender roles. For religion. For who constitutes a genuine "American." And many other categories. These are deeply embedded prejudices, transmitted at a cultural level and operating largely independently of conscious choice. And they come with a host of collateral implications: white test takers, for example, tend to show less trust toward blacks than toward whites, are less likely to invest in business ventures with them, and so on. Mahzarin Banaji and Anthony Greenwald, the two cofounders of Project Implicit, wrote in their 2013 book, *Blind Spot: Hidden Biases of Good People*, that black men experience these biases everyday, "whether they are walking down a street, trying to hail a cab, entering a store, applying for a job, for housing, for a loan."[47]

Millions of these tests have been taken since the IATs went online in the mid-1990s, and they consistently show people to be more biased than they assume themselves to be, responding measurably slower to word pairings that buck their stereotypes than to pairings that bolster them. We imbibe stereotypes all the time, and without our even being consciously aware of them, they, at a very fundamental level, become part of who we are. "It threatens the notion of social justice," Banaji averred. "If we do not even know that we are biased, what hope do we have of fixing it?"

At the University of Virginia, Greenwald ran a study showing participants images of armed black males and armed white males. At speed, the participants then had to make a decision to shoot or not shoot the image. Greenwald found his subjects were not more likely to shoot the image of the black man than the white. So far, so good. But, when he then showed images of *un*armed men, he found that his test subjects *were* more likely to shoot the black man than the white. In other words, because of implicit biases, the assumption of innocence had broken down.[48]

Other researchers have conducted variants of these shoot/don't shoot lab experiments. When, in the early 2000s, a research team from the University of Colorado at Boulder and the University of Chicago set up a study exploring split-second "shoot decisions" involving images of black men and white men who might or might not be carrying guns, they found that exposure to news reports of violent black criminals made the participants more likely to shoot even unarmed black men, whereas exposure to stories about violent white criminals did not increase the likelihood that they would opt to shoot the white people shown on their computer screens.

Subconsciously, the test subjects were being influenced by stereotypes: since young black men are routinely portrayed as being violent, any encounter, such as media exposure, that links black people to violence, amplifies the impact of that stereotype at the most basic, neural level. See an image of a black man, with, for example, a cell phone or wallet in hand, and the observer will too often assume it to be a gun—especially after repeated encounters, via the media, with images of violent, armed, young black men. "Participants respond quickly and accurately when targets conform to cultural stereotypes (armed Blacks, unarmed Whites). . . . Stereotypes systematically bias reactions to stimuli in the shoot/don't-shoot task," the authors subsequently wrote, in an article published in the *European Journal of Social Psychology*. "But [participants] respond slowly and inaccurately when targets violate these stereotypes (unarmed Blacks, armed Whites)."[49]

"Black Americans have every social reason to be suspicious of the police, and white Americans do not," argued Sheila Jasanoff, a science and technology expert at Harvard University's Kennedy School of Government, who studied the ways in which risk gets understood and acted upon in different cultural contexts.[50] "People certainly associate racial groups with more hazard than they might actually pose," Dale Hattis, research professor in public policy at the George Perkins Marsh Institute at Clark University, believed. Hattis, whose research explores how judgments of risk are constructed, continued, "People tend to generalize from cases that they find salient. The machinery of generalization allows these kinds of biases to creep in."[51]

In an era of 24/7 "breaking news," tweets, rant radio, and the like, as a culture we are, increasingly, primed to respond, with every fiber of our beings, to our basest fears.

"The transmission of danger information is one pathway to the acquisition of a fear," explained Alec Pollard, director of the Center for Obsessive Compulsive Disorder and Anxiety-Related Disorders at the St. Louis Behavioral Medicine Institute and a professor emeritus of family and community medicine at St. Louis University.[52] "And if that information is amplified and emotionally or factually exaggerated, you're more likely to get that fear. To overcome the repeated media presentations and distortions is really hard." If you are repeatedly subjected to endlessly looped news stories suggesting your children are likely to be victims of a school shooting, that fear becomes hard-wired into your brain's neural networks. If you repeatedly are told that a particular demographic—black men, say, or religious Muslims—are inherently dangerous, ultimately your brain will likely respond to such individuals much as a phobic brain responds to the things it is afraid of.

To the extent that racism or religious hatred is fear based, Pollard hypothesized, it literally alters one's brain chemistry, triggering responses from the amygdala whenever the affected person sees an image of a particular sort of individual. "If you were raised a racist, you can learn to perceive a class of people as safe—probably in very much the same way that people overcome phobias. But there is still a part of your brain that will still perceive them as inferior or dangerous." And those neural connections are particularly easy to reactivate. One can spend years

working on reducing one's racist beliefs, but a few sensational
crime reports on local TV showing young black men assaulting people who look like you, and all your fear instincts kick
in again. You can familiarize yourself with Muslim neighbors
and coworkers, but a dramatic television ad, such as the ones
Donald Trump ran suggesting all Muslims were somehow a potential threat and justifying the "temporary" barring of Muslim visitors from the United States, will likely reactivate all your
original feelings of fear and suspicion. "Safety learning is not
resilient like danger learning," Pollard explains. "It's fragile and
has to be reinforced. It's a survival issue: I don't want to give
up my apprehensions about a category of things too quickly,
because I could die."

Add it all up, and we have created what might be termed
an *Egosyntonia*, a community bound together by fear, chemically primed to react with fight-flight-or-freeze fear impulses,
and politically predisposed to tolerate deeply unpalatable activities—from the waterboarding of terrorism suspects to the
shooting of young men suspected of criminal activities—just so
long as those activities make us feel safer.

If we are told often enough that something or someone or
some type of person is bad—what the geographer and risk-anal-
ysis expert Roger Kasperson terms the "social amplification of
risk"—eventually our brains internalize it to such an extent that
the mere presence of something or someone fitting that category triggers all of our ancient fight-flight-or-freeze responses.
In other words, as the noted anthropologist Mary Douglas concluded in her writings on the cultural theory of risk, our worldview helps shape our sense of risk. When a person buys into a set
of understandings about what and who is dangerous—whether
those assumptions are peddled on the local television news or

discussed around the water cooler at workplaces—they are, in a much larger sense, buying into a broader cultural package.

"People are always trying to calculate the probability that something bad will happen," noted the risk-perception consultant and Harvard University instructor in environmental management David Ropeik. But why we deem one set of ills to be worse than another is inherently subjective. "How we calculate risk depends in part on cultural inputs. We align with one another in order to keep ourselves safe."[53] In his 2010 book *How Risky Is It, Really?*, Ropeik noted that we are, as a society, absolutely terrified of murderers, yet few of us are beset by terrors about tripping while walking, or falling in the shower, or being poisoned by radon gas, despite the fact that thousands more Americans die from falls each year than die at the hands of murderers, and that the EPA estimates that lung cancers associated with radon exposure kill twenty-one thousand Americans annually.[54]

Fear, noted Mary Douglas, is an extraordinarily effective glue binding communities together. It creates its own sets of priorities, its own rituals. It serves to denote who is a part of the in-group and who is an outsider. It acquires a force independent of its truth or the accuracy of the ideas that fuel its expression. "Ideas about separating, purifying, demarcating and punishing transgressions have as their main function to impose system on an untidy experience," Douglas wrote in her 1966 book *Purity and Danger*. "It is only by exaggerating the difference between within and without, above and below, male and female, with and against, that a semblance of order is created."[55]

Chapter Five

The Business of Fear

In 1971, when the Anxiety and Phobia Treatment Center opened its doors in White Plains, New York, with a mandate to treat the vast array of anxieties that modern-day Americans were succumbing to, it was the only such center in the country. Today institutions such as this exist all over the United States. Many are nonprofit, catering to clients regardless of their ability to pay, but many others aren't. In fact, designing products for America's fearful, anxious, and depressed multitudes has become a booming business: "Anxiety treatment centers can be very expensive, costing thousands of dollars by the time you've left the program," wrote the editors of the *Calm clinic.com* website. "The initial assessment alone often costs anywhere from $350 to $500, and the hourly fees for individual and group therapy may be $150 to $400 per hour. Additional fees apply for lodging."[1]

Forty years after the APTC started treating phobias and other fears and anxieties, the National Center for Health Statistics reported that the usage of antidepressants had increased in the United States by a stunning 400 percent in the previous two decades.[2] By that year, nearly one quarter of all women in their forties and fifties were on antidepressants. Whites were between three and four times more likely to be on these medications than were blacks and Hispanics. Roughly half of those diagnosed with depression also suffer from anxiety. Add in antipsychotic drugs and drugs for Attention-Deficit Hyperactivity Disorder, and the American Psychological Association estimated that by 2010 22 percent of adults in the country were on psychotropic drugs.[3] While not all of these medications were intended to deal with fears and anxiety, there was a high overlap.

In 1999, the Anxiety and Depression Association of America commissioned a report, *The Economic Burden of Anxiety Disorders*, which estimated that forty million American adults suffered from anxiety disorders, with medical impacts, lost work days, and other financial consequences, costing the American economy $42 billion per year.[4] Since then, the prevalence of widespread anxiety in society, or at least its diagnosis, has only grown, as have suicide rates. In 2016, the National Center for Health Statistics reported that the country's suicide rate had jumped 24 percent between 1999 and 2014, and that the number of suicides per year was accelerating upwards rather than stabilizing.[5] Some recent studies have suggested as many as 30 percent of adults in the United States and Canada now have anxiety disorders. Not surprisingly, several of the best-selling pharmaceutical products, the sales of which net Big Pharma billions of dollars annually, are intended to make users less anxious.[6]

The Anxiety and Depression Association of America, which serves as a sort of coordinating institution for anti-anxiety providers around the country, had approximately 1,500 members as of early 2016. One of its missions, according to Vice President of Communications Jean Teichroew, is to explain to the broader public that, "anxiety disorders are real and treatable." Another is to convince sufferers that "there are treatments available, and you can cope and lead a full life." Across the country, thousands of anxiety treatment centers serve vast numbers of clients. Any self-respecting city in the country, these days, has an array of such clinics to choose from, some residential, others outpatient. These clinics are now a core part of the American medical infrastructure, catering to an ever-growing number of anxious and depressed patients.

And the United States isn't alone. In Canada, the Moods Disorders Society estimates that between 4 and 5 percent of the population are depressed on any given day, and that 9 percent of men and 16 percent of women are suffering from one or another form of anxiety disorder.[7] As of 2015, Canada's health system was spending 14 percent of its budget on prescription drugs, with antidepressants being among the most commonly prescribed. In fact, for Canadians age twenty-five to forty-four, they were *the* most prescribed pharmaceuticals.[8] In the United Kingdom, a report released in 2014 found that the number of antidepressants prescribed to patients had soared from fifteen million in 1998 to forty million in 2012, with the increase picking up steam after the 2008 financial crash.[9] In Germany during this period, the use of antidepressants went up 46 percent in a four-year period.[10] In Ireland, the *Irish Examiner* newspaper found that 331,368 people, out of a total population of 4.7 million were on antidepressants in 2015.[11] In Iceland, a country that routinely ranks near the top of global "happiness" surveys, an OECD study found that one in ten residents, averaged across all age groups, was taking antidepressants on a daily basis.[12] Only the United States tops that.

At the same time as usage of antidepressants and anti-anxiety medications has increased around the globe, so the number of people who take their own lives has also grown. Globally, groups that monitor suicide data estimate that suicide rates have increased by a startling 60 percent since the early 1970s.[13]

Two things seem to be happening here. As a species, we are experiencing a vast, painful, existential moment, one that is saturating our collective brains in fear-generated glutamate, norepinephrine, cortisol, and glucose. One that leads to increased levels of depression, anxiety, and suicide. And, in tandem with this, an awful lot of businesses have made the bottom-line decision to cash in on these fears, phobias, and the general sense of angst by marketing vast amounts of drugs and therapy regimens aimed at making us all feel better. Those of us living in countries with health systems comprehensive enough to be able to fund a widespread distribution of feel-good pills are being successfully sold a Brooklyn Bridge. Companies have a huge profit motive in the peddling of anxieties, fears, and phobias, and the notion that wonder drugs—equivalent to the author Aldous Huxley's fictional "soma," in his dystopian novel *Brave New World*—can instantly solve these problems.

Paradoxically, many of the drugs prescribed for disorders such as ADHD, drugs such as Ritalin and Adderall, actually trigger the release of norepinephrine. "It is possible that taking stimulants could increase one's risk of developing PTSD when exposed to trauma," wrote Richard Friedman, director of the psychopharmacology clinic at the Weill Cornell Medical College, in an opinion piece for the *New York Times*.[14] Friedman reported that a study of active duty soldiers found that the increasing use of prescription stimulants correlated with increases in PTSD.

We feel anxious and so we take more drugs to take the edge off our emotions. And, oftentimes, those drugs—or the withdrawal if we come off of them—end up ultimately making us feel even more anxious and even more off-kilter.

Perhaps we are moving from what the sociologist Barry Glassner famously termed a "culture of fear" to something even more insidious: an *identity* of fear. We are caught in a feedback loop in which we are taught to fear anything and everything, to in many ways define ourselves fundamentally by what we our anxious about, miserable about, and fearful of. Our brain chemistry changes to reflect this omnipresent angst, the continual chemical red alert conditions make us feel bad, and so we seek medical intervention to reverse these unpleasant sensations. And those medicines in turn make it more likely that we will, down the road, experience uncontrollable sensations of fear and panic.

"Writing a prescription to treat a mental health disorder is easy," wrote the author Brendan Smith in a 2012 article published on the American Psychological Association's website. "But it may not always be the safest or most effective route for patients. . . . Today, patients often receive psychotropic medications without being evaluated by a mental health professional."[15] Often, however, patients *are* evaluated, and treated, by a rash of newly minted experts in anxiety, fear, depression, phobias, and so on. These conditions, it turns out, represent something of a gold rush for innovative therapists.

In Northern California, phobia specialist Dr. Howard Liebgold ran classes and workshops on "over 200 phobias," and set up a company named Angelnet to sell a huge range of products to his fear-consumed clients.

Liebgold was something of a legend in the world of anxiety and phobia treatment, known affectionately as "Dr. Fear." One could be treated at his string of Phobease clinics for everything from "agrizophobia," fear of wild animals, to "anuptaphobia," which is a fear of staying single. It turned out that an awful lot of people could be labeled phobic of something or other: chaetophobes are fearful of hairy creatures, while caligynephobes fear beautiful women. Hobophobes have a terror of rootless, homeless people, while pagophobes are fearful of ice and frost. One could even, apparently, be treated for syngenesophobia, which is a fear of one's relatives. "I'm Dr. Liebgold and I suffered from many different phobias for many years," Howard Liebgold announced to customers on his Angelnet website. "I finally found a simple cure, and honestly, it was life-changing."

Doctor Fear died in 2013, but the store, along with his inspirational sales pitch, lives on. There's the $175 course, complete with CDs and DVDs, on curing phobias. "If you are anxious or shy or have panic attacks or fear public speaking, driving, flying, bridges, elevators, shopping malls, supermarkets, leaving home, escalators, social contacts, buses, trains, subways, crowds, being alone, insects, animals, doctors OR any of the over two hundred recognized phobias OR suffer recurrent, disturbing thoughts OR have to perform endless ritualistic behaviors, you owe it to yourself to take the Home CD & DVD Course and start your cure," the sales pitch tells prospective customers. There are MP3 downloads, inspirational books, CDs of the doctor's lectures on specific phobias.[16] It's all marketed with a delicious lack of irony.

IF THE PREVALENCE OF fear and deep-rooted anxieties among its residents, especially pertaining to violence of one form or another, were a true measure of the level of risk that a society faces, twenty-first-century America would be one of the most dangerous places on earth, possibly even one of the most dangerous places in human history. And yet, of course, it isn't.

True, looming in the background of our daily lives are the risks of vast calamity—ecological collapse, climate change triggering rising sea levels that swamp major cities, nuclear war, direct impact by a large asteroid, a global pandemic spread at vast speed by air travelers from one continent to the next. These are huge challenges that, arguably, should actually cause more fear, more soul-searching, than they do. Were they to occur, they would shatter our civilization and cause untold devastation. Yet, with the exception of climate change, which is indeed already a rolling catastrophe, each day that goes by without those civilization-ending cataclysms is, in the United States, generally marked more by stability and routine than endemic horror and chaos. The very fact that a child's being kidnapped by a stranger merits headline news coverage speaks to the fact that most days in most places no such kidnappings occur. That a few Americans being infected by ebola is enough to dominate a news cycle similarly speaks to the rarity of the events. That the destruction of Flint, Michigan's safe public water supply in 2014–2015 sparked outrage partly speaks to the almost gothic horrors of the lead poisoning that occurred, with official connivance in that impoverished city; but it also speaks to the fact that the overwhelming majority of cities in twenty-first-century America, unlike most other cities in most other countries in most other time periods, do not have dangerous drinking water. Were Flint's experience the norm, it would not have made the headlines.

True, the United States does have far more mass shootings than does any other wealthy democracy—and not coincidentally it makes guns easier to purchase, and ammunition easier to stockpile, than do any of these other countries. True, it has a much higher homicide rate than other First World democracies. But compared to a slew of non–First World countries around the globe, from South Africa to Mexico, Brazil, El Salvador, and Honduras, from Russia to Afghanistan, Pakistan, Iraq, Yemen, Syria, and Sudan, it has far lower violent crime rates, fewer murders as a percentage of its population, and a government and law enforcement infrastructure far more capable of protecting its people.

In fact, viewed as one country among many, at one particular moment in time, the United States of the early twenty-first century is among the richest, and in many ways securest, societies in human history. The murder rate in 2014 was only 4.5 per 100,000, higher than a hundred years earlier, and higher than in Canada or the United Kingdom, say, but, after a nearly quarter century decline in crime rates, massively below what it had been in the more recent past.[17] The 2014 numbers compare with a murder rate of 9.5 per 100,000 in the country as a whole in 1993, when a more than two-decade-long rise in violent crime in America crested, and more than 25 per 100,000 in New York that year.[18] And they very favorably contrasted with a murder rate in Honduras, in 2012, that the United Nations' Office of Drugs and Crime calculated at a staggering 90.4 per 100,000; in Venezuela of 53; in South Africa of 30—countries where a brutal combination of poverty, political corruption, desperate economic conditions in places oftentimes ruined by drug wars, and, in the case of Latin America, free trade agreements with the United States and centuries of oligarchical rule have created a perfect storm of violence in recent years.[19]

Although the number of murders in a slew of large American cities ticked upwards in 2015 and 2016, they still remained far below what they had been in those same cities in the 1980s and 1990s. And despite the epidemic of fear that pervaded daily life, they were far lower than most other societies in history. In medieval Europe, historians estimate that in cities such as London and Amsterdam each year about 50 per 100,000 died a violent death at the hands of others.[20] These are rates seen today in only a handful of small, impoverished, drug-and-gang-dominated countries. Moreover, of those who didn't die violently in the medieval world, most died prematurely of a ghastly array of diseases and infections that today are cured with a few days' worth of antibiotics.

Compared to the slums of Johannesburg, Panama City, Tegulcigapas, Rio de Janeiro, or Caracas, even the most violent of American cities comes out far ahead. As for the calm streets both of wealthy central-city zip codes in Manhattan and of deep suburbia, they are positive oases of tranquility.

And despite the hype to the contrary, the number of kids per thousand kidnapped by strangers in the United States and either held for ransom, sold into some form of slavery, or murdered, is extremely low. In October 2002, the National Incidence Studies of Missing, Abducted, Runaway, and Thrownaway Children (NISMART) published a large-scale study, based on tens of thousands of interviews, which concluded that somewhere between 60 and 170 kids were taken annually in what were called "stereotypical kidnappings," the kind that involved a stranger, where the child was transported far from where they lived, was held overnight, and was either killed or kept by the kidnapper.[21] A study from a decade earlier found slightly higher, but broadly similar, numbers.

In fact, the vast majority of the tens of thousands of children kidnapped every year are taken, temporarily, by family members, often in custody battles, or involve teenagers leaving their homes, without permission, with friends or acquaintances. None of these are "good" crimes—they are, for the families concerned, terrifying—but since almost all of these cases resolve peacefully, they aren't in quite the same lethal category as the "stereotypical kidnappings" detailed by NISMART.

For the victims and their families, these "stereotypical kidnappings" are life-wreckers. They are as awful, as violent, as predatory, as any crime can be. But in terms of the overall societal risk such crimes pose, unlike in many other, poorer, and more violent countries, where gangs and warlords substitute for the power of the state, and where children are routinely kidnapped and held for ransom or turned into child soldiers, in the United States the numbers simply don't add up to an epidemic of kidnappings.

Crunch the data, and you find that children in the United States are much more likely to die of Sudden Infant Death Syndrome (SIDS) or of an asthma attack than to be kidnapped and murdered by a stranger on the streets of the city in which they live. The Centers for Disease Control and Prevention estimates that about 1,500 infants die of SIDS each year in the United States.[22] Researchers believe that many, although not all, of these children die not because of some mysterious, unexplainable systems failure in their bodies, but because their parents have laid them down to sleep in unsafe positions. As for asthma, 3,600 Americans die of the disease each year, many of them children, and more than 2 million emergency room visits are triggered by asthma attacks annually.[23]

Children are also almost as likely to die in their bathtub as to be kidnapped by a stranger: in 2012, the United States Consumer Product Safety Commission estimated that between 2006 and 2010 434 children under the age of five had drowned in bathtubs, buckets, toilets, and other bath-related products.[24] And the National Institute of Health has found that nearly 80 Americans each year die of reactions to hornet, bee, and wasp stings, and between 15 and 30 die in any given year after being attacked by dogs.[25] Nearly 1,000 Americans each year are killed in accidents involving falling off animals they were riding or in a crash while riding in a vehicle being pulled by an animal.[26]

Again, none of these statistics are intended to minimize the horrors of children being kidnapped and/or killed. But they are intended to help us calibrate risk. Were we thinking in a cold, calculating, rational way, we ought to be far more concerned about taking our children to visit an air-polluted town such as Fresno for a few days than letting them walk to their neighborhood playground alone.

Yet run-of-the-mill risks like those from air pollution don't generate the same sorts of headlines, nor do they inspire the same sort of gut-level terror as do child snatchings. That a child-kidnapper is the epitome of evil is a given; rightly, we feel nothing but rage toward them and disgust at their actions. We do not generally feel the same way toward a parent with too many chores to perform who occasionally leaves a child in a bathtub unattended and, after one gamble too many, returns to the bathroom to find their child has drowned. Absent other, opinion-altering circumstances, we are predisposed to view the latter as a tragedy and to feel deep pity for the bereaved parent. Yet simply because one event carries far more moral culpability, its perpetrator meriting far more moral opprobrium, than another doesn't, per se, mean that it is more likely to occur. In the telling, however, that distinction is too often lost.

In 1998, the Mayo Clinic studied parental attitudes to an array of risks. The researchers found that one-third of parents

reported worrying frequently about their children being kidnapped. They worried more about this threat, which in absolute
terms was extraordinarily low, than about car accidents, drug
addiction, and a slew of other situations that were actually far
more likely to take their children's lives.[27]

OVER THE PAST SEVERAL hundred years, since mathematicians
Blaise Pascal and Pierre de Fermat worked on probability theory
in the mid-seventeenth century, and, then, a century later,
Thomas Bayes developed a method of modifying probability
estimates in real time as events unfold and influence our understanding of the likelihood of given situations occurring, humans have perfected the mathematics of calculating risk. In so
doing, we have provided tools for wealthy, First World countries
to create vast infrastructure devoted to anticipating, and tamp-
ing down, an array of risks throughout society.

"The notion that the future is more than a whim of the gods
and that men and women are not passive before nature" was
one of the great liberating events in human history, wrote Peter
Bernstein in his book *Against the Gods: The Remarkable Story of
Risk*.[28] "The capacity to manage risk, and with this the appetite
to take risk and make forward-looking choices, are key elements
of the energy that drives the economic system forward."[29]

Using all of this accumulated knowledge, this newfound
understanding of the probabilities of risk and danger, we have
improved public health, decreased mortality rates, cured diseases
that in the not-too-distant past were invariably fatal, created social security systems to tamp down financial risks faced by the
elderly, and invented insurance mechanisms to buffer industry
and agriculture from the effects of everything from shipwrecks

to droughts. We have made workplaces safer and elevated consumer safety to a fine science. We can create actuarial tables that predict how long we will likely live and how much money we will need to save annually to meet our retirement needs.

And yet, increasingly, despite all of this technical capacity, all of this specialized knowledge, ours is a society in which we make fundamental decisions affecting our well-being and the safety of others based on deeply flawed understandings of risk and of fear: of who and what is "risky," of what constitutes dangerous activity, of how best we can protect those we love. We are not, it seems, all Bayesians when it comes to making complex economic or political or personal health decisions. Since it is bad news that makes the headlines, and since out-of-the-ordinary events tend to dominate the news, it is the exceptional cases of kidnappings and murders, of pedophiles and psychopaths that make the perception-shaping headlines on a daily basis. Watch too much television news, in particular—where the "If It Bleeds, It Leads" maxim has long dominated—and your worldview is likely to be skewed toward fear and panic; you are likely to come to feel besieged by what Trump termed "American carnage" and to start taking countermeasures to deal with that sensation.

Anxiety, historically, has been understood as something chronic; fear, by contrast, has been thought of as acute. It's about the here and now, about immediate split-second responses, about the postponing of analysis until calmer times. But what happens when these acute responses become chronic—when fear of specific events and people becomes a backdrop to everyday life, when everything seems to involve an unacceptable level of risk, and when the damage to analysis and reason becomes permanent?

Chapter Six

All They Didn't Do Was Hang Him from a Noose

loyd Dent found out the answer to that question one January night in Inkster, Michigan, when he had the bad luck to run afoul of a brawny police officer who seemed to be itching for a fight. William Melendez was so predisposed to think the worst of someone who looked like Floyd—black and male—that he simply assumed, because of all his many years' experience in the field, that the fifty-seven-year-old was up to no good. We know he assumed that because he said so in Judge Sabrina Johnson's courtroom on March 18, 2015, when he was questioned by Dent's attorney, George Rohl, about why he had stopped Dent on a traffic violation and then savagely beaten him. Rohl asked whether Melendez had planned on stopping Dent regardless of whether there was anything wrong with his driving, and the officer answered, "I planned on conducting an investigation, yes."[1]

"He made it very clear under oath that he racially profiled my client," Rohl, a somewhat flamboyant, sports-obsessed, fast-talking attorney, recalled a few months later, as the city was

145

getting ready to settle a lawsuit filed on Dent's behalf, and with
Melendez himself heading toward a trial that would eventually
result in him being convicted of assault and misconduct in office and sentenced to between thirteen months and ten years in
prison. (On appeal, the judge allowed for Melendez to serve his
time in a boot camp rather than a prison.)

What really got Rohl's goat about Melendez's behavior was
that none of it was covert; the erstwhile officer simply wasn't
ashamed of what had transpired. He had profiled Dent and,
presumably, many, many other people, and, said the attorney,
he "did so proudly."

Moreover, even though Melendez was heading to boot
camp, where he would likely reside for the next several years,
his conviction was an exception. In the vast majority of cases
involving extreme acts of force by officers against suspects, either no charges are brought, or if they are, juries decline to find
them guilty. All too frequently, in these cases, there is a racial
dimension to the violence. The research project Mapping Police Violence found that in 2015 more than three hundred black
people in America were shot dead by police officers; at least a
third of these individuals were unarmed at the time. The researchers also concluded that the rate at which unarmed blacks
were killed by law enforcement was five times higher than that
for unarmed whites.[2]

AFFECTIVE BIAS—THE SKEWED SENSE of perspective that comes
with hearing or seeing about particular events so frequently that
it changes the way you evaluate risk—is bad enough when it
comes to economic and personal health choices, to individuals' decisions over whether to fly or drive, whether to vaccinate

children against a nasty, itchy disease or gamble on the strength of those kids' immune systems to succeed in navigating the germ minefield. But it becomes truly destructive when public policies and practices are shaped based on power imbalances—be they racial or class-based—and the fears that tend to accompany vast disparities in access to power and to economic security. When we jump to the conclusion that poor people, or black people, say, are inherently risky simply because of who they are and of what their status in life is, we open the door to policies and practices that dehumanize them. We end up legitimizing peculiarly violent or coercive responses based on nothing more than hunches that they are planning to inflict harm.

Over a number of years, Phillip Atiba Goff, a research psychologist at UCLA, and his team analyzed the language used by police officers when calling in information on crimes and on suspects. Time and again, he found, the officers were more likely to use dehumanizing language when talking about African American suspects, no matter what their age or what sort of crime they were suspected of having played a part in. And he also found that once they started using dehumanizing language about a suspect, they were then much more likely to increase the level of physical force they used in dealing with that person.[3]

In other research, dating back to 2008, Goff found that white participants in his studies oftentimes implicitly associated black people with apes, and in so doing came to tolerate higher levels of force by the police against African American suspects, including children, than they did when the suspect was white. "A growing literature," Goff and his fellow authors wrote, "demonstrates that individuals tend to associate out-groups and out-group members with nonhuman animals more than they do members of their in-group. . . . In this research, White participants who were subliminally exposed to images of apes before watching a video of police beating a black man were more likely to endorse that beating, despite the extremity of the violence."[4]

Two thousand miles east of Goff's Los Angeles–based center, in a psychology lab at the University of Chicago, Jeni Kubota, her colleague Jasmin Cloutier, and several other researchers were researching just such scenarios. What happens in a white American's brain when you pair an image of a black face with a word that indicates violence? All the expected parts of the brain connected to fear and threat responses kick into gear. What happens in that same brain when you pair the black face with a word that bucks stereotypes, say a word like "peaceful"? Well, unless the brain belongs to a person who has long made a conscious effort to tackle his or her own prejudices, the brain does a sort of double take, finding it hard to interpret information that doesn't immediately fit with patterns and associations long used to associate black people with violence.

Why do we do a double take when we see a very elderly, frail-looking person engaging in a challenging athletic feat? Because the act doesn't fit our images of the elderly. It tells a story we aren't primed for, and we get confused. Our interpretative tools aren't fully equipped for such an image. We have to ponder it, work out what is happening, fit it somehow into our existing schema. "The mechanism by which we make sense of information that doesn't fit our expectations—you have to work harder to understand what's going on," explained Cloutier.

By extension, the Montreal-born psychologist mused, what happens in real life when people long used to thinking in terms of negative stereotypes about groups are confronted with manifestly different narratives? Did Barack Obama's election as president, for example, serve to shred negative images that many white Americans had of African American males? Not remotely, said Cloutier. "People thought that when Obama got elected our implicit associations [of black people] would get much better. But people with prejudicial views don't regard Obama as an exemplar but as a weird fluke. People work hard to discount an exemplar who doesn't fit their expectations." Even if they recognize the achievement of the individual, they end up saying something like, "He's not like the rest of them."[5]

A YEAR OR SO before Floyd Dent's run-in with Inkster's finest, Kubota had asked for white volunteers willing to have their brains studied under fMRIs while they were shown a set of images and given small electric shocks to accompany some of the images. It was a common research method in neuroscience—pairing an image that in and of itself was innocuous with the infliction of pain—and was known in the field as fear conditioning. Kubota's team showed some of the test subjects images of the faces of young white men and gave them an electric shock each time. And then they showed them black men and didn't give them a shock. As expected, after a while the parts of the brain associated with fear began lighting up on the MRIs each time a white face appeared on the screen. Also, as expected, fear wasn't detected when they saw a black face. Then the experimenters reversed the scenario, so that the black images were accompanied by an electric shock and the white ones weren't. Again, as expected, the subjects stopped showing signs of fear when they were presented with a white face and instead began to fear the black faces.

So far, so predictable. But here's where things got weird. When the researchers reversed the order of the test, so that their subjects first learned to associate black faces with the infliction of pain and white faces with the lack of pain, even when the order was then reversed the subjects continued to show fear of black faces. Their amygdalas remained in overdrive, their heart rates went up, their cortisol levels increased. "Even though the black faces are clearly safe now," Kubota recalled, and even though when asked about this the test subjects clearly could verbalize that they were being shocked when shown white faces, "you still see them have these neurological and physical responses of fear to the black faces. It's about groups related to danger."[6] Groups defined by the dominant culture as out-groups, as dangerous, have always been "processed in the brain the same way as other fear stimuli, like spiders and snakes, are processed. That's an old system; it keeps us alive. But that system can be co-opted by cultural meaning, and different groups can be processed as being in that fear–relevant class."

EEG research shows that humans process the basic racial category of people they see incredibly quickly. Within 120 milliseconds, says Kubota—literally faster than the blink of an eye—we have already decided whether a person in front of us is black, brown, or white. "And that activates a whole bunch of stereotypes. We see a young black man; we access all our stereotypes, and we don't have to see an individual. It's pretty efficient." So pervasive are broad-brush cultural assumptions that researchers have even found that young black men themselves, when confronted with an image of a young black man, jump to negative conclusions. They start making assumptions about violence, danger, and aggressiveness.

WHEN WILLIAM MELENDEZ SAW a black man driving a shiny new gray Cadillac at night in a crime-ridden neighborhood, he took a gut-check decision, based on his experience, that the driver must be a criminal and therefore had to be taken down.

In all probability Officer Melendez, a large, beefy man, his cheeks jowled, with the beginnings of a double chin, with short, heavily gelled brown hair and ear-length sideburns, didn't think that all suspects deserved to die. But nor was the self-professed "Robocop," who claimed to have made more than two thousand drug collars over the decades, averse to using fists and boots, Tasers and guns on suspects should they get on his bad side. He had, over the years, as a police officer in Detroit and elsewhere, wracked up a long list of complaints, mostly involving the use of unnecessary force. And although he had not previously been convicted of any crimes as a result of these actions, the police departments for which he worked had paid out plenty of cash to settle civil complaints.

Unfortunately for Floyd Dent, a Detroit resident who was visiting a friend in nearby Inkster, one frigid Wednesday evening in January 2015, shortly after nine o'clock, his presence in the neighborhood was more than enough to set off Melendez's internal alarms.

Dent, a fifty-seven-year-old long-time employee of the Ford Motor Company whose son, recently out of the military, was in training to become a law enforcement officer and whose ex-wife was a retired IRS investigator, was driving his late-model Cadillac through a poor neighborhood lined with run-down apartment complexes and unsavory motels. Some of these businesses, just down the street from Inkster's new police station and courthouse, were under law enforcement surveillance for the rumored drug-selling activities of their residents. He had been, he said, delivering some bottles of liquor to a housebound, blind friend in one of the apartments nearby. With hindsight,

it wasn't the smartest of moves. Dent's license had been suspended because of a number of unpaid tickets, and Dent, a fit,
goateed African American man, who looked far younger than
his fifty-seven years—he was roughly six feet tall, a muscular
213 pounds—must have seen, as he drove, the several police cars
in the vicinity. He must have known, given all of the media attention over the proceeding months and years to stop-and-frisk
police strategies, and to the large number of cases where black
men and boys had died at the hands of the police in cities from
Ferguson to Detroit, from New York to Cleveland, that he was
essentially wearing a target on his back.

What he almost certainly didn't know was that social conditioning can actually change how the brain processes information and imagery, especially in situations where very rapid
responses are required. Which, it turns out, is especially bad
luck for black men, who can be carrying just about anything
and yet still be seen by others to be holding, or reaching for, a
gun. Our brains get so used to seeing images in the media of
black men carrying weapons and engaging in violence that nonconscious threat responses can be triggered in the brain and the
body simply by seeing a black man.

Threat detection circuits, wrote New York University
neuroscientist and psychologist Joseph LeDoux in his book
Anxious, "trigger a general increase in brain arousal and the expression of behavioral responses and supporting physiological
changes in the body," which in turn generate feedback loops
further concentrating the brain's energies on dealing with the
perceived threat. "Brain activity then comes to be monopolized
by the threat and by efforts to cope with the harm it portends.
Threat vigilance increases. . . . Brain activity related to all other
goals . . . [is] suppressed." Even absent a conscious feeling of

fear, once the brain's threat-detection systems have been acti-vated, all of our survival instincts, honed over eons of evolution-ary time, kick in.

Over the years, going all the way back to 1999, Melendez had, as a narcotics officer, picked up numerous lawsuits for ex-cessive force and at least nineteen claims that he had violated the civil rights of suspects in Detroit, before, a few years into the new century, the Motor City police finally cut him loose. By that point, lawyers estimated, he had cost the city in excess of $1 million in legal fees and settlements. Since then he had drifted, trying, mostly without success, to find work in several nearby towns before finally landing in Inkster, where the then police chief, Vicki Yost, remembered him from their work together in Detroit. She had, in fact, also been named in several of the lawsuits against him. In one instance, a man in Detroit had allegedly attempted to carjack two officers, one of them being Melendez. In the chaos that followed, Yost's partner had shot the supposed carjacker dead. Nothing had resulted from the in-vestigations that followed—except that Detroit's attempt to fire the officer had failed and, ultimately, he had won a promotion.

Yost offered her old pal a job. It was a bleak assignment; the size of the Inkster police force had shrunk by two-thirds since 2008—even while its accumulation of military-surplus vehicles had continued apace—and pay for the remaining offi-cers worked out to somewhere in the range of $15 an hour, not too much more than that of a fast food worker. Like fast food workers, too, Inkster's police were essentially working without benefits. Not surprisingly, the caliber of these men in blue left something to be desired; they were, said local attorneys who were involved in suing them, known as "throwaway officers." Morale in the force was low, and brutality was commonplace.

In recent years, the twenty-five-square-mile city, with a population, roughly 90 percent African American, of not much
more than twenty-five thousand, in the buffer zone between the
chaos of Detroit and the affluent, mall-dominated suburbs to
the north and west, had in fact spent roughly as much settling
civilian lawsuits against the actions of individual officers as it
had paying those officers in the first place. The city's legal team
estimated that each year it was spending roughly $1.5 million
in settling lawsuits filed against its twenty-five police officers.
There was, recalled city attorney Jim Allen, sitting in his law
office in downtown Detroit, the case of the police officer who
walked into a gas station and Tasered a person for no reason.
There were beatings. There were allegations of drugs being
planted on suspects. In fact, so awful was Inkster's police brutality reputation that, by the time of Dent's encounter with Melendez, it could only get catastrophic liability coverage: the first
$2 million of any case would now have to be paid out of pocket
by the city's cash-strapped taxpayers.

William Melendez sat in a police car, his binoculars trained
on the parking area of one particularly scuzzy-looking motel.
The lot was small, surrounded by a rusting white-painted fence
topped with ornate red spikes. The inn was also painted red and
white. It looked to have about six rooms and was run-down,
cheap, everything about it signifying moral and physical disre-
pair. The kind of place where rooms were probably rented out
by the hour. Next to it was a low-end liquor store, and across
the street was another liquor outlet, this one attached to a "nov-
elty" adult store.

The officer kept watching the inn, waiting for some sort of
action that would justify a police intervention. Later, he would
claim that he had seen Dent's vehicle exit the motel lot after, he

believed, the driver had been involved in a drug transaction. (But also later, somewhat diminishing the trustworthiness of that initial report, after they had beaten Dent to within an inch of his life and confiscated his car, the police would also claim to his enraged family that they had encountered Dent walking down a dark street, hopped up on heroin, a dope needle still in his arm.) Melendez radioed another car, and they began following Dent. On video footage from the dashboard cameras, one can see the police trailing Dent's Cadillac along Oakland Street, past apartment complexes on the left and small, detached private homes on the right. One can see them hanging back, following from a distance as he drove. Waiting. Waiting. Until he did something that would allow them to turn on their sirens and chase him down. One can see Dent approach a stop sign at John Daly Street and not quite make a full stop. And then, half a block further on, one can see the lights go on, bright, dominating, the blues and reds reflecting off the piles of snow along the edge of the road. There's something of the hunt in this footage, an impression of the carnivore, high up on the food chain, stalking prey.

Dent saw those flashing lights in his mirror. He must, too, have heard the sirens. He knew he had a suspended license, and he also knew the reputation of the Inkster police for violence. He knew that even if he had done nothing wrong, he had every reason to be afraid. And now, seeing those lights, he made a poor decision; instead of stopping immediately, on a dark stretch near no houses or businesses, he would drive—slowly— through the River Park intersection, with its wild, abandoned park on the right-hand side, just up the street to a lit area and pull over there. It would, he hoped, be safer.

And so that is what he did. He cruised down Oakland, put his foot on the brakes, and finally, a few hundred yards after the sirens had first gone on, with police from the nearby town of Dearborn Heights as well as state troopers now joining Melendez in pursuit, he stopped, an overgrown lot to the right of his car, the old, abandoned police station, bordered by tall cell phone towers, to the left, and, off the road a bit, a small sports tavern and the True Believers Baptist Church adjacent to it. It was freezing cold, and there were no people on the street. Other than the noise of the cars, the only sounds were those of the planes, flying low overhead, on the flight path into the Detroit airport.

The engine off, Dent started to open his car door, which was, he soon came to realize, mistake number 2.

The pumped-up Melendez, who had a local auxiliary officer-in-training with him in his car, who was, perhaps, particularly keen to show that trainee how, on the mean streets, one established who was the boss, was angry. Already suspicious of Dent's activities, he now saw a black man in an expensive car apparently trying to evade a police stop. His instincts, he would later tell a court under oath, told him that a black man in an expensive vehicle in a poor neighborhood couldn't be up to any good.

Melendez had already made a gut decision that he would bring the driver to heel. And now, his adrenaline pumping, he moved in. As Floyd Dent opened his door, the beefy officer, who spent long hours at the gym bodybuilding, reached into the car, pulled Dent out and onto the ground, and, within a few seconds of the car stopping, began punching him. Hard and fast. Again and again and again. Sixteen times to the side of the head in ten seconds.

Later, Jim Allen, whose father had been a senior police officer in Detroit and whose grandfather was one of the country's first officers to patrol his beat in a motor car, would look at the videos of that beating, of Melendez once again egregiously violating a suspect's civil rights, and shake his head in amazement. "I'm thinking to myself when I saw that tape, 'Motherfucker, you never learn.' Those sixteen blows in ten seconds was something that was difficult for me to overcome. I was sickened by it. I remember seeing it for the first time. I had a sick feeling in my stomach." Shortly after seeing the video, Allen urged the city to reach a quick settlement with Dent—which, later that spring, they did, to the tune of $1.4 million. *Don't even try to defend the case*, Allen warned the political leadership. *Since the whole thing was filmed, you can't win.* He hoped that Melendez would face federal charges. The whole rancid situation made him feel dirty, angry.

In fact, when he thought about it, what made that sinking feeling worse for the city attorney was the fact that all the other officers present during the assault had either piled onto Dent or held back and watched, not one of them trying to pull Melendez off his victim. It was, he thought, one of the starkest, most brutal displays of power he had ever seen, a terrifying example of what happens in an increasingly unequal society when some people are viewed as being disposable. "It's all part of a system of control and power and forced obedience," he said. "Police brutality is one symptom of a much greater problem. All of the consequences of inequality are playing themselves out where the rubber meets the road: police-civilian interactions. State power is interacting most frequently with the most weak people—who happen to be poor and mainly from minority communities. Where is the abuse of state power seen most clearly? In these sorts of interactions. This is the flashpoint. If you make it about the racist cops, the problem of inequality will never, ever be addressed. That's not to relieve the individual police officer of their moral responsibility to treat people with dignity. But their behavior is a product of inequality."

At the time, Floyd Dent wasn't pondering relationships between the classes and races. All he was really aware of was a
strong sensation that he was about to die. His nose was broken,
his right eye socket was fractured. Four of his ribs were broken.
His head had started swelling massively, the damaged tissues
saturated with blood. And, inside the skull, his brain, too, hospital doctors later told him, had begun to bleed. Dent was being
hit and stomped into unconsciousness. "What is wrong with
you?" he kept thinking of his attackers. Out loud, he asked,
"Why are you beating me like this? What did I do? Why are
you beating me?" Melendez said nothing.

Then, as Dent was down on the ground, bleeding, passive, the police officers—there were now about a dozen on the
scene (video footage showed nine, internal state investigators
estimated eleven, the prosecutor's office eventually calculated
thirteen)—started to Taser him: four times, at close range, the
barbs burning his chest, the electric shocks making him lose
control over his bladder. "Taser the motherfucker," he remem-
bers hearing someone say. They were, it seemed, almost goading
each other into an ever-greater frenzy. Melendez grabbed him,
pulled him up, put him in a chokehold, tried to strangle him. "I
told him three times I couldn't breathe," the middle-aged man,
at the wrong place at the wrong time, recalled. "I just gave up."
A little bit longer, and he would be another Eric Garner.

Dent felt himself slipping away. He was, he thought in horror, experiencing his last few moments of life.

Meanwhile, on the video, another police officer can be seen
reaching into his pocket, grabbing a baggie, and putting it into
the trunk of Dent's Cadillac. Later, this bag would be the evidence cited by the Inkster police department when they charged
him with possession of cocaine. Later still, however, the video of

the drugs being planted would be one of the reasons that prosecutors dismissed the charges against Dent.

Eventually, Melendez—who would subsequently, in explaining his actions, tell a local ABC television news reporter that Dent was "very erratic, screaming and yelling. There was 'I will kill you.' He was very erratic, very nervous"[7]—relaxed the pressure on Dent's throat, and several officers prepared to transport him to the precinct. "Leaned me up against a wall. I was hog-tied. Told me to face the wall. It was horrible. I don't like to remember it. I start crying. I'm fifty-seven years old, never thought I'd live to have this happen to me. I saw it in the sixties, but I'm fifty-seven—it was like I was dreaming."

Bleeding profusely, slipping in and out of consciousness, the bound, dazed, prisoner was driven to the precinct for processing.

Estimates on the numbers of Americans killed by the police each year are just that: estimates. The FBI doesn't compile national data on this phenomenon, and what numbers there are have mainly been generated by activist groups trawling local news reports. But in recent years some news outlets and other organizations have begun to study the numbers more carefully. The *Guardian* newspaper, in the United Kingdom, estimated that in 2015 US law enforcement agencies killed 1,058 Americans.[8] The Killed By Police project, which began tracking data in May 2013, using news sources from around the country as well as social media reports, calculated that between May 2013 and the end of that year, 772 people were killed by police in the United States. In 2014, they found 1,111 police killings. And in 2015, 1,207 killings.[9] Mapping Police Violence found that the police killed at least 346 African Americans in 2015, with at least 102 of those men and women being unarmed at the time of the fatal encounter. In only ten of those instances were any police officers charged with a crime, the project's researchers found; in only two of the cases were the officers convicted, and in only one was an officer actually sentenced to serve time behind bars.[10]

Perhaps most extraordinarily, the MPV team concluded that in seventeen of the one hundred largest cities in the country the rate at which black men were killed by the police was actually higher than the national murder rate. In St. Louis alone, with a population of 317,000, the police had killed sixteen African Americans since 2013. Just how out-of-whack these numbers are can be seen by contrasting them with the rarity of police killings in the United Kingdom: in the ten years from the start of 2006 to the end of 2015, government data shows that a grand total of nineteen people were killed by the police.[11] The UK population, roughly 64 million, is about two hundred times that of St. Louis. In June 2015, the *Guardian* newspaper reported that fifty-five people in Britain had been fatally shot by the police in the previous twenty-four years, whereas fifty-nine people had been shot by American police in the first twenty days of 2015; that in the two years of 2010 and 2011, German police had killed a total of fifteen people; that in the twenty years from January 1992 to December 2011, Australian police had killed a total of ninety-four people; and that Canadian police averaged twenty-five fatal shootings per year.[12]

Given the headlines in recent years, it's tempting to conclude that there is an unprecedented rash of police shootings, beatings, Taserings. The historical evidence doesn't entirely back that up. In fact, American law enforcement has long been far quicker to reach for the gun against suspects, and the numbers of people killed by American police have long been far higher than is the case in nations America tends to compare itself with.

More likely than an epidemic of police violence is that the same social media trends and mobile recording technology that make the country more fearful have also served to highlight, and to publicize, in recent years a dirty secret that has existed for as long as police forces in America have existed: levels of police-inflicted violence against certain demographics—mainly black and brown men, undocumented migrants, the mentally ill—that have long resulted in body counts unheard of in other Western democracies. In many ways, America's historical tolerance of uniformed violence more closely resembles that of countries such as Brazil—where more than eleven thousand people were killed extra-judicially by law enforcement agencies and paramilitary forces between 2009 and 2013[13]—than, say, Canada or the United Kingdom.

In recent years, the curtains have been drawn back by cell phone and iPad-wielding chroniclers on that secret reality, on what goes on in the friction zones that separate out the poor from the well-to-do, marginalized groups from the majority. And the resulting spectacle, both of the violence itself and of the refusal to acknowledge it, is an ugly one.

We have seen images of young children shot dead by the police in a playground in Ohio and in a car in Louisiana. We have seen footage of a man choked to death by the police in New York. We have seen videos of men and women around the country Tasered seemingly at random. We have seen numerous men shot dead after being pulled over for traffic violations. Then there's the image of a man killed by police in South Carolina who were on a stakeout for someone else, while he was waiting in his car for his child to return from school. There's the video stream of a bikini-clad teenager in Texas tackled to the ground by a gun-wielding officer for no reason other than that the pool party she was attending had gotten a little bit too noisy. There's the African American teenager in North Carolina Tasered in the foster home in which he lived after neighbors phoned the police to say that a black man was burgling the house next door. There's the story of the mentally ill man in Sacramento, California, who police officers first tried to run over repeatedly and then shot to death.

The list goes on and on.

AT THE POLICE STATION on Michigan Avenue, the video cameras kept rolling as the paperwork on Dent was filled in. Still handcuffed, he was made to take his shoes off; then, when an officer gratuitously threw them across the room, he was forced to hobble over to them and pick them up again. He was, over the course of more than half an hour, continually humiliated. He was also, it soon became clear, getting ever closer to dying. His T-shirt was saturated with blood; the swelling on his head was beginning to look catastrophic. Eventually, even Dent's tormentors were forced to a grim realization: if they didn't get him to a hospital, and quick, they would have a corpse on their hands.

And so Dent was once again taken out of the little police station building. He was put into an ambulance and driven down Inkster Road, past a series of housing units and small complexes; past a few low-lying, shuttered-for-the-night hair salons and liquor stores; past the New Jerusalem Missionary Baptist Church, the local Walgreens and CVS; past a couple gas stations, a tropical fish store, and the Cherry Hill Lanes bowling alley. They were, now, moving from Inkster's streets into those of the neighboring Garden City. Slowly, but surely, the surroundings were getting more affluent. The ambulance drove past a chiropractic center, an animal hospital, a White Castle. Dent, the medics, and the police escort passed more bungalows. Finally, on the left-hand side of the street, was Garden City Hospital. It was a three-story building, tan brick, with rectangular reflective glass windows. Around the back, under a gray concrete awning, was the ER entrance.

The officers made their prisoner get out of the ambulance. Barefoot, his shirt covered in blood, his head the size of a football, handcuffed, he had to walk over the hard-packed snow that covered the parking lot and into the hospital. There he was checked in, his arms and legs cuffed to a bed in the waiting area, and told that he couldn't call anyone to tell them where he was.

It was in that waiting area, not too long afterward, that Marlene Jordan encountered Dent.

Forty years old, Jordan had been a resident of Inkster since 1982, when as a young girl she moved there from Buffalo, New York, with her family. She was in the hospital that night with her boyfriend and her nineteen-year-old son, who had gotten into a fight with a friend and needed to be stitched up. The two men were sitting on a bench in the ER waiting area, and Marlene had stepped outside to phone her daughter. She hung up, walked back in, and her son said to her, "The guy over there said he was beat by the police real bad and he needs someone to call his family and tell where he's at."

Jordan, curious yet apprehensive, fearful, as are most people most of the time, to get involved in someone else's battle, went over to Dent's bed. He was lying, temporarily alone, while the police officer guarding him had stepped away. "Ma'am," he said softly. "Can you call my family? Inkster police pulled me over, pulled me out of my car and beat me up. Planted drugs in my car." She looked at him more closely, and the more she looked, the more horrified Jordan became. "Oh my God," she recalled, sitting at a Panera Bread café in nearby Dearborn Heights months later. "Floyd looked like he was near death. There was a white T-shirt on the chair by him, covered in blood. He was in a bed, sitting up at 45 degrees; his hands were handcuffed just like this, straight." She extended her arms rigidly outward to demonstrate what she meant. "His face was purplish looking. Bruising. Swollen. They had the lights off; it was kind of dark. He looked like he was dead."

Taking a chance, Marlene Jordan agreed that she would call his family. Quickly, quietly, his words blurred by the swelling in his mouth and face, Dent blurted out a few names and numbers. Jordan moved a decent distance from his bed, so that the police officers hovering around the waiting area wouldn't get too suspicious. She felt she had become part of a cat-and-mouse game. But she knew, from looking at Floyd Dent—who she thought, from his mumblings, was named "Denis," instead of "Dent," that she couldn't *not* make the phone calls. He gave her his father's number, his daughter's, his son's.

FLOYD'S FATHER, JAMES FAILS, was asleep at his home on an overgrown street on Detroit's West Side—a street that, like so many in the Motor City, had a smattering of lived-in homes among a greater number of abandoned lots, the old house windows boarded up, the grass waist high—when his phone rang. In his late seventies, missing the first joint on two fingers of his right hand, and deaf at the best of times, he struggled to make out what the strange lady on the other end of the line was saying. She asked him if he had a son named Denis. She told him that his son had been harshly beaten by the police. James couldn't make head or tail of what he was hearing. Eventually he put on his granddaughter, who was living with him. "All I heard was this whispering," James's granddaughter remembered afterwards. "She was whispering, telling me her name, said she was calling on behalf of Floyd and he'd been beat up by the police."

Dent's guards were wandering through the emergency room waiting area, and Jordan was fearful of attracting their attention if she spoke too long, so she hung up. She went back to the area near where Dent was being held. She watched, horrified, when he told the nurses and the police officers that he needed to pee: there was no curtain around him. She saw when they refused to take his handcuffs off. Watched as a nurse was brought in to hold his penis so that he could pee into a chamber pot. Saw the absolute humiliation on his face. She listened as the doctors explained to the shackled Dent that he probably had bleeding on the brain.

And then she phoned James's granddaughter, Floyd's niece, back. Over the next few minutes, she punched the number into her cell phone, to provide short, cryptic, updates, several times. By then, Floyd's immediate family, spread across several locales throughout the Detroit area, had all been woken up. They were phoning the hospital, the police station, lawyers they knew, and anyone else they could think of, desperately trying to get information. Nobody was telling them anything. Nobody was even acknowledging that Dent had been brought to the Garden City Hospital. At one point, Marlene phoned Dent's niece, who, on another phone, called her father, Dent's brother. With one phone pressed to the other, Marlene told him to hurry. "You better get here right away," she urged him. "Before they kill him."

"I felt like if I hadn't called his family, they *would* have killed him," Jordan recounted. "Pumped him up with drugs and said he was a drug addict."

That night, and for many nights afterwards, Jordan couldn't get out of her mind the image of Floyd Dent, his body bruised, bloodied, broken, chained. "My son told me he looked like Emmett Till," she explained, referencing the photos of the body of the teenage African American killed by a Mississippi lynch mob in August 1955. "All they didn't do was hang him from a noose. But they beat him to a pulp. He was chained up. His face, he was just staring at us: 'Please help me. Do something.'"

FLOYD DENT'S FATHER, JAMES, and his brother—who had seen Floyd earlier that evening and took a while to realize the phone calls weren't some sort of sick prank—left the family home in a hurry, drove out toward Garden City, rushed into the hospital. They were terrified. They didn't know if Floyd was alive or dead. Inside the ER, the younger man put James in a wheelchair and began hurrying him down the long halls, looking for someone in authority who could explain what was happening. No one would tell them anything. They couldn't find their relative.

James got out of the wheelchair and, frantic, tried to enter the ER treatment area via a back entrance. An officer stopped him.

Realizing that they were getting nowhere, James's son grabbed him, pulled him back toward the car. "Daddy, let's go!" he urged the old man. And, in a fury, they drove through the late night back to Detroit. They waited, for what seemed an eternity, until the morning. And then, as soon as the workday had begun, they started phoning attorneys.

When they rousted out of bed an attorney the family had worked with in the past, the lawyer told them they needed to get to the police station immediately, work out what he was being charged with and what bail they needed to raise, and get him out as soon as they could. Like Marlene Jordan, the attorney, hearing how savagely Dent had apparently been beaten and knowing the sinister reputation of Inkster's police, feared for Dent's life.

That first night, as Wednesday night slid into Thursday morning, a growing list of relatives drove out to the hospital. Each was told either that Dent wasn't at the hospital or that he was there but that they couldn't see him. Several times during that period, Dent was moved from one location to another, in a macabre game of hide-and-seek played out between the police and his family. When one nurse acknowledged to Floyd's daughter, Tracy, that her father was, indeed at the hospital, another nurse made the "cut it" sign across her neck, as if to say "shut up." The nurse immediately stopped talking. When Floyd's son, who, in one of the more bizarre twists in the story, had taken the test to join the state police earlier that Wednesday, tried to find out what was going on, a hospital security guard and two police officers told him that Dent was a prisoner and wasn't allowed any visitors. At one point, they tried to tell Dent's children that he'd been found with a needle in his arm. A doctor told Floyd's father that Dent was, indeed, in the hospital, that his head was massively swollen, and that he had tested positive for cocaine. "I said, 'Oh no! You're wrong now,'" James said angrily. He knew his son, and none of what he was being told computed.

Seriously scared that Floyd's life was in danger, the family hurried to find a bondsman and then frantically phoned one extended family member and friend after another, trying to raise the money needed for the bondsman to get Floyd out of jail.

Meanwhile, as the hours passed, as Wednesday morphed into Thursday, and then Thursday into Friday, all Floyd knew was that he was in a world of pain; that, cuffed to the hospital bed, the cuffs on so tight that the skin on his wrists suffered lasting abrasions, he was being whisked from one room to the next. He overheard some of the police officers, who kept walking in and out of his room to look at him, whispering about how his family was searching for him. He learned that the doctors at Garden City Hospital were pumping him full of all kinds of drugs in order to relieve the swelling on his brain. At one point, Dent remembered, through the haze of painkillers and other medicines, he saw an African American nurse come in. They talked briefly; he told her his story; she broke down in tears. The police, meanwhile, were urging the medics on, telling them to hurry up, to get him into a fit state to be moved from the hospital to court, where he was to be arraigned on drug charges as well as charges of resisting arrest and assaulting a police officer.

On Friday afternoon, after more than forty hours in the hospital bed, he was finally taken from the hospital and arraigned. Shortly afterwards, he made bail. The police threw his bloodied clothes at him and shoved him out the precinct door. His brother and his father, seeing the state he was in, seeing the police standing by and laughing at him, both burst into tears. "He was staggering," his niece recalled. "I grabbed him under the arm, said 'You alright?' I had him on my shoulder, and we walked out the door. And I put him in granddaddy's car, and we came on home."

There, the bleeding wouldn't stop. Floyd was dizzy, in agony. His family decided they had to get him to another hospital. At the Henry Ford Hospital, where they took him, he was given a more complete workup, a CT scan, and other tests. The scale of his brain injuries became apparent. He was tested for drugs again; this time around, the tests came back negative. A nurse told them, James claimed, that Dent was the seventh patient they had seen that day who had been beaten up by local police.

It would take months for Dent to recover, for his injuries to start healing and his psyche to start repairing itself. Even after the charges against him were dismissed, even after the financial settlement, even after Melendez's conviction, Dent felt fragile. His concentration wasn't what it used to be. He forgot things that he used to easily recall. Life for Floyd Dent would, he knew, never be the same again.

FEAR, PER SE, DOESN'T create a William Melendez. But it does create the conditions in which we tolerate him as a necessary evil, a side effect of a disordered world. It is in our friction zones—those strange, semilawless regions of our psyche and our geography where virtually anything goes so long as it's in the name of security—that such individuals flourish. It is in spaces such as Inkster, where thin blue lines hold poverty and its accompanying violence and dysfunction in check, that violence inflicted by armed representatives of the state, or by vigilantes operating with the imprimatur of public approval, becomes routine. In these friction zones, we are primed to err on the side of "security" over "justice," to give law enforcement organizations and individuals leeway to shoot first and ask questions later. Melendez had, after all, successfully beaten back numerous other complaints before, until finally he was tripped up by the presence of video cameras on the Inkster police car dashboards.

"The best way to make people obedient is to create a conflict vis-à-vis outside groups," explained New York University professor Yaacov Trope. "You are less concerned with issues of justice when there is an outside group, an enemy. It's the best way to create a docile populace."[14]

"People like Melendez," Jim Allen felt, "are tolerated by folks who are victims of inequality. Which is the vast fucking majority of people. Because they've been conditioned to fear Floyd Dent, people they don't understand, they've never met, they don't live next door to. Fear is inbred through mass media. Orwell had the idea—the use of mass media to spread fear is nothing new. It justifies Guantanamo Bay, Abu Ghraib, preemptive invasions, you name it. That's manufacturing consent. That's Chomsky from thirty-five years ago. We're a hair-trigger society. The stakes are much higher. Climate change. We feel as if we are on the precipice of a mass extinction event. What more do you need to trigger fear than that?"

For Allen, the violence was a form of societal indigestion, a consequence of a collective inability to digest the vast uncertainties of the modern world. For Floyd Dent's family, it was about something much simpler: it was about what happens when fear meets racism in a dark street, late at night, in a run-down neighborhood that most Americans neither know, nor care to know, about.

"They stereotyped him," Floyd Dent's son, the soon-to-be police officer, believed. "They figured: black man, driving a nice car, he got to be doing something wrong. They planted drugs, tried to destroy his character by saying he was on drugs."

Melendez gave a series of media interviews after the Dent case started making national headlines. He painted himself as a Dirty Harry–type character, a tough guy who, yes, maybe had bent a few rules but always, and only, in pursuit of the greater good. He insinuated there was far more to the story than met the eye, that he was a fall guy, that he should be considered a hero. He played to his audience: "I am a police officer who puts on a uniform for fifteen dollars an hour, with no benefits," he told ABC local news reporter Jim Kiertzner in April 2015. "I'd do it for ten dollars an hour—because it's important to me." Taking the role of victim, the erstwhile officer declared himself to be at the wrong end of a politically motivated, politically correct witch hunt. "I consider myself to be a political speed bump, with all the law enforcement negativity that is surrounding this country. It's a very stressful job, where you have to make split second decisions. It can affect your entire life. You're tying police officers' hands when you're Monday morning quarterbacking."[15]

MELENDEZ HADN'T EMERGED SUDDENLY, good one day, bad the next. The rage behind such a character is, I believe, slow-burning, fueled by fear and angst, and that fear, that anger is, in turn, given oxygen by the broader climate of unease in society.

The more an event is seen as being unpredictable, and as existing outside of one's personal control, the more we tend to fear it, explained Jennifer Lerner, a "decision scientist" at Harvard's Kennedy School of Government who works at the intersection of psychology, economics, and neuroscience. That's why we tend to fear ebola more than, say, motorcycle riding, even though far more Americans each year die in motorcycle crashes than of hemorrhagic fevers. Riding a motorcycle, we feel that we're in control, we feel that we have agency, that our destiny is in our own hands. And that feeling of control provides us with an illusion of safety. By contrast, with a disease like ebola, it is the randomness of the event, the impossibility of predicting who will be infected or when, that instills the fear of God into us. For similar reasons, says Lerner, we overfear the technology of nuclear power—the invisible nature of deadly radiation that would accompany an accidental leak from a power station, the impossibility of literally seeing the risk and of thus avoiding it, making us overcalculate the risk factor. Conversely, Americans don't generally spend too much time pondering the risks of nuclear war, despite the utterly catastrophic consequences that would result were such weapons to be unleashed in conflict. We underestimate this particular risk, probably because we assume that human control over whether or not to use such weapons renders the prospect of such a war unlikely.

With something as amorphous as "crime," or "terrorism," something we hear a lot about on our televisions and over social media, it's easy to gin up tremendous levels of fear. The more nonspecific a threat is, the more unpredictable it seems, and the more unpredictable it seems, the more viewers feel they lack control over the situation—that regardless of the choices they make it is a threat that could destroy their well-being, and that of their family, at any time and without any advanced notice. In other words, audiences fed a daily diet of crime and terror stories conclude that, in these areas of life, they lack agency—and thus they respond with fear. They also respond by embracing policies and actions, no matter how morally dubious, intended to lessen the risk that they face.

Lerner and her colleagues saw this in national studies that they carried out in the months and years following the 2001 terrorism attacks. "Risk perceptions," she recalled, of studies she worked on while a member of the faculty at Carnegie Mellon University,[16] "were erroneously heightened. People who tended

toward anxiety saw more risk." In 2003, Lerner and three colleagues published a paper in the American Psychological Society's journal *Psychological Science* exploring Americans' estimates
of risk during these fraught months. They found that, on average, their respondents estimated they had a 20.5 percent chance
of being personally hurt by a terror attack within the next year;
those same respondents, when thinking of other people, estimated that the "average American" had a 47.8 percent chance of
being hurt by terrorist actions over that twelve-month period.[17]
These figures were, it turned out, wildly off. Had nearly half
of Americans been hurt by terrorism, there would have had to
have been 150 million terrorism casualties in the period from
September 12, 2001, through mid-September 2002. In fact,
during that year domestic terrorism victims—those who were
sickened or died during the anthrax attacks—were numbered
in the dozens.

Lerner and her team also found that different personality
types responded differently to terrorism attacks. People with
underlying anxiety traits responded with more fear, believing
that they, personally, were under threat. People who tended toward dispositional hostility responded instead with anger, not
necessarily believing that they were about to be killed by terrorists, but primarily wanting revenge. Disproportionately, women
responded with fear and men with anger. But both the fearful
and the angry were willing to support huge changes in order
to reduce the likelihood of future attacks. "The national security environment in Washington," Lerner remembered, recall-
ing meetings she had with security officials over the years, "was
willing to support torture. Because they felt such extreme fear.
'We have to do everything we possibly can to keep the planet
alive.' They were receiving all kinds of information every day

that was in fact terrifying. And they had no way to really know what might happen next."

At least in part, police officers mostly get a free pass when inflicting violence on suspects because the public has been conditioned to always be afraid, to permanently go through life on edge, in what the firearms trainers call "condition yellow." If we're willing to condone torture by military and intelligence officials to stop possible future terrorist attacks, why not also police use of fists and Tasers and guns to stymie possible future crimes? After all, Lerner's research has found that in addition to most Americans hugely overestimating the likelihood that they will be victims of terrorism, they also dramatically overestimate the likelihood that they will be victims of violent crime. In the same study that detailed misperceptions about the risks of terrorism, Lerner's team found that respondents believed the average American had a 43 percent likelihood of being the victim of violent crime.[18] In fact, in 2002, there were just over 7.4 million violent crimes recorded in America, roughly one-twentieth of the number that would have occurred had that calculation of risk born some approximate relationship to the realities on the ground.[19]

Time after time, we let someone like Melendez get away with extraordinary acts of violence. We turn a blind eye, figuring most of the guys at the wrong ends of his anger had it coming to them. They might not have done what he said they did, but they probably did something equally bad. Gangbangers don't generally elicit much public sympathy when they get beaten. They are, after all, the stuff of our worst nightmares.

But finally Melendez goes too far—he takes his furies out on the wrong person, a fifty-seven-year-old long-time employee of Ford Motor Company, with a large family to provide him with support, and with a record no dirtier than a series of unpaid tickets and a suspended driving license. Then, at last, that silent majority—the people who so often manage to square their own moral circles by justifying police violence in the name of preserving social stability—can no longer ignore the problem.

And that's when the questions become more awkward: Why were so many people in a position to know better in denial for so long? Why didn't anyone long ago take this police officer off the streets? Why was he continually given the benefit of the doubt?

The answer to all of these questions, I suspect, is that we are scared enough in our daily lives to feel that the devil we know is better than the alternatives—so long as that devil's violence is largely directed at *the Invisibles*, at those with no power, whose stories we have long chosen to ignore or to demonize, whose very existence we have regarded as somehow less than fully human.

That's how a twelve-year-old African American child, Tamir Rice, in a poor neighborhood of Cleveland, can end up shot dead by police officers who mistakenly thought he was toting a real gun instead of a toy. "Black children are afforded the privilege of innocence to a lesser extent than children of other races," Phillip Goff and his colleagues concluded. "Black boys are seen as more culpable for their actions (i.e., less innocent) within a criminal justice context than are their peers of other races. In addition, black boys are actually misperceived as older relative to peers of other races. . . . Dehumanization of Blacks not only predicts racially disparate perceptions of Black boys but also predicts racially disparate police violence toward Black children in real world settings."[20]

That's how a Staten Islander, Eric Garner, can be choked to death by police officers while they were arresting him, not on suspicion of a heinous, violent offense but rather for selling black-market cigarettes.

That's how an African American driver, Philando Castile, can be shot multiple times by police officers who had pulled him over for a minor traffic infraction.

It's how a seventeen-year-old African American youth, Trayvon Martin, in the wrong place at the wrong time, can be killed by a local neighborhood watch vigilante in Sanford, Florida, early one winter evening—and how that vigilante, George Zimmerman, can then be acquitted at trial.

And it's how the African American teenager Renisha McBride can be shot dead by a homeowner when she knocked on a door in Dearborn, Michigan, for help late one night in November 2013 following a car crash. Theodore Wafer, the person opening that door, shotgun in hand, didn't see a real person, in trouble, seeking help; instead he saw a stereotype, assumed that he was in imminent danger, and opened fire.

In each instance, the shooters and the chokers claimed that, in the fraught moments leading up to the confrontation, they feared for their lives. That they had to use violence to bring an unpredictable situation to a close. "This guy looks like he's up to no good or he's on drugs or something," *Mother Jones* magazine quoted Zimmerman telling a police dispatcher shortly before he shot Trayvon Martin. "Now he's coming towards me. He's got his hand in his waistband. And he's a black male. . . . Something's wrong with him. Yup, he's coming to check me out. He's got something in his hands. I don't know what his deal is. . . . These assholes, they always get away."[21]

In Martin's hands, it subsequently became clear, was not a gun but rather a pack of Skittles and an iced tea.

Chapter Seven

Not Quite Human

In the late 1990s, I wrote several articles about a rogue police unit on the south side of Chicago that had decided to torture known gang members in order to extract murder confessions from them. Over a period of many years, the police, under the command of an officer named Jon Burge, had used an array of deeply unsavory techniques on their victims: these ranged from electric shocks to mock executions, from burns to beatings.[1]

One gang member, whom I interviewed in prison while researching these articles, explained how the torture unfolded. After being picked up on suspicion of having committed a murder, he was, he told me, taken to an isolated lot and suspended by his arms, which were handcuffed behind his back, a torture technique used by the Israeli security forces and known in the trade as "Palestinian hanging." Then, he continued, the officer opened the boot of the car, took out a shotgun, showed him the shell, and said, "Look at this, nigger." The officers forced the gun into his mouth, and one of them reportedly told the gunman to "blow that nigger's head off." Immediately afterwards, the officer pulled the trigger. Through a sleight of hand, the shotgun shell had been removed from the barrel: when the trigger clicked, no

bullet ripped his face apart. Instead, the officers started laugh-
ing. "I've had a gun pulled on me before," the man recalled, "but
I knew the guy wasn't going to pull the trigger. In my lifetime,
I'd never experienced anything remotely close to this."

Three times, he was mock-executed, and still he wouldn't
confess. And so, he recollected, the officers took his handcuffs
off, recuffed him with his hands stretched out above his head,
laid him down on the backseat of the car, pulled his trousers
and underwear down, and stuck a cattle prod on to his testicles.
"It was a burning sensation that seemed to go all through your
body. A stinging, a burning that just wouldn't go away. After
about the fourth time, I lost count. They said, 'He's a strong
nigger,' or something, and they turned it up. The pain got to the
point where I certainly couldn't handle it any more, and I told
them that I'd say whatever they wanted me to say. I was humiliated and hurt so bad. They liked their work; they enjoyed what
they were doing; they had a ball."

For years, as one murder after another was "solved," Burge's
unit was lauded for its detective work. Astonishingly, despite
many of the convicted prisoners having told their attorneys that
their confessions were coerced, and despite rumors swirling in
poor, African American communities in Chicago that a regi-
men of torture had been unleashed, the torture squad continued to operate with impunity for almost twenty years. It wasn't
that the information that could have brought their actions to a
close wasn't available; rather, it was that no one in a position of
power was willing to tie all the loose threads together and call
out Burge's team for their terrifying tactics. And, perhaps as
importantly, because the people crying foul were known "bad
guys," their allegations weren't taken seriously. Had middle-class
suburbanites, one after another, alleged such acts of torture,

the outcry would have been immediate. But when poor black men from economically marginalized neighborhoods, many of them already with long crime raps, spoke out, their voices were dismissed. *Sure, they might have gotten it a little rough*, the rationale behind this veil of silence seems to have been, *but they knew the rules of the street*. What would clearly qualify as torture if inflicted on a wealthy white man was regarded by Chicago's establishment—until, finally, after decades of allegations and a growing chorus of media coverage, it was forced to act; until, finally, one prisoner after another was granted a retrial; until, finally, Burge's reputation crumbled and his unit was disbanded—as no more significant than playground fisticuffs when carried out against impoverished black men.

It's that same assumption that allows us to rationalize the use of torture, and in some cases, indefinite detention, against terrorism suspects. "You're not a man, and you don't deserve respect. Kneel, cross your hands, and put them behind your back," the long-time Guantanamo Bay detainee and author Mohamedou Ould Slahi, a suspect originally from Mauritania, reported his interrogator telling him, during the time in which he was held in an Afghan facility, run by Americans, in mid-2002, before being transferred to the Cuban prison camp. At that site, he witnessed men being hung from the ceiling by their hands and their faces being slammed against the floors. "I obeyed the rules," Slahi wrote, "and he put a bag over my head. My back was hurting bad lately and that position was so painful." "You're going to be sent to a U.S. facility," the interrogator purportedly told Slahi. "Where you'll spend the rest of your life. You'll never see your family again. Your family will be fucked by another man."[2] When Slahi denied being a member of any terrorist group, the interrogator "put the bag back on my head and started a long discourse of humiliation, cursing, lies, and threat. I don't really remember it all, nor am I ready to sift in my memory for such bullshit. I was so tired and hurt, and tried to sit but he forced me back. I cried from the pain. Yes, a man my age cried silently. I just couldn't bear the agony."[3]

One can only waterboard, beat, sleep-deprive, and hang by the hands people whose humanity is in doubt, people who, in the minds of the torturers and the society that condones that black art, have placed themselves outside of the rules of civilized conduct, and, by extension, outside of the community of humans from which morality flows.

Those who carry out torture, wrote Ariel Dorfman, the Chilean playwright, essayist, and long-time opponent of General Pinochet's violent dictatorship in his home country, in his 2004 collection, *Other Septembers, Many Americas,* always argue that they inflict extreme pain on their victims only out of necessity. They never claim the mantle of the Inquisitor "in the name of evil," Dorfman noted, "but in the name of safety, the common good, the necessary things that have to be done so that we can all sleep quietly at night. It's up to us to reject that fear and insist that we do not want anyone hurt in our name."[4]

We justify these vile acts by asserting, evermore loudly, evermore insistently, that times have never been so perilous. "Safety at all costs" is the classic authoritarian argument. And when it becomes embedded in a culture, it generally affects social choices in a vast array of ways. At the extreme, it leads to the embrace of torture. More generally, though, it leads to a stunning intolerance of, and desire to shame, those who reject dominant ideas about security and public safety.

Take, for example, the story of Debra Harrell, a forty-six-year-old woman in North August, South Carolina. A few miles to the south from where Harrell lived, just the other side of the Georgia state line, the town of Augusta was home to the 8,500-seat James Brown Arena, named in honor of the great soul singer, who had grown up there. But its northerly twin in South Carolina, where Harrell lived and worked, had none of that glamour. It was a small, rural community, near the Savannah River, part of the cotton-, corn-, soybean-, and peaches-growing region of Aiken County. By landmass the county was South Carolina's fourth largest, at 1,073 square miles slightly larger than the entire state of Rhode Island. If it was well-known for anything, it was for the training of racehorses; the county hosted a Triple Crown: the Aiken Trials, a steeplechase, and the High Goal Polo Game, which routinely drew large crowds, and tourists with full wallets, to the region.

Like the rest of the Palmetto state, Aiken County was reliably conservative, with local voters in the GOP primaries in the spring of 2014 outnumbering participants in the Democratic primary by a ratio of roughly six to one. The county council was dominated by Republicans, and in March of that year, one of the few local Democratic voices, councilwoman Kathy Rawls, had announced that she was switching parties and joining the GOP. The Tea Party had a large presence in the county.

It was also a county with a long history of racial repression, and with an equally long history of using the criminal justice system to intimidate black residents. In 2009, the journal *Crime, History, and Societies* published an article by the Montclair State University historian Jeff Strickland. It noted that after the Civil War, "Aiken County was the most volatile place in South Carolina. Scholars have long treated the region as one of the most violent in the entire South, a place where southern honor thrived. Aiken County alone had twenty-nine rifle clubs with an average of fifty men enrolled in each. Former Confederate General Wade Hampton and the Red Shirts waged a state-wide operation of violence, murder, and intimidation against African Americans to discourage or eliminate Republican political participation and resistance to white political ascendancy."[5] Whites murdered blacks, yet it was blacks who, all too often, ended up in the state's postwar chain gangs and prisons. Throughout the post–Civil War South, as the late-nineteenth-century investigative journalist George Washington Cable discovered, the criminal justice system became one of the most brutal props behind what was termed White Redemption and, then, the system of Jim Crow.

In 2014, 71 percent of the county's residents were white, and most white voters in this part of the country were deeply conservative. Just over a quarter of the population, including Debra Harrell, was African American. Like in so many other parts of the country, black people in Aiken County were disproportionately likely to end up involved with the criminal justice system and therefore to spend time in the Aiken County jail on Wire Road in the town of Aiken, a new jail that, on any given day, had an inmate population somewhere between 375 and 450, or in one of South Carolina's twenty-five prisons. State Department of Corrections data showed that 64 percent of all prisoners in the state were African American.[6]

Over the past quarter century, the prison population in the state had more than tripled. And over the past thirty years, criminal justice spending in the state had increased by upwards of 500 percent—a trend largely in keeping with the rest of the South and, to a slightly lesser extent, much of the rest of the country.

For weeks throughout the summer, Harrell's nine-year-old daughter, off from school for the holidays, had accompanied her to work. She had sat for hours in the McDonald's, playing computer games on the family's laptop, while her mother served fast food to a steady stream of diners. A crew person, explained a job advertisement for the outlet, had duties that included "Greeting customers with a smile," and "Preparing all of McDonald's World Famous food." Throughout South Carolina, which has no state minimum wage legislation and where minimum wage workers thus earn only the federally mandated minimum, a starting worker at McDonald's earns between $7.25 and $7.77 an hour.

A few days earlier, someone had broken into Debra's house and stolen the family's laptop. The girl now had nothing to keep her occupied during the work day, and she asked her mother if she could, instead of going with her to the McDonald's, spend time in Summerfield Park. It was a large park, with a playground, a splashing pool, swings—and, Harrell's attorney would subsequently note, a breakfast and lunch program—for the kids. The girl spent a lot of time in that park with her friends, and Debra, thinking it would be a healthier place for her daughter to while away the days than the inside of a fast food restaurant, said yes. She gave her daughter a cell phone so that they could stay in contact with each other and told her daughter to come to the McDonald's at lunchtime; although it was more than a one-mile drive from the park to the restaurant, if you cut across the park on foot, it was only a five- or six-minute walk.

For the first two days, everything went smoothly. Then, on the third day, a woman in the park, concerned that the little girl was alone, asked her where her mother was. When she said that Debra was at work and that she was playing unaccompanied, the woman called the police. By that evening, Debra had been arrested for "unlawful conduct towards a child," a class E felony that could in theory result in a prison sentence of up to ten years; the daughter had been taken in by social services and was heading into the foster care system; local television stations— playing on public fears of unaccompanied children being kidnapped or raped—were running breathy stories about how a tragedy had been narrowly averted by the speedy intervention of North Augusta's law enforcement agencies; and McDonald's had set in motion a response that, within days, would result not in affordable day care services being set up for the children of its employees but in Harrell being fired from her job.[7]

The whole saga was an exercise in irrationality, a case study of what happens when common sense is given a backseat to hysteria. North Augusta wasn't a violent crime hotspot; rather it was a sleepy backwater. By far the most common forms of crime were burglary—such as the one that had resulted in Harrell's laptop being stolen—theft, and car theft. In 2012, North Augusta's violent crime rate was 134.4 per 100,000, compared to a US average of 214. Only twice in the last fourteen years, once in 2002, and again in 2009, had North Augusta's rate outpaced that of the country as a whole. In 2012, the county seat of Aiken had seven murders; North Augusta, by contrast, had two. In the entire year, its Department of Public Safety recorded two rapes. And while eighteen registered sex offenders lived in the city, that still produced a lower sex offender to general population ratio than was the case for South Carolina as a whole. The town was an unassuming little place where houses sold for an average price of $124,000, and where most days the local paper, the *Aiken Standard,* covered stories about the Lions Club, local high school sports teams, and debates over small-town tax proposals rather than real-life local crimes.[8]

Yet, like so many rural areas in modern-day America, it had, over time, developed a healthy dose of hysteria when it came to crime and punishment. Fear of crime paid, as Sheriff Hunt, who had successfully lobbied for massive annual increases in criminal justice and law enforcement expenditures, knew all too well. Add into that mix distrust of poor, black single mothers, and Debra Harrell's situation was a tragedy waiting to happen.

When a passerby spotted the girl unattended and called the police, all hell broke loose: the police picked up the girl and arrested the mother, local news swarmed the area reporting on a tragedy averted—despite the lack of any indication that the girl was at risk—and CPS removed the girl from her family home, an action likely far more destabilizing and damaging to the child's well-being than her having been left to play in a playground.[9]

NOT SURPRISINGLY, IN THIS era of angst, Harrell's story wasn't unique. There was the thirty-five-year-old African American woman in Phoenix, Arizona, who left her two young kids in her car while she went for a job interview at an insurance company. She was arrested, prosecuted for child endangerment, and sentenced to eighteen years' probation.[10]

There was Lisa Deckert, also in Arizona, who left her kids in the car, the air condition running, on a cool morning in October 2013, while she popped into a store to buy dog food for the family pet. When she came out of the store a few minutes later, she found her car surrounded by police and a fire truck, and her kids screaming in terror.

Deckert was charged with child endangerment. She had three court appearances, spread out over a six-month period, was fined several hundred dollars, and then was mandated to take eight hours of parenting classes. During this whole process, a child protective services team showed up at her home and asked her daughter extremely invasive questions in an attempt to find out if she'd ever been hurt by her parents. Deckert, who had no family living nearby in Arizona to take her kids should she be sent to jail, found the ordeal almost unendurable. "It's insane," she recalled. More than a year after the incident, she was still jittery. "You're not free to be a parent; it's a joke. We're raising our kids in fear." Deckert had become extremely anxious and depressed; she was worried, even when she pumped gas, about leaving her kids in her car. She was having nightmares about her kids being taken away from her by child protective services.[11]

In Florida, CNN reported in August 2014, a woman was arrested after giving her seven-year-old son a cell phone to call her with if he got into trouble and letting him walk to a playground unaccompanied. In Ohio, a father was arrested after his boy got off the church bus that he was supposed to attend a local youth group in and instead went off to play, unaccompanied by an adult, with friends.[12] In Houston, a woman went to meet a prospective employer for a job interview in a food court at a mall. Having no child care, she took her six-year-old and two-year-old along with her, left them at a McDonald's table in the food court barely thirty feet from where she was sitting, and proceeded with her interview. Shortly after she was told that she had the job, a police officer approached and arrested her.[13]

Then there's the story of Danielle and Sasha Meitiv, and their two children, Rafi and Dvora.

Danielle is a climate scientist, Sasha a physicist. Both in their forties, they look younger than their years, he skinny and goateed, she with corkscrew curly hair. They dress casually, in jeans, fuzzy socks, batik shirts. And both seem playful, inquisitive, somewhat theatrical individuals—even their family name, Meitiv, is, it turns out, a creation. Sasha, who grew up in the latter years of the Soviet Union, in a university town outside Moscow by the name of Chernogolovka, had a last name of Luvkovsky; Danielle, who grew up in Queens, New York, was Luttenberg. When they got married, they felt that Luvkovsky-Luttenberg was too much of a mouthful, and so they came up with a new name: Meitiv, meaning, in Hebrew, "He Does Good." It is a word that is frequently used in Hebrew blessings and is a part of the Meals on Wheels logo in Israel.

The Meitivs, along with Danielle's father, Jean, live in Silver Spring, a neighborhood of DC near the end of the Red Line metro, in the gray zone where the city gives way to the affluence of Maryland suburbia. The houses are mid-sized, the side streets leafy green. They live down one of those side streets, a fifteen-minute walk from the metro station, in a house whose walls are covered with maps, with kids' artwork crayoned directly onto the house paint, with Japanese silks and other eclectic art. The kitchen, its furnishings pinewood, is decorated with posters of root vegetables and peppers, its shelves stacked with cookbooks. On the kitchen table, they keep bowls of freshly picked tomatoes, fresh-out-of-the-ground yams. On the ledge above the sink is a bowl full of wine-bottle corks. Next to the sink are a jar of Miso and a bottle of avocado oil. Higher up, on that wall, hangs a painted Mexican pottery lizard.

There isn't a television in the Meitivs' home; they both believe that television does a pretty good job of rotting the brain. There is, however, a large Black Lives Matter sign planted firmly in the front yard. There isn't much evidence of caffeine in the house either, but there is an abundance of herbal mint tea.

All of which makes the Meitivs seem a touch granola-crunchy. So it isn't entirely surprising that their parenting decisions have, over the years, reflected a desire to get away from the mainstream, and to let their children explore the world for themselves. By the time Rafi was eight or nine and his sister five or six, the Meitiv parents were letting their children head out together, during daylight hours, to the nearby parks and cafés—without adult supervision. The kids learned to cross streets safely, learned directions, learned about gauging situations and people. In short, they acquired the skills needed to, ultimately, take them into adulthood.

Above all, Rafi and Dvora's peregrinations involved them navigating a world beyond their own leafy street. For the neighborhood in which they live isn't only residential. On the main avenues are restaurants, car repair shops, markets, Laundromats, even a few vacant lots. Many immigrants live here, in apartment buildings along those main drags, including a thriving Ethiopian community. It is, in short, mixed-use, mixed-income, and mixed-race. It's a part of that great American melting pot that, in times gone by, used to make citizens proud but now, too often, fills them with fear and dread.

Which is how the Meitivs first got into trouble.

In November 2014, when Rafi was ten and Dvora was six, the kids were walking back from their school bus stop with Danielle when they asked if they could stop off at the playground a block from their home. Since Danielle needed to cook dinner, she said they could stay at the park while she cooked.

A few days later, there was a knock at the door. When Danielle opened it, she encountered a pair of child protective services officers. One of her neighbors had, apparently, phoned them to report that the kids were playing unaccompanied. *Were they in the park alone the other evening?*, CPS asked. When Danielle said that they were, the officers told her that according to Maryland state law she was not allowed to leave them unaccompanied in a public space. Danielle looked this law up and saw that it specified that kids were not allowed to be left alone in buildings—but that it didn't mention outdoors. She phoned CPS and gave them her analysis of the law. A few weeks after that, the case was closed.

Weeks later, toward the end of December, Danielle was out of town, attending her cousins' fiftieth wedding anniversary party in New York, and the kids asked Sasha to drop them off, on their way home, at another nearby park to play. Half an hour later, three police officers picked the boy and girl up, made them get into a squad car, and drove them back to the Meitiv residence. When they got to the house, the police wouldn't let the children go inside; instead, they called for backup. "My kids were scared," Danielle recounted, retelling the story that her husband and children had told her after she returned to Silver Spring. "There were six police officers and five police cars— Saturday afternoon, in front of my house. My husband in flip flops." Repeatedly, the police asked Sasha for his ID, which he said he didn't have to show them since he had done nothing wrong and was in his own home. "My son calls me crying, saying, 'Mommy, the police are here, and I think Daddy's going to get arrested.'"

In the event, Sasha wasn't arrested, but once again Child Protective Services turned up on their doorstep—this time with a detailed "safety plan" that they insisted Sasha sign on the spot or they would summarily remove the children and place them into foster care. The plan stipulated that they would not let their children "be left unsupervised by an adult *anywhere.*"

Over the next several months, the Meitivs were repeatedly investigated by CPS for child abuse or neglect. They were threatened with prosecution, their house was inspected, they had to provide the names of all adults living with them, and, without Danielle and Sasha's consent, their children were interviewed at their school by CPS officers.

For Danielle, the whole thing was an absurdity, "a Kafkaesque outcome." *How ironic,* she thought: she had trained her kids to navigate the neighborhood safely; she had taught them how to cross streets and how to interact with adults. And the only time the children had ever been interfered with by strangers was that evening, when they had been detained against their will, "abducted" as she put it, by police officers and then social workers.

The Meitivs, unlike so many other parents who have faced similar situations in recent years, had the resources and the determination to fight back legally. They repeatedly pushed back against the CPS allegations and repeatedly asserted their rights to let their children play unaccompanied. Two months after the safety plan had been foisted on them, they received something of a vindication in the mail: a "notice of investigation closing" from the Maryland Child Protective Services agency. The charge of neglect had been found to be unsubstantiated, and the case was being closed.[14]

Two months after they had been given the all clear, however, on an early spring day in 2015, the troubles began again. The family had spent six hours cooped up in their car, driving back from visiting Sasha's parents in the town of Ithaca, in upstate New York—Sasha's father was on the faculty at Cornell University. The kids were cranky and wanted to stretch their legs. So as they neared home just shy of four o'clock that afternoon, Sasha and Danielle decided to drop the kids off at the corner of Cedar and Ellsworth Streets, to let them walk over to the local park for a while and then head back to the house for dinner. The park was a fixture for local kids, with two small playgrounds and a couple tennis courts.

Rafi and Dvora played happily for forty-five minutes and then, as they had promised their parents they would do, began heading for home. They walked over to Fenton Avenue, with its Ethiopian restaurants and bakeries, to buy some snacks to munch on the way back; they stopped in at Kaldi's Café, but didn't have enough money for what they wanted to buy—and so they continued walking. A minute later, they stopped at the corner of Wayne Avenue and Fenton to pet a guy's dog. The man allowed them to play with his dog for a while, and then, for no discernible reason, as they left to continue their short journey home, he suddenly decided to call 911 to report that two kids were walking unaccompanied in the area.[15]

As Rafi and Dvora walked through a little parking lot, a police car raced up, the officers jumped out of the car, and the two children were ordered into the vehicle. Had common sense played a role, the police officers would have simply offered them a lift home. Instead, they were held, incommunicado, for two and a half hours, from 5:15 to 7:45 that evening, while their parents frantically worried about their whereabouts. At 7:45 the children were handed over to Child Protective Services, and from 7:45 to 10:45 pm, well after the children were normally asleep, the agency refused to hand them back to Sasha and Danielle.

Again, ultimately the Meitivs weren't prosecuted, but their sense of security was shattered. "I find it terrifying," Danielle said simply. "All because my children were walking outside on a sunny afternoon. People have completely lost their minds."

Vindicated or not, over the next several months, as their story did the rounds, the family still faced a wrathful online response. When word got out on social media about the Meitiv family, the Facebook mood quickly turned nasty. One woman, in slamming Danielle and Sasha for their parenting choices, referenced a child murder that had occurred in the neighborhood nearly three decades earlier.[16] Danielle, the poster noted, was "incredibly stupid" for not recognizing the fear, and the roadmap to identifiable dangers, inspired by such a story. "What's wrong with you? Don't you have a survival mechanism?" was the gist of many of these Facebook postings, although they were, frequently, far saltier, laced with foul language and woven through with bile.

MEANWHILE, NO ONE HURLS invective at the Meitivs, or any other parents, when they take their kids by the hand, walk them down the front yard's path and out to the street and the family car, strap them into their car seats, and set off on a drive to the mall or the supermarket, to visit family or to go on a vacation— despite the fact that far more children die in car accidents than are killed by strangers while going on walks to the local park or café, despite the fact one doesn't have to search archives dating back thirty years to find stories involving local children who have died horrible deaths while sitting in automobiles being driven by their parents, older siblings, or babysitters. In fact, according to the Association for Safe International Road Travel, 1,600 children age fifteen and under—children too young to drive who are, therefore, being driven by others—die on American roads each year.[17] In 2013, 465 people died on Maryland's roads; by contrast, the number murdered in the state that year was 387.[18] Since 235 of those killings occurred in the single city of Baltimore,[19] that means the entire rest of the state saw 152 murders, a fraction of the numbers killed, to so little notice, on the state's roads.

In Arkansas, Wyoming, Alabama, Montana, and Mississippi, the annual road-death rate tops out at well over 20 deaths per 100,000 residents.[20] No state in the country has a murder rate anywhere near that level. And yet, overwhelmingly, it is violent crime that scares people more than automobiles.

The relative rarity of violent crime has, paradoxically, made it seem that much more menacing, precisely because when it does occur it is that much more headline-grabbing. By contrast, the frequency of fatal car accidents largely inures us to both their likelihood and their devastating impact. Moreover, a car accident is just that, an accident—although frequently one involving alcohol, drugs, distraction, or just plain bad driving; whereas a kidnapping, a rape, or a murder involve human agency—at its most malign and perverse level.

And that's where our limbic systems kick in. We too often assume the worst is waiting in the wings and, with our stomachs clenched and our blood pressure soaring, make our most fundamental decisions accordingly. "Before we do anything with our kids, we go through this religious catechism where we imagine all the worst things that could happen," averred Lenore Skenazy, a feisty New York–based author who made waves in 2007 when she decided to let her young son, Izzy, who had been obsessed with the city's subway systems for as long as he could remember, roam New York City, and ride those subways, unattended.

Critics denounced her as the worst mom in the country; for Skenazy, however she had made a judgment that her son was responsible, mature, and, as she and her friends were when they were children decades earlier, quite able to handle the city's streets without nonstop supervision. Skenazy went on to spearhead what became known as the Free Range Kids movement and to become a full-time commentator on what she regarded as the absurdities of modern risk-averse culture. "Parents feel and are told that they must have their eyes on their children either physically or technologically, or outsourced to a preapproved adult like a coach or a teacher. It is so completely hysterical—a combination of the bogeyman plus insurance. It's a Gordian knot. The idea of constant surveillance being the only good parenting thing is so entrenched. We live in a zombie apocalypse where anybody who approaches our children is going to kill them and any product they use is going to hurt them. My job is chronicling an absurd culture. I feel like I'm a blind person groping my way through the culture."[21]

Unable to process the truly extraordinary systemic risks we have to navigate, we deflect our focus, expending huge amounts of energy trying to literally remove all risk from our daily interactions. The risk-free society is a utopian dream, and as with all utopias, in attempting to implement it we move quickly into dystopian terrain.

Skenazy talked of a study, she couldn't remember from where, of the temperature of lunches that preschoolers were bringing with them to school. It found that a whopping 97 percent were at an unsafe temperature. When the report was released, it generated sensational headlines: "Deadly School Lunches." "Sack Lunches and Danger." Sitting on a bench on the grassy grounds where her family's somewhat ramshackle, ship's-cabin-like wooden cottage bungalow resides—the bungalows, lined up in rows, used to serve as the living quarters for a Catskills summer camp that first was run by German Bundists, then, from World War Two onwards as a Jewish camp—Skenazy, in jeans, a brown velvet zip-up sweater atop a striped blouse, blue socks with brown shoes, and a straw boater hat with a black ribbon, laughed dismissively. Skinny, short, and full of nervous energy, she moved her hands expressively as she talked. This was the sort of thing that made her mad as hell. "Some kids are eating tepid sandwiches. So what?! Nobody has died of tepid lunches."

The Free Range Kids advocate collected these sorts of stories—stories that don't make any rational sense, tales of crime and punishment in which the punishment is frequently far worse than the offense itself. She talked of a woman who contacted her after she got screamed at by a neighbor for reading a book while she sat in the front yard with her young children. "Put that book down," the neighbor screamed at her. "Your kids could be kidnapped."

Once the founder of the Free Range Kids movement got on a roll with these stories, she was hard to stop. One after another, the bizarre tales tripped off of her tongue.

She talked of a woman in Illinois who left her two toddlers in a car—not on a hot day, but on a 50 degree day—while she did an errand for ten minutes. The woman was convicted of child abuse, and the kids were placed on a child abuse and neglect registry. In some states, parents can be sent to jail for up to a year for leaving their kids alone in a car, which, Skenazy pointed out, "is ironic, since you're in trouble for leaving your kid alone in a car for a minute—and now you're in jail for a year."

"Fear," Skenazy concluded, "is a virus. And it's easiest to spread from our media and what we've decided is news and what we decide to make our TV shows and movies about."

In 1964, RICHARD HOFSTADTER published *The Paranoid Style in American Politics*. In it, he detailed how American politics had, over the generations, produced a discouraging number of profoundly paranoiac movements and individuals. The paranoid style, Hofstadter believed, brought in its wake a self-contained worldview: history didn't just sometimes generate conspiracies—plots, say, such as that which led to Julius Caesar's assassination, or the secret gatherings of revolutionary agents in 1848 Vienna or pre-1917 Russia—but was actually at a core level *shaped* by conspiracy. In such a world, conspiracy became the driving force behind all of the vast political, economic, and cultural changes shaping modernity.

Thus, in the decade after the end of the Second World War and the onset of the Cold War with the Soviet Union, for the John Birch Society any and every change was the product of an international Communist conspiracy, one that roped in not just the usual lefty suspects on campuses and in art circles but even senior Republican Party figures. Birch Society founder Robert Welch went so far as to name President Eisenhower as being a part of this conspiracy. In the best-selling book *None Dare Call It Treason*, the author John Stormer asserted that the US Congress was complicit in a planned Communist takeover of the United States. Senator Joseph McCarthy talked ominously about Communists infiltrating the top levels of government, academia, and media. The House Un-American Activities Committee held hearings to root suspected leftists out of their positions as producers of popular culture in Hollywood.

"Political fear," wrote the political scientist Corey Robin, in his 2004 book *Fear: The History of a Political Idea*, "depended upon illusion, where danger was magnified, even exaggerated, by the state. Because the dangers of life were many and various, because the subjects of the state did not naturally fear those dangers the state deemed worth fearing, the state had to choose people's objects of fear. It had to persuade people, through a necessary but subtle distortion, to fear certain objects over others."[22]

Fear has, at various moments in history and in various countries around the globe, come to occupy a disproportionately large role in shaping cultures and polities. In fourteenth-century Europe, for example, as the bubonic plague swept through countries, killing a vast proportion of the population, local leaders whipped up mobs against scapegoat populations: Jews, lepers, and purported witches were tortured and killed by the thousands, as populaces sought an explanation for the calamity that was befalling them. Not having a germ theory of disease, they looked to Satanic dealings, conspiracies of poisoners, outsiders seeking to pollute and contaminate the communities in which, however precariously, they lived. Albinos in parts of Africa have long been hunted down and killed by neighbors terrified of the dark forces they supposedly represent. Six hundred years after thousands of Jews were burned to death in towns throughout the Germanic lands, paranoiac, barbarous, totalitarian regimes in Germany and in the Soviet Union unleashed the unspeakable horrors of religious Holocausts and forced famines against populations they feared were undermining the coherence of the state. Fear of racial "contamination" led to the abominable regimes of Apartheid South Africa and, in the United States, the Jim Crow South. Fear of spreading Communism was used to justify the bloodthirsty actions of military juntas from Indonesia to Honduras, Chile to Greece.

A generation after Hofstadter highlighted the role of the paranoid style in American politics, and decades after the state had marshaled its full resources to teach Americans to fear anything and everything even vaguely linked to Communism, in the 1990s the sociologist Barry Glassner wrote a book titled *The Culture of Fear*. Glassner's premise was simple: increasingly, we were fearing things that really oughtn't cause us great alarm, and that fear was one of the few common, shared experiences that tens of millions of Americans could relate to. Fear was, as the seventeenth-century political philosopher Thomas Hobbes had predicted it would be, the glue binding the various institutions and individuals contained within the modern state together. It was a foundation on which entire political and cultural projects were being built; on which the worldviews of countless individuals rested. A problem that Hofstadter had located in the realm of politics, and one that had, generally, been kept to the fringes of the political process, had, now, spread into the broader realm of mass culture, affecting daily decisions and individual priorities at least as much as it influenced national political choices.

A generation on, again that culture of fear has flowered. What Glassner glimpsed as something in embryo is now ripening, or metastasizing, into maturity. There are companies that market bullet-proof backpacks for children, so that their parents can send them off to school with slightly more confidence that, if they were caught up in a school shooting, they would escape unhurt. There are anti-ebola hygiene kits marketed to suburban American families. There are tiny, waterproof GPS tracking devices that go into kids' bags and allow parents to track exactly where their young children—children too young to carry smartphones—are at every minute of every day, the nuts and bolts of a surveillance systems now so omnipresent that, were George Orwell himself, creator of the modern dystopia *1984*, to be resurrected he would surely keel over again in shock at the extent to which his nightmares had been realized and even improved on.

In one suburb after another, teenagers are subject to curfews—partly because so many parents are so fearful about the supposedly omnipresent risks that now face their children, and partly because, as a society, we have become so fearful of the children themselves—and of what they will do and to whom if we let them out after hours to explore their worlds.

Suburban Americans increasingly behave as if they are living in the South Bronx—and not the South Bronx of the early twenty-first century, which is actually quite a calm, safe place, but instead the burning, out of control, crime-besieged South Bronx of the late 1970s and 1980s. Meanwhile, inner-city residents, where a vastly disproportionate number of America's street crimes actually occur, and by extension where residents are disproportionately likely to be victims of crime, are increasingly policed and controlled as if *all* of their residents are criminals—with, as a result, one example after another of police brutality, which, in turn, leads to spiraling community reactions against that officially sanctioned violence.

The result, from Ferguson to Baltimore, from Baton Rouge to Minneapolis, has been mass protest and civic unrest—and a set of events that, seemingly inexorably, has led to an almost choreographed dance of destruction involving burning vehicles and storefronts, the acrid smell of tear gas, the spectacle of heavily armed and armored police, advancing behind walls of Plexiglas shields, to disperse crowds of angry, disempowered youngsters. There have been curfews and checkpoints, as well as die-ins and freeway takeovers. And from one city to the next, there have been, and likely will be in the years to come, rhetorical battles over how to understand, and to describe, the unfolding events. One person's riot is, after all, another person's rebellion.

When Missouri's governor, Jay Nixon, mobilized the National Guard to patrol the streets of Ferguson following days of protests against the police killing of a teenager, Michael Brown, in the summer of 2014, a majority of whites polled by the *New York Times* and CBS supported the decision; meanwhile most black respondents said it would make a bad situation worse.[23] In December of that year, pollsters commissioned by the *Washington Post* and ABC found that six out of ten whites were confident that the police were held accountable for their actions; by contrast, only one-quarter of blacks felt that way. And while only 28 percent of whites thought the police were too prone to use deadly force, nearly three out of four blacks thought they were too quick on the draw.[24] The following spring, as protests against perceived police brutality picked up steam, another poll showed the extent of the racial divide on this issue: more than half of whites polled thought the protestors were "people seeking an excuse to engage in looting and violence." Only a little over one-quarter of black respondents felt this to be the case.[25]

As these events get more news coverage, suburbanites, whose streets are, in fact, far *less* likely to be the scenes of either crime or of civic protest than are poorer, more urban settings, hunker down, their televisions and smart phones, their iPads and talk shows all telling them to be scared of the chaos lurking oh so very near to their horizon.

Fear, and the violence unleashed by that fear, has become the hinge upon which our deepest divisions and societal anxieties are mounted, the set design for the stage upon which the theater of twenty-first-century American life plays out.

ALL OF THIS IS, I believe, a phenomenon tied both to the rise of an all-pervasive and deeply sensationalist media and, as importantly, to the rise of a grossly unequal society.

The United States in the early twenty-first century is a place of stark inequities: in 2016, *Forbes* magazine published a list of the twenty-five countries globally with the most billionaires. Fifth on that list was Russia—a country long associated in Western media with the rule of an elite oligarchy—with 77 billionaires, who together had $282.6 billion in wealth. Fourth was India, with 84 billionaires controlling $248.4 billion. Third was Germany, with 120 billionaires in possession of $469.1 billion. Second was China, at 251 billionaires and $593 billion. But far, far out in front was the United States. With 540 billionaires, it had more super-rich individuals than those next four highest countries combined. And with those billionaires among them having a whopping net worth of $2.399 *trillion*, those billionaires controlled one and a half times more resources than did all those billionaires in China, Germany, India, and Russia put together.[26]

Meanwhile, roughly one in six Americans, and more than one in five children in the country, were living below the government-defined poverty line.[27] Among African American and Latino communities the poverty rates were even higher: fully 26 percent of African Americans and 24 percent of Latinos lived below the poverty line.[28]

One of the consequences of that inequality is a maldistribution not just of income and of opportunity, but also of perceptions of risk and fear. Increasingly, those without are seen by those who have as representing danger, risk, as being worthy of fearing. They are, in many ways, the Great Unwashed of our age, perceived to be as dirty and as germy, as violent and as unstable as were their antecedents in Victorian London. Thus the poor, the addicted, the undocumented, the homeless, the mentally ill—as well as the communities disproportionately lived in by the poor—all are seen as potentially destructive of the broader social order. And those who don't buy into the narrative of unfolding chaos and all-encompassing, omnipresent danger—middle-class families, for example, who dare to let their kids play alone in the great, scary outdoors or crime victims who urge understanding and forgiveness in place of punishment and vengeance—are vilified for exposing themselves or their young to the potentially predatory tendencies of the poor, the sick, the perverted waiting to take advantage of any sign of weakness.

The more unequal our society becomes, the more common understandings—shared experiences between rich and poor—cease to function. At a certain point the bonds of empathy collapse, to be replaced by suspicion and fear. And once that happens, those who can increasingly do opt out of public spaces, ceding the public sphere to people and groups seen as "dangerous" and risky, people with nothing to lose, desperadoes stumbling along on the very margins of society. Fear becomes the solvent dissolving the glue, the shared bonds, of a caring community. And, in turn, it becomes a new glue holding together alternative, more coercive power relationships. It is the product of inequality and at the same time the incubator of ever-greater inequality, both the legitimator of existing power structures and also the guarantor that hierarchies will remain in place.

That skewed understanding of risk runs the gamut—from grossly exaggerated estimates of the dangers of letting children play outside through to grossly exaggerated notions of the dangers to individuals and society posed by the mentally ill, by undocumented immigrants, by young black men, by inner-city school kids and so on.

Increasingly, in a twenty-four-hour news cycle, in which the smallest events can get magnified and broadcast globally within minutes, in which everyone can tweet and blog and otherwise electronically opine with only a modicum of facts to support the underlying stereotypes and fears, we are a limbic society. In other words, as our society gets evermore complex, demanding more powerful analytical tools from each and every member, too often we end up taking shortcuts, using only the parts of our brains neurologically decked out to make the quick decisions needed by hunted and hunter in a primitive, pretechnological world.

And taking shortcuts, we tend to judge people either as members of our group—the in-group—or as outsiders, potentially threatening, rapacious members of an out-group. We start thinking tribally. And we become easy fodder for demagogues. In a distressed, angry state, psychologist Darcia Narvaez explained, humans often look to a person who says, "I will save you. I will save you. I'm the only one who can do it." Turning against others to explain one's own feeling of discomfort, and looking for a super-hero to make all good in the world again, thus becomes a safety valve. "You don't want to feel bad," said Narvaez. "You want to feel better." And you feel better, in this instance, by defining yourself in opposition to some "other," alien group.[29]

Back at the University of Chicago, Jeni Kubota talked, with amazement, about a study she did on what researchers call the Ultimatum Game. In this game, you are presented with a stranger who is given a set amount of money—ten dollars, say. That stranger can then offer you a portion of the money. If you accept what he or she offers you, both you and the stranger get to keep the money. If you reject the offer, neither you nor the stranger get anything. Rationally, it's a no-brainer: even if the stranger offers you the paltry sum of one cent, you're financially better off saying yes. At least you get the one cent.

Kubota's team found, however, that rationality didn't hold sway here. If you believed the offer was insulting, you might nix it just to spite the stranger. And here's the kicker: white participants were far more likely to take umbrage, and to seek to stick a finger in the eye of the stranger even at their own financial cost, when the offer came from a black or Latino stranger than when it was from a white stranger. "Even though it's irrational to *ever* reject an offer, people are much more willing to take a hit to themselves to punish an out-group member than an in-group member," the psychologist explained. "Even when it comes at a personal cost. If you can find these irrational behaviors even in these silly economic games, you can imagine how irrationality functions at a systemic level. This violation of rationality is really fascinating."[30]

In a world of Twitter and 24/7 cable news, there is a real risk that such irrationality becomes the norm. There is, after all, no equivalent to the slow food movement in the media world today, no cultural mechanisms that allow us to take a deep breath, step back a few feet, and carefully digest the news that we are presented with. Instead, living within our personalized social media bubbles, we are expected to reach conclusions and change our behavior in response at near-warp speed. And so, to accomplish this, we rely on neural processes in the nonconscious, nonanalytical parts of our wonderfully complex brains, on ancient fight-flight-or-freeze response mechanisms honed over hundreds of millions of years of evolution, to make split-second decisions in our highly technological, interconnected, and engineered twenty-first-century society. Not surprisingly, as a result, we often get things horribly wrong. We flood our brains with the chemicals of fear, and then we make decisions about our evermore complex surroundings.

And modern neuroscience has demonstrated that those decisions in turn enter into our biological feedback loops: the more we are socially conditioned to fear certain types of individuals and behaviors, the more our brains are flooded by chemical releases in given situations, making it evermore likely that we'll respond in knee-jerk ways in the future. In other words, Facebook and Twitter, Instagram and Fox News may literally alter our most basic biochemical response systems.

As a result, we come to fear not what is really likely to affect us but what we are *told* is likely to affect us: hence the fact that almost everybody my age at some point developed a healthy fear of being eaten by sharks while swimming in the ocean. Not because we all knew shark victims—National Geographic has estimated that only nineteen Americans are attacked by sharks annually and that, on average, only one American every two years dies as a result of these attacks[31]—but because we had all seen the movie *Jaws*. I suspect an earlier generation of movie goers was similarly scared off of low-end roadside motels, not by a genuine rash of serial killings but by the power of Hitchcock's *Psycho*.

Most of us these days also don't spend a huge amount of time obsessing about the possibility of nuclear war, despite the fact that the *Bulletin of the Atomic Scientists* has long set its Doomsday Clock at just a few minutes to midnight—meaning that many of the best minds in the nuclear science community fear that there is imminent risk of one or another country or terrorist group either intentionally or accidently precipitating a nuclear apocalypse.[32] In 2010, a CNN poll found that nearly two-thirds of Americans were either not worried at all, or only mildly worried, about nuclear war,[33] despite the fact there were now more nuclear powers than at any time during the Cold War, and despite the fact that security analysts continued to worry that stockpiles of nuclear weapons and nuclear materials, especially in the countries of the former Soviet Union, were not properly secured against theft.

In 2015, the California-based Chapman University conducted a nationwide survey of American fears. Topping the list of fears reported by respondents: 58 percent were afraid of government corruption. Way down the list, at 33.6 percent, was fear of nuclear attack. That was 3 percent less than the percentage of Americans who feared gun control (not guns, mind you, but the *control* of guns), just over 2 percent less than the percentage who feared Obamacare, and only 0.6 percent more than the percentage of Americans who feared reptiles.[34]

At least in part, citizens of the early twenty-first century, unlike the early atomic-age generations—many of whose denizens *did* think about, write about, and, by the hundreds of thousands, protest the possibility of nuclear war—don't invest a huge amount of time thinking about the dangers of nuclear weapons because, after the Cold War wound down without those weapons having been used in combat, much of the media stopped talking about them. Out of sight, out of mind.

THE SAME LOGIC HOLDS for an array of other things that, argued consumer advocate Ralph Nader, we *should* be very much afraid of. Poorly designed car safety systems, for example, or highly profitable but extremely toxic pharmaceuticals marketed without adequate attention paid to long-term health risks faced by patients. Things that do occasionally grab the headlines—though only when something doesn't just go a little bit wrong but spectacularly misfires—but on a daily basis tend to be ignored, replaced in the public consciousness by the soothing imagery produced by well-financed marketing departments.

"Many producers [of pharmaceutical products] fear that if the numbers were available people would think that the risks are bigger, the benefits are not that great, the uncertainties are larger," noted Carnegie Mellon psychology professor Baruch Fischoff, head of an advisory committee to the Food and Drug Administration. "People would rather sell the impressions than sell the facts."[35]

For Nader, the result of us being sold impressions over facts was a great popular willingness to ignore real-and-present dangers, or what he called "corporate-sponsored mayhem." The Occupational Safety and Health Administration (OSHA), calculates that roughly fifty-eight thousand American workers die each year as a result of workplace accidents, one hundred thousand Americans die as a result of medical malpractice, sixty-five thousand die because of air pollution, and more than forty thousand because they lack medical insurance and thus their illnesses are left to run rampant. Every single day in America, Nader said, between two hundred and two hundred and fifty people die of infections they picked up while in hospitals. And yet these massive fatality rates "are never discussed in elections or in Congress. It's all about street crime and terrorism." In fact, he continued, "Far more people get killed by adverse effects of medicine than from street drugs."

You can, however, put a face on street crime, in a way that it's much harder to do with something like toxic chemicals. It's easy for the local television news to run a sensational story on a local gang or a spate of heroin overdoses. It's much harder to get an audience to care about chronic asthma in poor, polluted communities or the daily drip of staph infections, one here, another there, coming out of hospitals around the country. "The styles of violence a culture has," Nader had come to believe, "are very correlated with distributions of power, in terms of what violence is reported and remedied, and what violence isn't reported and remedied."[36]

WE ARE CONDITIONED TO fear stereotypes more than complex, but far more lethal, multifaceted events—social, economic, technological, and climactic trends, say—and the result is frequently something akin to madness. Hence the Jan Morgan phenomenon: the woman who owned a gun range and refused to let Muslims in because she was convinced that *all* Muslims were potential terrorists, and that if she let *any* Muslims in to her business, she would court a massacre.

There had been *no* Muslim-orchestrated terrorist attacks in Arkansas at the time Morgan made her decision to bar Muslims from her range—though if one were watching Fox News, the most available of news channels in the South, in the early years of the century, one could be forgiven for thinking such massacres were a daily occurrence. Meanwhile, the state, awash as it was with guns and with heavily armed locals, did have one of the highest gun-inflicted murder rates in the country, and one of the highest gun-inflicted suicide rates,[37] with the vast majority of these deaths not being meted out by Arkansan Muslims.

Facts, however, often don't seem to matter as much as gut feelings. And when it comes to the crowd's gut, Muslims in contemporary America, black teenagers, foster kids, undocumented immigrants—all are the sharks in our popular imagination: movie-set horrors ready and willing to attack.

Meanwhile, I don't know too many people with an absolute phobia of walking in meadows in the Northeast, despite the fact that far more people are sickened by East Lyme disease, carried by ticks that live in these meadows, than are attacked by sharks. Perhaps that has something to do with the fact that to date there hasn't been a Hollywood blockbuster on Tick Attacks. Nor has there been such a movie on slippery showers, uneven sidewalks, or two of the truly great silent killers, radon poisoning—which, as mentioned earlier in this book, the Environmental Protection Agency estimates triggers lung cancers that kill twenty-one thousand Americans each year[38]—and carbon monoxide poisoning. And despite Hollywood's propensity to script horror flicks about exotic killer bugs, ebola-like creations that melt the walls of blood vessels and turn humans into gooey, bloody blobs, I can't recall any Oscar-worthy film on pneumonia; this despite the fact that pneumonia is still one of the most potent killers of weak or elderly human beings.

Our fears, in short, simply don't match up to the realities of the risks we face. We fear things that come with a particularly ferocious ick factor (ebola and the dissolving capillaries being a case in point) or people the media focuses particular attention on, such as ideologically inspired zealot terrorists, rather than the more mundane and commonplace maimers and killers of thousands—be they flu viruses or pneumonia bacilli, workplace accidents, disgruntled lovers, or invisible toxic gases.

THAT DOESN'T MEAN THEY'RE the wrong fears. From the perspective of those marketing fear, they're the exact right fears:

fears that keep society divided and justify those social divisions; fears that sell an awful lot of useless security and monitoring products—from the sight- and sound-monitoring widgets that saturate every middle-class household with a new baby through to tracking systems allowing you to see what your possibly wayward spouse is doing and where, every minute of every day; fears that distract us from the deeper, bigger, more systemic problems facing our society. They are the baubles of a culture lacking the attention span to really grapple with the larger crises of a complex, high-tech, bureaucratic system.

A lot of writers in recent years have written about the wrong way of fear: from Glassner's classic *The Culture of Fear* in the 1990s, through to Daniel Gardner's post–9/11 *The Science of Fear.* These writers aren't wrong, but they're missing a larger story.

The real story is how America has reinvented itself as a society so divided, so insecure, and, in many ways, so unhappy with daily existence that to feel better we *need* that fear. It's the drug that gives us meaning. It provides us with a storyline to help interpret our daily realities. It allows us to say "I (or we) would do this, but . . . ," and that "but" then is followed by a litany of reasons why things are so goddamn awful that change and reinvention will have to be postponed.

In twenty-first-century America, fear and risk have emerged as paralyzing matrices, as a form of kryptonite within which our best impulses too often get frozen in place and stifled.

Chapter Eight

Drilling for Disaster

As the Meitivs knew all too well, children are peculiarly affected by that matrix of fear. They are seen both as potential victims—of random sexual predators, of gun-toting homicidal maniacs, of bullies and gangs, of drug dealers and pornographers—and also, in many instances, as potential menaces. To both protect them and protect others from them, they are, as a result, now policed and watched and monitored as no other generation of kids in American history has been.

In most parts of the world—in countries like Switzerland, with a far lower violent crime rate than the United States, and also in countries such as Mexico, with a far higher violent crime rate—children are given levels of autonomy unheard of in modern America.

Until late into the evening one can see groups of kids playing, unsupervised, in the streets of any Mexican city. In Switzerland, during the morning one can see preschoolers walking through the streets to kindergarten. They are trained, from a young age, how to cross the streets by themselves, and, oftentimes, they wear colorful tags hung from their necks to signify to passersby that they are very young, very small, and ought to be extended any help they might need. In Japan, children as young as six or seven routinely navigate crowded public transport systems on their way to and from school. Were those same children to be put on trains and buses in the United States, they would almost certainly be stopped and taken in by the police, and their parents would be turned over to the tender investigations of Child Protective Services.

When my family was staying in Valparaíso, Chile, learning Spanish, we took it for granted that children would roam the streets by themselves. How else would they get to school in a city where most residents didn't drive cars? How else would they entertain themselves in a city where most residents can't afford endless after-school programs and lessons? How would they stay cool in a city where most buildings don't have air conditioning?

As the sun went down and then was replaced by the darkness of night, one could see, and hear, children playing in the alleyways and along the hilly streets: playing soccer or tag, or just running around with other kids their age. It was part of the rhythm and soundtrack of daily life in Valparaíso. It was, one sensed, as important a part of life for these children as was what happened behind the locked doors and gates of their houses.

The contrast with our California neighborhood was stark. There, despite the fact we live near a light rail station, and close to a major boulevard along which buses drive on a regular basis, cars line up along all the residential streets for the half hour before the local high school lets out at three o'clock. The teenagers driven to and from the school each day, have, I would guess, never been allowed to test their own navigation skills by using light rail or buses with no parent present to supervise. I suspect one could take the process one step further, too: many of these kids have grown up utterly cocooned, never allowed to do anything or go anywhere without adult supervision. They will go to college or enter the job market largely unprepared to make even the most mundane of decisions unaided. The rationale for this? That it's a dangerous world and kids should be spared as much interaction with it, for as long as possible, as parents, teachers, coaches, and others can organize.

Every few weeks, our kids are subjected to "lockdown" drills, our age's equivalent to the inane duck-and-cover drills of the Cold War—in which hiding under a wooden desk was supposed to provide kids with protection from the hundreds or thousands of kilotons of explosive power unleashed by a hotter-than-the-sun, city-leveling thermonuclear explosion. When the lockdown alarms are activated over the school PAs, teachers immediately shut and lock their classroom doors; they count their children to make sure none are out in the yard or on bathroom break; and they email or text the school principal's office to let them know that all children are accounted for. While they are doing that, all the children in the classrooms either hide underneath their desks or line up along walls not visible to a potential attacker looking through the door's window from the outside. They are taught to stay absolutely silent during these drills, so as not to draw the attention of a marauding gunman. As the drill unfolds, the school principal and his or her assistants quickly parade through the school, testing each door to make sure it really is locked.

Afterwards, drill over, the children—who have spent the last several minutes hiding from potential killers seeking to destroy them, their friends, and their teachers—are supposed to get on with the school day, and continue with their classes, as if nothing out of the ordinary has happened. It is, of course, an absurdity. Exposed to such an extraordinary stress-invoking situation, those children will carry that stress forward with them. "When the stress response systems are active," Darcia Narvaez wrote in her book *Neurobiology and the Development of Human Morality*, "we become necessarily more self-focused, more attuned to danger to ourselves, and ready for offense or defense in the face of threat." She explained, "Active aggression or passive withdrawal or some combination will feel 'good' or 'right' to the individual actor. In this case, there is little room for compassionate or thoughtful response. When a person operates from the survival systems or continues in a 'threat-down' mode after a stressor is passed, he will interpret innocent events as threatening, as chronically aggressive kids do when someone accidentally bumps into them."[1]

Put a child through enough lockdown drills, and you will teach that child to regard life as little more than a series of potential deathtraps. You will, eventually, teach that child to jump at their own shadow.

Even setting aside the long-term risks to children's psychic well-being, in the short-term, too, these drills are not risk-free. In March 2015, Rick Montgomery, a journalist working for the *Tribune News Service*, reported that a nursing home worker in Colorado had sued a school district, presumably for the mental trauma and terror she suffered, after she accidentally stumbled into the middle of an active-gunman drill. In Missouri, four teachers got so uncomfortable with these drills that they contacted a local county prosecutor to explore their legal options. And in Iowa, more than twenty-five teachers sued for workers' compensation after being injured while training with fellow school officials to wrestle role-playing gunmen to the ground.[2]

In many instances, veteran school security experts worry that the new procedures themselves can endanger the people they are supposed to protect: anti-intruder doors were installed in some schools in Ohio without overrides built in, making it hard for first responders to reach stranded kids in, say, the event of a fire; and making it easier for teenagers to rape fellow students in a classroom that they have managed to temporarily put on lockdown. There are anecdotes from around the country about teachers being injured during lockdown drills. And at the Kaimuki Middle School in Hawaii, a lockdown drill involving a teacher running through the school wielding a hammer, in imitation of an attacker, drew criticism after several young kids were traumatized by the sight of their seemingly crazed teacher on a rampage.

At one local school near my house, in a calm suburban neighborhood—a school that has experienced only two genuine lockdown situations in the past twenty years, one when a murder victim's body was dumped in a property across the street from the school, the other when a potentially dangerous stray dog made its way onto campus—a teacher, under extraordinary stress in her personal life, got so confused by one of these drills that she thought there really was a gunman on the campus. "Run!" she screamed at her terrified young students. "Run!" And sent them caroming through the hallways in search of safety.

In rural Shelbyville, Indiana, which FBI data shows to be the third-safest midsized town in the state,[3] administrators became so obsessed by the possibility of random violence that in the summer of 2015 they installed a $400,000 security system in the high school, complete with cutting-edge locks on all the doors (allowing a state of instant lockdown to be imposed), omnipresent cameras, and smoke cannons embedded in the ceilings to disorient would-be attackers.

Shelbyville had had zero murders and four reported "forcible" rapes in the period from 2010 through 2013, the most recent years for which data was available to administrators when they agreed to install the security system. It had had eighteen cases of aggravated assault and six robberies.[4] In fact, in the previous few years, the most lethal use of force in Shelbyville had been by the police, who shot dead an armed man at the end of a nine-hour standoff in September 2015, the month the school security system went into effect.[5]

But Shelbyville's low-crime rate didn't serve to put the brakes on the school security plan. On NBC's local news affiliate, WTHR 13, local school superintendent Paula Maurer announced, "It used to be that education was the number 1 thing that schools did. Now we need to keep our students safe first."[6] And so one of the safest cities in Indiana now had a school security system, paid for with government grants, that could have paid the salaries of roughly nine teachers, in a city where the average teacher's wage was just over $43,000 per year.[7] Teachers wore panic buttons around their necks, the pressing of which would trigger a campus-wide lockdown. The police, watching on cameras from miles away, could set off smoke alarms and fire alarms, in select areas known as Hot Zones, to disorient any intruders who happened to make their way onto campus.

"I'm all for technology and innovation," the anchor opined at the end of the splashy, laudatory five-minute segment on the new school security system. "But it makes me sick to my stomach that it's come to this."[8] Of course, had his news team dug a little deeper, he would have realized that things *hadn't* really come to such a pass after all. Shelbyville was a small, sleepy town with small, sleepy town problems. But now it was a small, sleepy town with a bells-and-whistles school security system just in case the unimaginable were to happen, and a populace primed to believe—because their local news had told them it was so—that their kids' high school was a likely war zone.

When I contacted the superintendent for a comment, she emailed back to tell me that "for the safety of the students" the school district's board of trustees had instructed officials not to participate in any more interviews about the security system.[9]

THE SCHOOL SECURITY INDUSTRY has now become huge business, in the same way as the country's prison systems were massively ramped up in the 1990s and 2000s despite falling crime rates.

One can trace this back to the mid-1990s, when President Bill Clinton's administration, seeking to prove that Democrats could be as doggone tough on crime as Republicans, asked Congress to fund thousands of "school resource officers," making the presence of often-armed police a daily reality in schools around the country. Thousands more police were also funded by city and state grants to school districts. At the same time, one school after another, especially in inner cities, brought in airport-style metal detectors and "clear bag" policies so that school officials could easily check everything that students were bringing into the schools.

Not surprisingly, as schools increasingly came to resemble prisons, so more and more students ended up being arrested in school settings. In cities such as Stockton, California, where even nonpolice "resource officers" were granted arrest powers, hundreds and finally thousands of kids acquired arrest records for minor, oftentimes status offenses.[10] Sometimes the confrontations engendered by the presence of these officers could be horrendous. In October 2015, for example, students filmed an officer in a South Carolina school violently tipping a teenage girl backward out of her chair and onto her neck, before dragging her across the floor and arresting her—for the relatively benign offense of using her cell phone during math class.

Two decades on from the legislative beginnings of America's school security fetish, things reached a whole new level of bizarreness. After the tragic December 2012 Sandy Hook massacre, in Newtown, Connecticut, one company after another rushed to take advantage of the opportunities presented by the red-alert levels of fear around school violence—in the grand quack tradition of patent medicines and promised elixirs of youth. As a result, a huge number of utterly inane products entered the market, despite the paucity of evidence that many of them have any impact at all on crime and mortality rates.

It is, said school security specialist Kenneth Trump, longtime president of the Cleveland-based National School Safety and Security Services, something akin to a feeding frenzy, "overnight experts, gadgets, and gurus who have popped up out of the blue. Every time we have a high profile shooting we see another business or product, well-intended but not well thought-out." After the Columbine massacre, Trump recalled, there was a "fairly reasonable conversation" about security; by contrast, in the years following the slaughter at Sandy Hook "it's been the worst I've seen in thirty-plus years, in terms of people responding emotionally and businesses preying on the emotions of people who are afraid."[11]

Take, for example, Bullet Blockers, a company working out of Lowell, Massachusetts, that manufactures and markets bulletproof backpacks for elementary school children—the ones for young girls come in a pretty raspberry pink or purple plaid; the ones for boys in red, black, blue, and camo—bullet-proof jackets, bulletproof iPad cases, and even bulletproof white boards for use in classrooms. "As a human you have the natural tendency to save yourself by putting something up in front of you," explained Ed Burke, the company's cofounder, in promoting his iPad cases. The company even marketed a "survival kit," complete with fire starters, first aid guides, cold compresses, and other items that would allow a child to survive a prolonged school lockdown.[12]

Burke wouldn't tell me how many individual items of each product his company had sold, but he did say that "since the Paris attacks [of November 13, 2015] our business has grown 80 percent, and continues to grow." In other words, a terrorism attack overseas was serving as an extraordinary marketing opportunity for a US company largely catering to parents scared to send their young kids off to school each morning.

"Thank God, [none of these products] as yet" had come into play in a school shooting situation, he told me evasively. But "they've been tested randomly, to test ballistic capabilities." One can only ponder the psychic damage done to young kids kitted out by terrified parents in bulletproof jackets and backpacks before they are sent off to school each day.

Meanwhile, the self-defense group known as the ALICE Training Institute, based out of Medina, Ohio, began marketing the idea of training elementary school kids in the art of throwing heavy objects, such as cans of food, at gun-wielding attackers. "It comes out from the business community, who think they see a dollar, a sales opening," said Trump dismissively. "I increasingly believe we walk a thin line around reasonableness."

In Long Island, New York, an entrepreneur named Derek Peterson established a tech company start-up called Digital Fly. It developed a software capacity, using Google Maps, that allowed schools to monitor all social media postings around a school or in an entire school district, within a radius chosen by the school. The intent, which would be eerily familiar to government spy agencies the world over, was to use keywords to drill down into communications used near schools, looking for potential shooters or bombers, bullies, or would-be suicides. The postings of anyone within that catchment area, be they students, local residents, or simply people passing through, were monitored. "My software will identify it," Peterson explained enthusiastically, either oblivious of, or indifferent to, the extraordinary privacy implications of his work. "The school administrator will get emails. At that point every school has a different policy—they get the parents, the police involved. I provide you with a hammer; here's the tools to build the house."

When I spoke to him in the winter of 2016, Peterson claimed that his technology was being used in more than fifty schools around the country, as well as in some schools in Ireland and in South Africa. His ambitions were large: "It could go global. We're hoping it does. I'm a serial entrepreneur; this is right in my sweet spot. How do you put a price on protecting little ones? Unfortunately we live in a crazy world where kids are targeted. So any way we can protect children, I'm all for it."[13]

Like Burke and his backpacks, Peterson acknowledged that he had no real way of knowing how well the implementation of Digital Fly was working—although he did claim it had helped head off two suicides in New York City schools. But since he only charged schools $1.50 to $2.75 per student, it was cheap enough that he hoped schools would figure it was worth adding to their tool kit just on the off chance that it worked. He toured the country, telling PTA meetings that his product was as cheap as one can of soda per year for each kid, and then he provided a patter on how if even one bloody nose was avoided, it was money well spent. "Right now, there are fifty million K through twelve matriculating students, just in the US," he said, as he pondered his company's future. "The sky is the limit."

THE SCHOOL SECURITY INDUSTRY is a classic example of what goes wrong when the private profit motive meets popular fear. Money that could be spent on, say, the hiring of teachers and the buying of up-to-date textbooks is, instead, diverted into the buying of a seemingly endless array of security products that, in the vast majority of instances, will never be used. For, despite all the hyperbole, in actual fact school shootings and other lethal attacks on school grounds are almost vanishingly rare. Since the mid-1990s, a total of around nine hundred murders have occurred inside American schools, averaging out at about forty-five per year.[14] Since more than fifty-five million children are enrolled in schools in the United States, these numbers mean that in any given year a child has a less than one in a million chance of being killed while at school. Compare this to a national murder rate of just shy of five per hundred thousand, or sixty per million, and schools start to look like an oasis of calm, about sixty times less lethal than their surroundings in the broader community.

Even in the 2012–2013 school year, which encompassed the horrors of the Sandy Hook elementary school massacre, the National School Safety Center estimates that a total of thirty kindergarten through twelfth grade students were shot dead in schools in incidents that didn't involve gang-on-gang violence or students committing suicide.[15]

In fact, far more children die in the United States each year of the flu or pneumonia, from drowning, or as a consequence

of road accidents than die in school shootings. The CDC estimates that, depending on the severity of the flu season, annual
flu deaths in the United States range from a low of three thousand to a high of forty-nine thousand.[16] Of these, in an average
year a little more than a hundred flu fatalities in the country
are children. In the 2009–2010 season, however, nearly three
hundred fifty kids succumbed to the disease.[17] Globally, more
than nine hundred thousand children under the age of five die
of pneumonia every year, an invisible catastrophe few American
media outlets cover and few Americans are, as a result, aware
of.[18] More children die from encephalitis or other complications
triggered by insect bites. More kids die from sports-related injuries. And by huge orders of magnitude, more die from asthma
in deeply impoverished and polluted communities, the asthma
worsened by the presence of toxic pollutants in the air they
breathe, pollutants that range from pesticides to diesel particles
to mold spores that flourish in slum housing.

Yet none of these causes of death—many of them slow-
moving disasters that are both more difficult to comprehend
in the aggregate and less easy to sensationalize in news headlines—result in the sort of mass hysteria that has been seen in
recent years around the prospect of school violence. And, by extension, none of these have resulted in the emergence of quack
industries designed to assuage fears while conveniently relieving
individuals and institutions of large sums of money that could
better be spent elsewhere.

IN LARGE PART, THIS has happened because of how we mentally
categorize events such as school shootings or outbursts of terrorist violence. We think of them as crimes—which, of course they

are. But we don't think of them as public health disasters—which, given the interplay of mental illness and easy access to weaponry, in the case of nonpolitical mass shootings, and fanatical political beliefs that emerge as states fail and as wars spread, in the case of terrorist-related shootings, of course they also are.

Viewed as stand-alone crimes, it is absolutely no surprise that, say, the grotesque mass killings in Paris on November 13, 2015, or the shooting of school children in Sandy Hook a few years earlier, are understood as world-changing events. That they dominate the news cycle for weeks and months on end, and fundamentally change how ordinary citizens go about their lives and how political leaders shape their domestic and international agendas. That they result in the spending of tens of billions of dollars to invest in security apparatus designed to stop the next attacks and render safe public spaces shown to be terribly vulnerable.

Recall Dr. Sally Winston's idea that the anxious brain is a brain incapable of correctly calibrating risk. It sees the stakes in play—dead children, terror victims on city streets—but not the actual odds that these events will be visited on your child's particular school or your particular favorite restaurant or sports venue or shopping mall or concert arena. The anxious brain is predisposed to "sticky" thoughts, to ideas that once embedded in consciousness are almost impossible to shake off. And nothing embeds an idea in one's head more than around-the-clock television and social media news coverage. When a crime like Sandy Hook or the Paris massacre occurs, our attentions are riveted, our fear levels crescendo, and our chemical responders hit the scene running. We become cortisol and norepinephrine fiends. We viscerally feel that these events could happen to us, that they are likely to happen to us, that only by the grace of

God have they so far *not* happened to us. As the news cycle rolls on, as one headline and one ghastly story follows the next, as one survivor after another is interviewed, or one relative of a dead victim followed by another relative is asked to convey their grief, we lose the ability to weigh the odds.

"When we're making these complex decisions," explained University of California, Berkeley, psychologist and neuroscientist Sonia Bishop, "we are bombarded with people saying, 'This is the case, this is the case.'" It's very hard to discount things you hear again and again."[19]

Trapped in the echo chamber that inevitably accompanies a school shooting or a terrorism attack, our default assumption is to assume that the events are of a far bigger magnitude than they in fact are and, moreover, that we, and those we love, are in immanent peril. Were they instead seen as public health disasters, however, and placed in the context of other far more lethal outbreaks, these events would not produce either the individual adrenal rush or the level of international panic that they currently generate. For in the cold light of day, and without minimizing the agony that they cause, in actual fact the numbers of people killed in these attacks pale in comparison to a slew of other causes of premature death around the world.

The same day that 20 children and 6 adults were murdered by Adam Lanza in Sandy Hook, somewhere in the region of 4,000 people globally died of tuberculosis.[20] More than 300 of those who died were children. That same day, globally another 3,500-plus people died of HIV/AIDS. In Russia, Poland, Kazakhstan, Korea, Portugal, Peru, and several other countries, rampant alcoholism was reducing each resident's life in the early years of the century by an average of five years. The same day that 130 people died at the hands of ISIS fanatics in Paris, roughly the same number of people died in the United States of drug overdoses. The same number had died the day before and would die the day afterwards.[21] In 2015 as a whole, roughly 50,000 Americans would die of drug overdoses—many of them taking powerful pharmaceuticals such as oxycontin and fentanyl that they had become addicted to after being prescribed them by their doctors.

In Afghanistan, in 2012—the year of the Sandy Hook massacre—the United Nations estimates that more than 12,000 children under the age of five died of respiratory infection and other lung diseases caused by what epidemiologists term "household air pollution." That translates to nearly 33 kids dead every day of preventable respiratory diseases resulting from the fact that people too poor to be able to afford safe heating and cooking technologies were burning woods and other fuels that spewed potentially lethal particles into the air their children breathed. More than 6,000 children under the age of five died of the same cause in Burkina Faso and in the Ivory Coast; more than 5,000 in Burundi, in Madagascar, and in South Sudan; roughly 4,400 in Zambia; nearly 3,400 in Guinea; about 3,100 in Zimbabwe; more than 2,700 in Haiti.[22]

Maybe the difference is simply one of intent? After all, thousands of children may die each day of TB, diarrhea, cholera, and other illnesses, but is this not simply an unfortunate act of nature, one vastly different in its moral implications from the heinous decision on the part of crazed or fanatical gunmen and bombers to sow mayhem in a particular place and against a particular group of people?

Partly, the answer to that question is yes. But it's also the case that many diseases kill their victims not because there is no known cure, but because the victims do not have the financial

resources, or their countries do not have the medical infrastructure, to link sufferers up with effective medical interventions.
That's why poor children in Third World countries tend to die
of diarrhea, whereas affluent kids in First World countries get
prompt rehydration treatments and recover within a few days.
Globally, sixteen thousand children under the age of five die
every day, according to data collected by the World Health Organization, a huge proportion of them from treatable conditions
such as diarrhea.[23]

It's why a diagnosis of HIV in a wealthy country today, and
especially among the more affluent members of that society, is
an announcement that an individual has a chronic disease for
which they will have to take expensive medications for the rest
of their lives; whereas that same diagnosis in many poor countries, or poor communities within generally rich countries, is a
statement of imminent death. It's why drug-resistant TB tends to
flourish in countries, such as Russia and the United States, that
incarcerate a large proportion of their population in overcrowded
prisons, where airborne diseases rapidly spread, and then release
infected individuals into poor communities with minimal access
to quality medical care. It's why children in poor countries are
far more likely than children in wealthier lands first to be exposed to toxic air in their own homes and communities and then
to die as a result of the pollution-induced lung diseases. In the
United States, environmental campaigners have long studied the
disproportionate impact of asthma on low-income communities,
positing a range of causes from slum-housing conditions to the
presence of pesticides in poor rural neighborhoods, to the situat-
ing of diesel transit depots in impoverished urban districts.

The Harvard University medical anthropologist and physi-
cian Paul Farmer, renowned for his work among impoverished

communities in Haiti, in parts of the former Soviet Union, in many countries in Africa, and elsewhere, has long been fascinated by the ways in which societies divvy up access to basic resources and social goods such as medical care. He has found that the poor tend to suffer disproportionate health impacts not just in a country such as Haiti but also in a wealthy democracy like the United States. "The liberal political agenda has rarely included the powerless, the destitute, the truly disadvantaged," he wrote in his 2003 book *Pathologies of Power*. "It has never concerned itself with those properly classified as the 'undeserving' poor: drug addicts, sex workers, illegal 'aliens,' welfare recipients, or the homeless, to name a few. . . . The drama, the tragedy of the destitute sick concerns not only physicians and scholars who work among the poor, but all who profess even a passing interest in human rights."[24]

That we tolerate such a maldistribution of basic resources, both between countries and within them, means that there is an element of human choice and of intent when mortality rates soar not across the board but among select demographic groups. That the death rate for adult men in Russia increased by 49 percent in the four years after the fall of the Berlin Wall and the end of the Communist system of governance cannot be consigned to random chance.[25] Whatever other benefits accrued Russians, and citizens of the other one-time member states of the Soviet Union, as Communism was replaced by crony-capitalism, longevity wasn't among them. In fact, as inequality rose dramatically in the years after the Soviet Union fell apart—the Gini coefficient, used globally as a measure of inequality, increased in Russia from 27 in 1990 to 52 in 2001—so too did the death rate. In 2004, the British epidemiologist Sir Michael Marmot estimated that across the one-time Soviet Union as a whole, as life expectancy plummeted, an additional four million deaths

had occurred during this period.[26] In Russia itself, the number
of additional deaths caused by what we might think of as forced
capitalism-ization was somewhat comparable to the numbers
who died in the famines and organized killings in the Soviet
state of Russia that accompanied Stalin's forced collectivization
program in the 1930s—though nowhere near as high as the
numbers who died in neighboring Ukraine in the '30s. That's
not to diminish the scale of the atrocities under Stalin, which in
their deliberate, calculated nature, surely rank among the worst
crimes against humanity of modern times, but it is to say that
less obviously criminal actions can, in their impact, also cause
large-scale, and avoidable, human suffering.

A shockingly similar trend emerged among non–college-
educated whites in the United States in the last decade of the
twentieth century and the first years of the twenty-first. While
most of the population saw huge gains in life expectancy, for
white men with at most a high school education, life expectancy declined by three years between 1990 and 2008; for white
women without a college education the decline was even more
precipitous: fully five years.[27] Not coincidentally, this was the
population group suffering the most catastrophic economic
changes as the economy globalized, losing earning power, jobs,
and status; seeing increases in long-term unemployment; frequently forfeiting access to health care as they lost employment
or ended up working part-time in jobs that no longer came with
benefits. It was a population at particular risk of drug addiction,
stress, the health impacts of a poor diet, and so on.

Such conditions, Farmer wrote, create "pent-up anger born
of innumerable small indignities, and of great and irremediable
ones. Structural violence generates bitter recrimination, whether
it is heard or not."[28]

All of this means that the notion of agency alone can't be the reason we are so horrified by large terrorist attacks and so disinterested in chronic public health disasters. For if agency was sufficient to trigger public horror, the economic policy choices in both Russia and the United States over the last quarter century, choices that have generated extraordinary wealth for some and extraordinary insecurity, and escalating death rates, for many, would on a daily basis be generating headlines and a growing clamor to deal with this scandalous state of affairs.

That we spill far more ink on attacks that kill dozens rather than complicated societal changes that affect millions brings us back to the way such events are covered. When a mass shooting occurs, the world's media descends on the scene, and within minutes a global audience is watching, in horror, on cell phones, tablets, computer screens, and TVs. The impact of the event is easy to visualize, and the pain of the victims correspondingly easy to empathize with. But when a disease like diarrhea or malaria or tuberculosis takes its routine and deadly toll, or when collapsing public health infrastructure hugely lowers the life expectancy of millions, by and large the media stays away. No audience is generated. And the seeds of panic aren't sown.

None of this is to minimize the scale of the atrocities carried out by groups such as Al-Qaeda and ISIS; rather it is to complicate a story, familiar across the globe at this point, which highlights certain kinds of death, meted out by particular groups and in particular wealthy places, while downplaying other, more "routine" but oftentimes equally preventable deaths that ultimately truncate far more lives. "Corporate-originated death and injury is given a low place on the ladder," Ralph Nader avers, discussing how the media prioritizes coverage of fatalities. "Terrorism is top of the list."[29]

We are more likely to care about events that can be boiled down to a sound bite or a few seconds of vivid visual coverage. And we are more disposed to be outraged by the sadism, the deliberate cruelty, of a bloodthirsty act of terror, say, than the cool, dispassionate, bottom-line calculations that corporations frequently make, and that too often for comfort also result in huge, and preventable, loss of life.

That we are so conditioned to trust, or at least live with, big corporate institutions is probably why drug scandals that cause mass fatalities rarely remain long in the public consciousness.

Take the Vioxx scandal, for example. Medical experts have estimated that, by conservative calculations, between 1999 and 2004 roughly sixty thousand Americans died as a result of complications triggered by taking this drug, which was marketed by the pharmaceutical company Merck, despite an abundance of warning signs that there were problems with the medicine, as a miracle weapon in the fight against arthritis. That's twenty times as many fatalities as the number of people who lost their lives on 9/11. It's more than one thousand times as many as the numbers killed in the Orlando nightclub massacre in June 2016.[30]

Thousands upon thousands of the men and women who were prescribed this drug—often by doctors who were being heavily courted by Merck, often after the patients themselves had seen seductive ads on television touting the drug's miraculous healing properties—succumbed to heart attacks or to strokes. Yet beyond a few big lawsuits and some congressional hearings, the scandal quickly faded from public view. The world's priorities did not shift in the wake of this catastrophe, public finances weren't reordered to reflect a new regulatory "war on corrupt pharmaceutical companies," and national resources weren't marshaled to ensure that subsequent disasters unleashed by Big Pharma could never again occur.

Ask most people today, more than a decade on from the drug's withdrawal from the market, what the Vioxx catastrophe was, and they'll shrug their shoulders, unable even to hazard a guess. Ask them, by contrast, what happened on September 11, 2001, and almost all of those questioned will be able to give a generally reliable answer.

Every few weeks parents at my children's schools will get notices, such as the one I received by email in the spring of 2015, informing parents of kids at the elementary school my son attends, about a slip in the rules: in my case, it was from our kids' after-school program helpfully informing us that an elementary school kid had reached under the desk and inappropriately touched another elementary school kid, that the "appropriate authorities" had been notified, and that an investigation was under way. What once would have been dealt with by talking with the child had, in this era of paranoia, been promoted to a full sexual-abuse investigation involving deeply prepubescent protagonists and a vast city and state bureaucracy.

In the suburbs of Salt Lake City, a chain of Montessori schools, traditionally attractive to parents because of the educational philosophy's emphasis on creativity, art, and play, markets itself to prospective parents by highlighting their security systems: fingerprint recognition software controlling entry through the front doors; cameras monitoring each classroom, with the images displayed in the foyer for parents to browse; a ten-foot-high fence blocking all views into the play yard.

There is an insanity, a claustrophobia, to this way of raising children. And it only makes sense if one's surroundings are
viewed through thick lenses of fear and risk, if one assumes the
worst is always waiting just around the corner, waiting, stalking,
spying out opportunities for carnage.

For one of the investors in the Montessori school-chain
outside of Salt Lake, a man who, in his previous career had
worked extensively within the criminal justice system, it was a
fear of sexual criminals that was the animating impulse behind
his emphasis on security. He believed that roughly one-third
of all of Utah's prisoners were in prison for sex offenses, and
that of those almost two-thirds were pedophiles. He also was
convinced that one could extrapolate those numbers onto the
national stage, meaning that nearly seven hundred thousand of
the country's two million-plus jail and prison inmates were sex
criminals.[31] When they got out of prison, he feared, these men
would go after young children in schools such as the one he was
now involved in.

He was partly right but largely wrong. It *was* true that the
number of prisoners convicted of sex crimes in Utah was increasing—though not up to the one-third mark he posited; the
federal Bureau of Justice Statistics calculated that, nationally,
12.2 percent of all inmates were behind bars after being convicted of rape or sexual assault, and it did not provide an estimate as to what proportion of these were convicted of crimes
against children.[32] Utah *did*, it is true, have a higher proportion of prisoners who had been convicted of sex crimes. But that
wasn't because there were vastly more sexual predators today
than in the past; rather it was because over the past few decades
Utah, like many other states, had massively expanded the defi-
nition of sexual offenses. It was, for example, one of thirteen

states requiring someone convicted of public urination to register as a sex offender, and one of twenty-nine states that now considered consensual sex between underage teenagers to be a serious enough offense to also merit inclusion on the sexual offender registry.

On the other hand, unlike Alabama and four other states, it didn't require men convicted of soliciting a prostitute to register as sex offenders.[33] And at the same time as it had created catch-all felonies around acts like public urination that in the past were largely ignored, the state had massively increased the length of sentences handed out for sex offenders. Attorneys in the state-referenced cases where a man had been given a thirty-year-to-life sentence for touching his daughter's genitals, despite the fact the girl, caught in the middle of a messy divorce between her parents, had dramatically changed her testimony between the time she was interviewed by the police and the time she testified in court. In another case a gay man in an email flirtation with a man he thought was twenty-one but who was in fact underage was sentenced to two to ten years in prison for receiving emailed photos of the teenager's penis.[34]

Not surprisingly, as more sex offenders were sent to prison and fewer were released because of these longer sentences, the proportion of Utah's prisoners who were sex offenders increased. It was a simple case of mathematics.

In the eyes of the school official, however, society was facing an unprecedented epidemic. It was why he had urged his architects to design a school with high concrete external walls, somewhat reminiscent of the walls surrounding a prison yard, separating the children from the glorious mountain views outside. "Kids can't escape," he explained. "But more importantly, people in parking lots can't look in and see who's inside.

One-third of our criminal justice system is full of sex offenders; and most of those offenders are pedophiles."

OVER THE PAST SEVERAL decades, educational bureaucracies around the country have embraced "zero tolerance" rules that have had the effect of removing young children from their schools, and criminalizing huge numbers of them, for often-times ludicrously insignificant breaches of school regulations. Locked in place in the name of public safety, these rules have, instead, for more than a generation simply contributed to the schools-to-prison pipeline.

Disproportionately, the victims of this zealousness have been kids from poor families and/or students of color. Zero tolerance is the working-class and black flip side of the middle-class and white helicopter-parenting fiasco. It's the notion that certain children—especially those without parental resources and wherewithal to fall back on—are so risky to the broader society that they must be sacrificed for the broader good, that they must be monitored by in-school police officers rather than counselors and teachers, that they merit being handcuffed or even Tasered and arrested when they get into trouble in their classrooms or the school yard. These children are suspended or expelled on a dime; they have the police called on them for actions that would, in years past, have simply resulted in a talking to from the teacher; and, frequently, they end up with a criminal record that will affect them for years and decades to come.

In a zero tolerance era, kids can be arrested on school premises for pretty much anything. In 2013, journalists from National Public Radio's "State Impact" project reported on a seventh grader in Hallandale, Florida, handcuffed and charged with misdemeanor battery after hitting a friend of his with a Tootsie Roll. In 2012, the journalists found, 13,780 students in Florida were arrested at school; more than half of them were African American.[35] Nationally, that year, more than ninety thousand students were arrested in their schools.[36]

CNN reported, in 2014, on an African American high school student, on the football team, in Farmington, Michigan, handcuffed, arrested, expelled from school, and sentenced to eight months' house arrest after getting into a tug of war with a teacher over a note that he had written, and didn't want to give up, on fellow football team members he wanted to tackle on the field.[37] The CNN report went on to document that more than half of all students arrested on school grounds nationally were either African American or Latino.[38] In 2016, a five-year-old in Colorado was suspended from kindergarten after bringing to school a plastic gun that shot out soap bubbles.[39] That was absurd, but not as absurd as the story out of Ohio, where a ten-year-old boy was suspended for pointing his fingers in a way that looked like a gun.[40] Or the case of the first grader, in Omaha, Nebraska, suspended for bringing a butter knife to school.[41] Then there was the kid in Pennsylvania who forgot to take his Swiss Army penknife out of his backpack before he went to school one morning and was expelled as a result. In that case, the courts overturned the school district's decision. And there was the first grader in Newark, New Jersey, who brought a fork-spoon-knife hybrid known as a "spork" to school to eat his lunch with and, until a public outcry forced the school district to reverse its decision, faced forty-five days in a reform school as a result.[42] But in many other instances such absurdities have remained in place. In Ocala, Florida, a ten-year-old girl was arrested for cutting her lunch with a knife.[43] And just outside of

Baltimore, a school suspended a seven-year-old boy for chewing his pop tart into the shape of a gun. When his family sued, the courts upheld the suspension.[44]

In an age of anxiety, one can, apparently, never play things too safe.

Chapter Nine

Strange Fruit Under
the Mesquite Trees

I n late March 2016, a series of powerful bomb blasts killed
nearly three dozen people at the international airport in
Brussels, Belgium, as well as in a train carriage pulling out
of one of the central city's busy stations.

Within minutes of the atrocity, then-presidential candidate
Donald Trump had taken to the airwaves and to Twitter. He
didn't make statements expressing moral and emotional solidarity
with the victims and their families. Nor did he talk about the extraordinarily complex political and intelligence challenges facing
multicultural Western societies in the face of ISIS's attacks. Instead, he used his platform to proselytize for torture. The recently
captured suspect in November's Paris attacks, Salah Abdeslam,
would, said the presidential hopeful, have talked "a lot faster with
the torture," and in doing so might have spilled the beans on his
Belgian confreres before they could launch their attacks.

Torture, beyond the waterboarding sanctioned by the Bush
administration, had, by that point in the campaign, become
Trump's leitmotif. Time and again he urged his crowds on by

dangling before them the prospect of violence for violence's sake. Time and again he flaunted his contempt for international norms by embracing torture—the word, for so long taboo, as much as the deed—as an official policy of state.

And yet he never defined exactly what sorts of state-sponsored torture he was advocating, exactly what actions he sought to make the courts, the military, and the general public complicit in.

As the Spanish Inquisition gathered steam, more than half a millennium ago, the fanatical grand inquisitor Tomás de Torquemada, wrapped himself in a mantle of faith and declared that he would torture to save souls and to destroy heretics. The Inquisition began by liberally employing *tortura del agua*, a technique the American military and intelligence agencies rebirthed after 2001 with the label "water torture." Later, when that was deemed not to have rooted out enough false believers, Torquemada's team moved onto more drastic methods. They tied victims' hands behind their backs and hung them from those hands by a rope. Known as the *strappado*, this technique inflicted excruciating pain and destroyed nerves, ligaments, and tendons in the arms and shoulders. When the *strappado* didn't gain the desired results, the torture teams progressed to the infamous rack, stretching the tied victim slowly, dislocating joints and destroying muscles, ligaments, and bones. Eventually, if the victim didn't talk, their limbs were literally ripped off of their bodies.

Other victims of the Inquisition were impaled through their anuses or their vaginas on the Judas chair. Still others had their thumbs crushed, their breasts shredded, their eyes gouged out.

The list of Inquisition torture techniques is long. The legacy is a stench that wafts through the centuries—an endless reminder of the horrors that a handful of fanatics can unleash on a civilization. Five-plus centuries later, Torquemada's name remains, rightly, infamous, a buzzword for cruelty and extremism.

In the eighteenth century, Enlightenment philosophers such as Cesare Beccaria and Voltaire sought to discredit torture as a legitimate tool of the state. It was, they argued, a relic of barbarism, both unjust and oftentimes ineffective. In the democratic age that, in fits and starts, was dawning, torture had no official place. It could not be a formal part of the legal system, nor could it be publicly defended by those claiming their right to govern from the people and their reason for governing to serve the people.

That didn't mean that torture disappeared. Far from it. But the Enlightenment critique *did* lead to a public rejection of the practice in democracies. Where it continued was either in totalitarian political systems or, in democracies, hidden deep in the shadows, used in extreme situations but never publicly acknowledged. The legal and linguistic wiggle room democracies created in the centuries that followed to insulate themselves from charges of torture speak to how much moral opprobrium was directed toward the practice.

Which is why Donald Trump and his supporters' extraordinary embrace not just of the acts of torture but of the word itself represented a watershed moment. Here was a man vying for the highest office in the land who wanted to turn into a moral good, to romanticize, acts of savage violence that for hundreds of years had been regarded as beyond the democratic pale. In speech after speech, his rhetoric normalized the extraordinary, making "torture" simply one more part of the state's standard tool kit, as run-of-the-mill as fingerprinting or a high-speed car chase. This truly was the banality of evil described by the sociologist Hannah Arendt.

In front of his adoring crowds, Trump played the tough guy well. They wanted theater, and he provided it. They wanted cathartic violence, and he offered it up to them in spades. He was like the mafia-type cinema figure who intimidates and thrills his audiences by talking about his enemies "sleeping with the fishes." But for all the bravado, the reality TV star cum presidential candidate never actually got down and dirty and explained to those audiences exactly what he would be asking them to do, when, as president and as commander in chief, he authorized "the torture" and a "lot worse than waterboarding."

Would he make them dismember ISIS recruits limb from limb? Would he order them to impale suspects slowly, on spikes? Would he, as did the Nazi Gestapo with their victims, have them hang terrorism suspects from meat hooks? Would he, as did partisans during the brutal Russian civil war that followed the 1917 revolution, have enemy fighters disemboweled, their steaming intestines, still attached to living bodies, nailed to trees? Would he order psychiatrists to use their skills to break the minds of dissidents and terrorists, as did Soviet medics under Stalin? Would he order soldiers to throw young men and women out of helicopters and planes, some to plunge into the ocean, others into volcanoes, as did the Juntas of Latin America in the 1970s and 1980s? Would he, as did Saddam Hussein, order soldiers and intelligence officials to pour acid onto victims or drill holes in their feet and hands? Would he insist that teenage recruits rip out toenails and fingernails, smash faces beyond repair, stomp on testicles, rape bound men and women?

Or would he, as did the rogue police unit in Southside Chicago, which I wrote about in the 1990s, go after suspects and force confessions out of them by tying them to scalding hot radiators, by mock-executing them, or by using the Vietnam

War–era "telephone" torture—in which electrodes were clipped to a victim's genitals and a wind-up device, like a field telephone, was then cranked to deliver devastating electric shocks?

These were not the sorts of questions that one normally asked of a leading presidential hopeful. But then again, no serious candidate for the American presidency—or for the leadership of any other functioning modern democracy—had ever fetishized torture in the way that Donald Trump came to do. No modern presidential candidate had declared entire races and religions to be the enemy. And no leading candidate had sung the song of fear as perfectly as did Trump to his angry, vengeful, and deeply fearful throngs.

In Trumpism, one saw a weaving together, in the early months of 2016, of a host of fears—of immigrants, of Muslims, of domestic crime and criminals, of changing cultural mores, of refugees, and of disease—and a host of deeply authoritarian impulses intended to rein in all of this chaos. In such a milieu it became acceptable to bash refugees fleeing appalling conflicts, or even to argue—as did several GOP hopefuls during the party's presidential primary process—that only Christian refugees from Syria ought to be admitted into the country.[1]

Less than two months after the November 13, 2015, terrorist atrocity in Paris, Trump released a half-minute television commercial. "The politicians can pretend it's something else," a narrator intoned, "but Donald Trump calls it radical Islamic terrorism. That's why he's calling for a temporary shutdown of Muslims entering the United States until we can figure out what's going on." After another few seconds devoted to the candidate's plan to build a wall to seal off the United States from Mexico, the footage cut back to Trump. His anti-immigrant solutions, he shouted out to an enthused crowd, would "make America great again."

Throughout the primary season and throughout the general election campaign itself, Trump ginned up his crowds by calling for the mass execution of terrorism suspects, by advocating collective punishment and "the torture," and by mocking Muslims for their dietary rituals and religious beliefs.

These words aren't just empty slogans. They come with consequences, legitimizing bigotries and hatreds long harbored by many but, for the most part, kept somewhat under wraps by the broader community. They give the imprimatur of a major political party to naked violence. In the five days following Trump's December 7, 2015, announcement that he would seek to ban all Muslims from entering the country, hate crimes against Muslims surged. When researchers at Cal State University, San Bernardino, analyzed crime data from the period, they found that there was a shocking 87.5 percent increase in such crimes against Muslims in that five-day period compared to the same week in 2014. Taken as a whole, in the twenty states the researchers looked at data from, anti-Muslim crimes increased by 78 percent in 2015 as compared to 2014.[2]

A demagogue such as Trump connects best with a scared audience, with a people so addled by fear that they cease to analyze rationally. Trump's appeal, as he barreled through his Republican primary season opponents and toward the general election, wasn't based on how he hewed to facts but on how he played to emotions. That many of his statements were, quite simply, spun out of air was far less important to his enthused crowds than that he seemed to connect with their anxieties about a world run amok.

It was the same playbook used by a slew of Tea Party political figures in the years leading up to Trump's eruption onto the national political stage. In mid-February 2016, Maine's

governor, Paul LePage, a self-made businessman who had gotten elected as a part of the Tea Party sweep of 2010, addressed
a town hall meeting in which he urged stringent restrictions on
the admission of Syrian refugees into his state. LePage—whose
political résumé was full of such controversial acts as ordering
officials to jackhammer a mural in the Department of Labor
showing in a positive light the strike actions of trade union-
ists, talking about African American drug dealers coming north
from New York City to seduce young, white Maine women,
and calling for drug dealers to be guillotined[3]—told the crowd
that these refugees were carriers of all sorts of diseases. "What
happens is you get hepatitis C, tuberculosis, AIDS, HIV, the
'ziki fly,' all these other foreign type of diseases that find a way
to our land," the governor announced, in an at best awkward
foray into medical science.[4]

The "ziki fly" LePage was referring to doesn't exist. It was,
commentators guessed, LePage's attempt to discuss the zika
virus, a mosquito-borne disease that was garnering international
attention at the time after being linked with epidemics of mi-
crocephaly and Guillain-Barré syndrome in a number of South
Pacific Islands and Latin American and Caribbean countries.
There was no evidence of zika epidemics in Syria, Afghanistan,
Iraq, or other Middle Eastern countries from which war-weary
refugees were fleeing. Nor was there any medical evidence that
TB, AIDS, and hepatitis C were "foreign" diseases from which
Americans, prior to the recent refugee crises, historically had
been immune.

THERE ARE, IN MODERN America, friction zones, spaces both
physical and psychological, where our dreams collide with our

nightmares, where opportunity and despair intermingle, where innocence and depredation collide. In these zones, along the US-Mexico border, where fears of invasion and of terrorism loom like grotesque caricatures over the broiling landscape; in our terrors about children being abducted, raped, or killed; in places such as Inkster that serve as buffers between decayed and desperate inner cities and wealthy and expansive suburbs; in the nightmares of a growing number of parents about vaccines converting normal, healthy, happy kids into zombies; in the anxious dramas we play out on airplane security lines as our joy at an interconnected global community collides with our horror of apocalyptic, death-cult terrorist organizations; in all these places different rules apply.

Out of these nightmares, demagogues like LePage or Trump can rise: would-be leaders who promise quick and violent fixes to deep and intractable problems. In the friction zones, anything, up to and including torture, goes.

It is on the border, for example, that undocumented migrants caught by the Border Patrol frequently have their faces pushed harshly downward into cactus spikes. It is in our suburbs that parents letting children out alone to play, or single mothers who leave children unattended while they head off to job interviews, can find their lives uprooted by inquisitive and hostile Child Protective Services personnel. It is in poor neighborhoods such as Inkster that men—and it is usually men, although, as the Sandra Bland case showed, poor women are not immune from this treatment—can be yanked from cars and savagely beaten by the police on nothing more than a hunch and a whim. It is in these friction zones that the veneer of civility crumbles and worlds are remade in ever-stranger, more brutal permutations. It is where our sense of order and stability collides with ever-shifting realities on the ground that our sense of decency is most aggressively undermined and our willingness to embrace unsavory policy choices and law enforcement practices, which in other circumstances we might shy away from as a community, is most viscerally displayed.

In the early 2010s, the psychologist Jennifer Richeson, then at Northwestern University, and her colleague, Maureen Craig, created a series of studies to explore the impact on their subjects of telling them that by the year 2050 the United States would be a majority-minority country. They found that, simply by announcing this demographic prognosis, the whites they tested immediately became more fearful of immigrants, more likely to support the Republican Party, and more predisposed to sign off on conservative policy responses. "Should White Americans (on average) respond to the changing demographics by becoming more politically conservative," they wrote, with prescience, in a 2014 paper published by the Association of Psychological Science, "the U.S. political landscape is likely to become increasingly racially polarized."[5]

BY THE MILE 19 marker on the Arivaca Road, in the Sonoran desert south of Tucson, Arizona, is a stumpy purple cross with a metal disc at its center, anchored by a pile of stones. It is all that remains to bear witness to the body of a newborn infant found dead there, by the side of the road—one of hundreds of anonymous victims on the migrant trails connecting Mexico and the United States. The cross was designed by a local artist and planted by a group of Tucson Samaritans, who walk the trails looking for migrants in trouble and who hold brief prayer services at spots where bodies—oftentimes just bones in the sand

and dirt, picked clean by vultures and desert winds, surrounded by cacti and mesquite trees—have been discovered.

Those bodies are the border's harvest of shame, the stench of decay in the ones found too soon for the vultures to fully do their work the signature of a morally bankrupt border policy. We build walls a few miles on either side of a populated settlement not to truly stop the flow of migrants but to push them ever farther out into the desert wilds. We make the crossing an odyssey, able to be completed only with the help of ruthless people-smuggling gangs, willing to trek their human cargo into some of the most inhospitable terrain on earth. Out in the high desert, the dangers of the crossing accumulate, the likelihood of pain, suffering, and death grows. Sow enough pain, reap enough bodies, and, the theory goes, the migrants will turn back and head home. It hasn't worked: still by the tens of thousands the migrants, desperate and impoverished, come.

Regardless of whether those bodies are found by the Samaritans—who began patrolling in the early years of the century as the border crisis intensified—or by the Border Patrol, that hateful smell cloys. "Thirteen years, I've seen a lot of dead people," remarked one uniformed agent, whom I talked to while he sat in his truck, cooling its engine, just the north side of the border fence in the tiny town of Sasabe—an area of the border notorious for both people smuggling and the seemingly endless flow of drugs. "Usually the first thing I think is, 'Can the smell get any horribler?' You think you'd get used to that smell, but you don't. It seems to permeate your nose for days. I think it's psychological. Like it's stuck in my nose-hairs or something. You take a shower, and it goes away. But anything will trigger it again."

During upswings in violence meted out between rival drug gangs, US Border Patrol agents would arrive at work and find mutilated bodies thrown over the fence from Mexico. Headless corpses. Corpses run over again and again by cars. Sometimes a local cowboy who worked a ranch near Sasabe would ride the fence line—an east-west scar, designed to separate north from south, thrown up in haste over the past couple decades, through the middle of a long borderlands within which a distinct culture, a fusion culture, a distinct third country has emerged over many, many decades—looking for the dead. At other times, though, the bodies turn up on the trails far out in the desert, beyond the ends of the symbolic, but ineffective, miles of fencing. There, when migrants sicken in the heat, or when lethally sharp cactus spikes pierce through tattered shoe soles and into the feet of walkers; when scorpions or rattlesnakes strike; when someone falls on a rock ledge and breaks a bone; when they drink bad water from fetid pools and the diarrhea takes them; or when they simply don't have the energy to keep pace with the group, the *coyotes* leave them to the elements. And those elements—in a land where for months of the year the sun heats the air to upwards of 120 degrees—are fierce and unforgiving.

With no food, a sedentary person, conserving their energy, can survive extended periods of time; with no water—the desert's most precious resource—in that heat they can die within a couple of days.

Which is why, as the deaths spiraled in the early 2000s, a number of humanitarian groups based out of Tucson began searching for the sick—they would either tend to these individuals on the scene or, if it was an emergency, call in Border Patrol, who could then get emergency services to take them, under guard, to a local hospital—and dropping water jugs along the remote migrant trails. After all, by 2008, the Tucson Sector of the border was the most lethal stretch of real estate in the

United States. Some months, upwards of thirty bodies would be found in Pinal and Cochise Counties alone. From October 2008 through September 2009, 420 bodies showed up along the southwest border. The following two years the number dipped just below 400 annually. From October 2011 through September 2012, it spiked at 477, and in the years following remained above 400.

These are fatality levels that dwarf the numbers killed along the Berlin Wall at the height of the Cold War. In Berlin, roughly eighty people were shot dead trying to cross that wall in the entirety of its twenty-seven-year existence. On the US-Mexico border, in the waters of the Rio Grande and on the desert floor, many times that number lose their lives every year.[6] Most die at the hands of the elements; some are murdered by the smuggling gangs; others, on both sides of the fence, are killed by bullets fired by Border Patrol agents—cases that, in the rare instances in which they go to trial, generally result in the Border Patrol being cleared of all wrongdoing. And yet, in our popular imagination, it is the Berlin Wall that stands out as the ultimate symbol of injustice—perhaps because that was a wall designed to stop people from leaving somewhere oppressive, and the walls and fences and sensors and helicopter patrols along the US-Mexican border are, by contrast, designed, at the behest of politicians and populaces who mainly live an awfully long way from that border, to stop people from arriving in a place defined by a dream. In such a discourse, fleeing an ideology is seen as heroic; fleeing endemic poverty is seen as criminal. By extension, lethally hemming people in, using bullets to prevent movement from one place to another, is, to our well-heeled psyches, more of a moral affront than lethally keeping people out, and using dehydration and heatstroke, as well as the threat of "aiding and abetting" charges against anyone who helps transport migrants northwards, as deliberate strategies of deterrent.

THE SAMARITANS WOULD DRIVE southwards through the vast, almost psychedelic desert landscape, in vehicles decked out with red crosses taped to their sides, along highways lined with Border Patrol agents and internal checkpoints; under skies patrolled by drones and helicopters; past creosote bushes, saguaro cacti, cholla cacti; and eventually along motion-sensor-saturated dirt tracks that led ever closer to the border, to the canyons and arroyos connecting the two countries, the trunks of their four-wheel-drive vehicles packed with cases of plastic gallon water bottles, along with bags of emergency food rations. They would park, fill their backpacks with the heavy bottles—each gallon jug weighed eight pounds—and with shoulders bowed under the weight, sweat soaking the long-sleeved shirts and long pants they wore to protect their skins from the cactus needles, they would walk deep into the desert.

For local author Kathryn Ferguson, who had once upon a time worked as a dancer in Germany, in Turkey, in Egypt, and elsewhere, the walks had become a core part of who she now was. They provided meaning, a moral contrast to the indifference and hostility with which so many people, on both sides of the border, viewed what went on out in the desert. "Darn it all," she said, as we headed far out into the arroyos early one June morning, as the thermometer began its daily climb up toward 115 degrees, 120 degrees. "I just love this desert. I can't be without this dust—sand and dust and canyons, sunsets, sunrises, horny toads, lizards." As she drove, and then walked, with the water bottles she would leave for migrants—far into the canyons, past old abandoned mines, through scrubland buzzing with a million insects, into a region, monitored by an alphabet soup of federal, state, and county agencies, so close to the border that our cell phones, picking up signals from a Mexican cell phone tower in what was rumored to be a drug cartel–controlled town to the south, went onto international roaming—Ferguson felt that she was making an impact, albeit a small one, on a vast, sometimes cruel landscape. "The borderlands are no-man's-lands," she had decided. "Frankly, out here anything goes. What happens out here on a trail, nobody sees. This world that we're in out here has its own laws. There are ways of dealing with people. It's about people surviving."[7]

At the dusty crossroads—faint traces of trails identifiable by the footprints left behind, the detritus of the camps providing clues to where people trying in the main to be invisible rest and eat and sleep along the routes—the Samaritan volunteers would drop their bags and, quickly, do a census of the old bottles left from earlier drops. Some of those bottles would be intact and empty—signs that their actions had, indeed, saved lives. Oftentimes, however, the plastic would be either sharply punctured, as if by a pin or knife, or simply slashed down the middle. The water would, of course, have run off—unused—into the sere desert earth; the bottle would be unusable for any migrant hoping to take a ewer with them to the next watering hole (there *are* a few small oases here, though many of them contain water that will quickly make those who drink it violently ill); and, perhaps most importantly, the Border Patrol and the myriad militia groups roaming the borderlands would, leaving these wrecked trophies, have made their point: that this is their land and governed by their brutal rules. Eighteenth-century Londoners, used to seeing the rotting corpses of executed pirates left hanging in iron bodysuits from bridges as a warning to others not to follow such a path, would have gotten the force of such imagery instantly.

There is something extraordinarily eerie about such a scene: slashed water bottles lying ragged, like strange fruit, under the mesquite trees, fragments of dreams—a cheap orange bead rosary, snagged strands of wool from a blanket—hanging, silently, from the branches above. In an art museum in Santiago, Chile, once, I realized that what in English are termed "still life" paintings in Spanish are termed "still deaths." Out in the desert, the temperature clocking in at 116 degrees, there was something utterly lonely, demonic, Still Death about the slashed bottles and the mesquite trees.

One finds such strange fruit, I believe, where empathy breaks down and where a critical mass of people and institutions cease to think of the condemned or the vulnerable as humans, with the same needs, fears, and desires as anyone else. When our assumptions of risk assume cartoonish proportions—every migrant is assumed to be part of a vanguard force preparing the ground for invasion, every water bottle left in their path a weapon provided the enemy—our responses to that risk all too quickly veer toward the inhumane.

The local chapter of the American Civil Liberties Union had documented numerous instances of such responses. Men, women, and children were being detained in "filthy, frigid, overcrowded conditions," in the words of ACLU attorney James Lyall.[8] Wearing jeans, a short-sleeved checked shirt, and black-rimmed spectacles, Lyall looked more like a social worker than a lawyer. He spent much of his time going into ICE detention facilities, interviewing detainees, trying to work out patterns of abuse. Many of the migrants told him that they had been "denied food, water, medical care, hygiene supplies, access to showers." In 2014, included among the prisoners, the ACLU identified 116 unaccompanied children. Migrants reported being "dusted" by low-flying ICE and Border Patrol helicopters out in the badlands, forced to flee ever further into the desert to escape the devil dust whipped up by the choppers' blades. Some of these people didn't make it; their remains were found days or weeks later. Others, separated from their guides, were rounded up, dehydrated and scared, by the Border Patrol. The strategy, said Lyall angrily, seemed to be: "If we increase the suffering of immigrants, that will deter them from coming back. It's profoundly sick and inhumane, and that's our national border control strategy."

The Border Patrol and other agencies deliberately dehumanize the border crossers. It's easier that way: after all, you put a face to a story, and suddenly you're dealing with all the accumulated pain and heartbreak of an individual in trouble. "You have to harden yourself," explained the agent sitting in his vehicle in Sasabe. "You can't put a face to it. I've been doing it a long time. I don't want to put a face to them." And so a language is cultivated that doesn't have room for the individual. Border Patrol and the US Marshals Service refer to "products" processed into holding facilities along the two thousand miles of the southern border. News reports describe the migrants as "illegals," "aliens," "criminals." Vigilante groups warn of "Third World invaders." Politicians talk of "hordes" and "swarms" of migrants. Lost in the mix is the story of these men, women, and children as individuals.

"They have been and are invisible," John Fife, the septuagenarian founder of Tucson's sanctuary movement, said sadly, speaking of the undocumented migrants he had worked with for so many years. "The general public has not viewed them as mothers, fathers, children, babies, families, human beings. That's all part of the process of exclusion and fear of easily identified populations."

Fife was a lean man, in blue jeans and an untucked white cotton shirt, hiking boots, and a cream-colored cowboy hat. On his left wrist was an ornate silver bracelet, adorned with a motif from the local Tohono O'odham tribe. He had been a pastor in Tucson since the late 1960s and, in the 1980s, had been one of the country's most outspoken voices in defending the rights of refugees fleeing US-funded wars and death squads in Central America. "Keep your head down, don't make any waves, any ruckus. Be invisible and you will survive. That's been taught for a long time."

The churchman and human rights activist had watched, horrified, as the first miles of border wall were built in the mid-1990s. He had read, also in horror, the first newspaper reports, in the late 1990s, of large numbers of deaths in the desert. And he had been just as stunned when, within a couple of years, the news reports disappeared—not because the deaths had stopped, but because they had simply become so commonplace that there was nothing newsworthy anymore in a body showing up here, another there. "As bodies piled up," he recalled, "the only people who knew about it were the medical examiner's office."

The staff in that office were overwhelmed by a tsunami of bodies, many of them in appalling conditions. Painstakingly, they tried to piece together who these people were and where they had come from. Whether they were Mexican or Guatemalan, El Salvadoran or Honduran. A 2013 report commissioned by the University of Arizona's Binational Migration Institute

and the Pima County Office of the Medical Examiner found
that one in eight of the victims recovered since 1990 were under
the age of nineteen. Nearly half were younger than twenty-nine.
And the deaths were becoming more frequent: the numbers
dying between 2004 and 2012 increased at a far greater rate than
the numbers intercepted by Border Partol, 500 percent faster by
some estimates. By 2006, with the migrants being pushed ever
farther out into the remote desert in the wake of stepped-up enforcement activities, resulting in it taking longer for their bodies to be discovered after they died, almost half of these bodies
were in such an advanced state of decomposition that the cause
of death could not even be determined.[9]

From 1999 until 2015, in the Tucson Sector alone, more
than 2,800 bodies were found. And, Fife said, that was likely
just the visible part of a much larger catastrophe. "Our experience out there is that three to five times more people die than
are found. The desert cleans itself up pretty fast. A body disap-
pears in two weeks, down to scattered bones." Conceivably, if
Fife's estimates hold true, upwards of 10,000 people, the vast
majority of them never identified, never buried, never properly
mourned, have died just along that few hundred mile stretch of
border in recent years. Untold thousands more have died along
the other four sectors of the border.

BUT NO MATTER HOW many people die, still the migrants come
north, the poorest of the poor, looking not for fortune but for
a few dollars a day as hourly laborers, picked up at informal
labor markets in empty lots and on early-morning Tucson street
corners. They sit and wait, in small groups, dusty-looking and
tired, their clothes tattered, their haircuts cheap. The lucky

ones. The ones who don't get picked up by Border Patrol and either dumped back over the border or, if they are among the unfortunate first few dozen caught each day, sent to an Operation Streamline courtroom and then to jail—as an exemplary punishment intended to further deter those who would dare to walk through the desert and into those labor markets in the promised land.

One could see the workings of Operation Streamline in the federal courthouse, in downtown Tucson, most weekday afternoons. Shortly after one o'clock several dozen men and a few women, almost all of them dark-skinned *campesinos*, almost all of them young, their hair cut short, each wearing low-end jeans or tracksuit pants, would shuffle, chained at the waist and hands, into the William D. Browning Special Proceedings courtroom. Over their ears were headphones through which they could hear translations of the English-language proceedings that would determine their fate. At one thirty, the judge would enter the room, its walls gray, its ceiling blue, with orange crossbeams, and the proceedings would begin.

Judge Bernardo P. Velasco was a large man, his pate bald, his chin sporting a heavy goatee. He wore a blue shirt with a pen protruding from the left breast pocket, a dark gray suit, a dull gold tie. On the fourth finger of his left hand was a big turquoise and silver ring; on the corresponding finger on his right hand, another ring. When he entered the courtroom, he visibly limped. Velasco was charged with instilling the fear of God into the men and women lined up before him. "Each of you has been charged with felony reentry, which is punishable by two, ten, or twenty years, depending on your previous criminal history," he intoned. And then he added that if they waived their right to a trial, instead pled guilty to a misdemeanor, and agreed not to appeal, the felony charge would be dismissed. Not surprisingly, virtually no one in an Operation Streamline hearing decides to plead not guilty.

Velasco calls out names in batches of seven, each individual assigned an attorney. One after another, they stand, plead guilty, and accept their jail sentences, which range from thirty days up to one hundred and eighty days behind bars. Each case takes approximately twenty seconds. Each group then shuffles out, the chains jangling around their waists and hands, to be processed and begin their sentences in jail. Half an hour after it has begun, the proceeding is over.

But the judge, it turned out, didn't enjoy this part of his job. He recognized the need to control the border, but nevertheless he felt sympathy for the young men and women caught up in Operation Streamline. As importantly, he felt that it was little more than symbol politics, unlikely to stem the flow of desperately poor migrants heading north. Velasco was burdened by what he called, as he inhaled on a white plastic nicotrole inhaler in the little office that he retreated to after court adjourned, "a tremendous disappointment in our country's inability to fulfill our idea of being a good neighbor. We've never been a good neighbor to Latin America. We've never secured our borders or improved economic conditions. Our country refuses to admit that we like cheap labor. We need to come up with a more rational immigration policy that reflects our mutual needs."[10]

Velasco commented scathingly on the notion, being pushed by Trump and his supporters, of building a wall along the full length of the border: "Hadrian's wall didn't work. The Berlin wall didn't work. The Gaza wall, they blew that son of a bitch up so they could go shopping in Egypt. The only wall that worked was the Great Wall of China. But we're too cheap to do that; it's impossible. We've got how many miles of ocean? You [have to] figure out a way to help people have a good economy down in their part of the world. If we'd spent the money we spent on the war on drugs on economic development, people might stay home and work."

ALL ALONG THE US–MEXICAN border, however, miles of high steel fencing were still going up. And in Texas, under then governor Rick Perry, in the winter of 2011–2012, heavily armored PT gunboats had begun patrolling the Rio Grande. They were, Perry averred, necessary to fight the smugglers and the large cartels that were bringing drugs and crime northwards. John Fife, for one, didn't buy it. The cartels, with their vast financial infrastructure and their ability to pay off law enforcement and border agents in both Mexico and the United States, would always find a way around whatever makeshift security arrangements were implemented at any one time on any one area of the border. But the ones who wouldn't find a way around, the ones most likely to get hurt by these new arrangements, were the poor migrants looking to escape the violence unleashed by the cartels and the long-standing poverty so many Mexican communities were trapped in. For Fife, the spectacle was deeply unsavory; in Texas, he said bitterly, one could now see "PT boats driving up and down the Rio Grande and defending against mothers with babies in their arms."

From California east to Texas, migrants were dying along the increasingly militarized border. And, too often, no one seemed to care. "Even some of my friends," Ed McCullough sadly recounted, "say [of the would-be immigrants], 'They're breaking the law, and they deserve to die.' It's just incredible.

The husband of one of my wife's best friends said that—so we haven't talked to him in a while."

For McCullough, an octogenarian retired University of Arizona geologist who had spent years walking and charting the migrant trails, finding injured, sick, or dead migrants far out in the desert, the two words he kept coming back to were "Why?" and "What?" Why did so many people risk so much trying to cross that lethal border? What were they leaving behind? What did they hope to find? And why were so many people so scared of them? The more he had studied the issue, the less sense America's approach to the border made to him. "If you take a look at what we're spending on the border fence, you're talking billions of dollars. If you spent that money instead on investing in the places in Mexico from where they come, they wouldn't come. Invest money in cooperatives down there."

But politics kept getting in the way of common sense. And the game of kabuki continued: the big talk on clamping down on the undocumented. The theatrics—aimed more at far-off voters who had never experienced the immensity of the border than at those who actually lived in the desert and knew the inherent porousness of the region—of building a few miles of fencing along thousands of miles of border. The brutality both of the people smugglers and of those whose job it was to hunt down the migrants. The passion plays of death in the desert and the routine exploitation of undocumented laborers who made it north. And, day after day after day, the immigration raids that separated parent from child, husband from wife.

IT WAS THAT FEAR, of being separated from her husband and her children, that had led forty-one-year-old Rosa Loreto to seek sanctuary at the old Southside Presbyterian Church in Tucson.

Loreto, who kept her brown hair tied back, her face rouged slightly, her neck adorned with a silver necklace, her eyes complemented by stylish glasses, had moved north to the United States in 1999, traveling from Hermosillo, in the Mexican state of Sonora, on a tourist visa and then staying on after it expired. Her husband, separately, had traveled the same route. In Arizona, he worked construction jobs; she cleaned houses. You could, she rationalized, make as much in one day in the United States as you would in fifteen days in Mexico.

A little more than a decade after they arrived, Loreto was stopped by sheriff's deputies one morning, about six o'clock, as she was driving to a job. When she couldn't produce her papers, the deputies called Border Patrol. Loreto spent the next two months as a prisoner at the Eloy detention facility, living in a large dorm with roughly fifty other people. Her husband, for obvious reasons, couldn't visit her. Neither could their two young children. In Eloy, prisoners who didn't follow the rules were put into isolation. It was, she says of the rumors, "a dark room, a dark place, 'the Hole.'" Only after the family managed to raise three thousand dollars in bond was she allowed, finally, to return home.

In 2012, Rosa Loreto received her deportation orders, and two years later, in 2014, she was given a deportation date. "It was very difficult, very sad. Because the children would say, 'I want to do this, do that. School starts in August.' But it's always pending: Will we have to leave? My children don't exist in Mexico; their schools are here. Their world, their home is in the United States. We have family to visit in Mexico, but it is not their home. Their friends at school, or baseball, the baseball moms, none know they don't have papers. I'm not a criminal; I'm part of society. I only came here for opportunity." In Mexico, she says, she would not have money for milk or shoes for her two children.

Distraught at the thought of having to leave her kids behind in Arizona while she returned to Mexico, and equally
horrified at the prospect of yanking them both away from all
that they knew and taking them with her, Rosa instead decided
to seek sanctuary in the church—a place with a congregation
known to locals for its activism around the issue of deportation.
In late 2014, she quietly left her family home and moved, alone,
into a small room out back of the old adobe church. The police
were reluctant to come onto holy ground to arrest her, but she
knew that as soon as she went outside its protective walls, she
was likely to be picked up and taken into detention. And so,
week after week, then month after month, she whiled away her
time inside, surviving on food and supplies donated by sympathetic church members, helping with chores around the church
when she could.

Rosa's husband and children would come to visit her every
few days, but most of the time she was by herself. "I couldn't
sleep," she remembered of those first initial weeks. "When my
family goes home—it's a tiny room, but it feels huge. I sit in a
chair and look around and feel alone." She missed cooking for
her children. She missed taking them to baseball practice. She
missed preparing her house for Christmas.

Gradually, however, she developed a routine. She would
stay up late into the night, thinking about her life and planning
what she would do if and when her immigration status was ever
resolved. She wanted to start her own house-cleaning business.
She wanted to show the government that, if given the chance,
she knew how to better her family's circumstances. Her family
would come visit every few days; they would sit on the floor of
the church and do puzzles together, or she and the kids would
snuggle up and read books. She would listen to the sounds of

the day laborers waiting outside the church for someone to come and hire them for a few hours of casual, cash-in-hand work; she would atune her ears to the sounds of traffic on the nearby freeway. And in lieu of paying rent to the church, she would help clean its kitchen and prepare meals for the local homeless population who would show up there for food.

In Greensboro, North Carolina, a million miles from Loreto and her protectors at the Southside Presbyterian Church, on June 15, 2016, Donald Trump was holding yet another "raucous" rally. He would, he promised, make America great again. And, in large part, his plan to do so involved deporting vast numbers of immigrants and making life as unpleasant as possible for many of those who remained. A writer for the *New Republic*, Jared Yates Sexton, heard the candidate railing against immigrants and Muslims. Sexton reported on the vendors selling shirts emblazoned with the motto "Hillary sucks, but not like Monica." He listened to the audience members screaming "bitch" every time Hillary Clinton's name was mentioned. He caught the sounds of Trump fans shouting "Kill them all!" when the candidate went off on the supposedly liberal media. And then, in the parking lot out back of the stadium, he overheard a man tell his wife, "Honey, immigrants aren't people."[11]

Chapter Ten

When Fear Doesn't Win

I n the spring of 2015, a meme began circulating on social media sites. "We had a war on drugs and got more drugs. We had a war on terror and got more terror. Let's have a war on jobs." It was, on the surface, nothing more than a light piece of satire. Yet those three sentences spoke to something important. Hysterias don't solve vast societal problems. Too often, overwrought responses generate more of the very conditions they were intended to vitiate, creating cycles of chaos and, at the same time, ever-greater curbs on personal liberty.

In the overhyping of risk, we have nurtured dystopia. And in dystopias, the currency of violence, be it individual or institutional, acquires a perverse prestige. "Fear," wrote Corey Robin, in *Fear: The History of a Political Idea*, "ensures that those with power maintain it, and prevents those without power from doing much, if anything, to get it."[1] Mass incarceration, omnipresent electronic monitoring of individuals' lives, a militarized border, political campaigns that target specific ethnicities and religions, locked-down classrooms, the routinization of brutal police tactics, the breaking apart of families in the name of safety, the expulsion of children from schools under the guise of stability: all are symptoms of a social system in deep crisis. So too is the epidemic of anxiety and the extraordinary reliance tens of millions of Americans now have on powerful psychotropic medications simply to get through each day.

Our fears have, quite literally, become embedded parts of our identity, and by extension, the drugs we use to take the edge off those fears, and the chemical changes to our brains that those drugs trigger, have become a part of what makes us who we are as individuals and as a community.

IN SEPTEMBER 2016, I took a flight from Sacramento to meet up with a team of psychologists at the University of Chicago who were studying how ideas about race and about social status interacted. On a warm, slightly humid, late-summer day, I walked south through the campus, past the elegant quad, with its lawn freshly mown in neat rows, past the gray stone buildings, the walls covered in ivy, the roofs decorated with gargoyles— late-nineteenth-century constructions masquerading as medieval European gems—to Beecher Green Kelly Hall, one part of which is home to the university's psychology department.

Over the following hour, I filled in some forms and talked with Brad Mattan, a postdoc recently arrived in Chicago after completing his PhD at the University of Birmingham in England, who had designed the study I was about to participate in. On Mattan's Letovo laptop, I took an Implicit Association Test—which, for the umpteenth time I had taken it, showed that I was subconsciously biased against black people. And, for the umpteenth time, I was horrified by this result, by the fact that, in taking the test, my brain noticeably slowed down when asked to identify images or words that were either "black" or "good," as contrasted with either "black" or "bad," or "white" or "good." I was horrified but no longer shocked; after all, I had taken several of these tests while researching this book, and I was by now all too aware of how prevalent these subconscious biases are.

At two fifteen that afternoon, Mattan walked me west across campus to the third floor of the medical building. There, in a small office equipped with a large computer, I went through a series of pretest preparations, including being taught to associate the color blue with "low status" and the color orange with "high status." Then I took my coat off, removed my keys, coins, and wallet from out of my pants' pockets, decoupled my belt from my jeans, and headed into the chilly MRI room. A technician swapped out my metal spectacles for a couple of red plastic-rimmed lenses that wouldn't be prey to the machine's powerful magnets, secured over my eyes by a Velcro strap attached at the back of my head, and another technician laid me down on the MRI bed, strapped on respiratory and heart monitors, gave me foam ear plugs and a large headset to protect my ears from the racket of the machine, attached a panic button to my torso, put two little widgets with buttons I could press in response to visual stimuli in my hands, and shunted me into the narrow MRI tube.

For the next forty minutes, as the huge machine banged and wailed and hammered away, sounding alternately like a jackhammer and an impossibly high-volume dentist's drill, I watched a set of images, some of black people's faces, some of white people's faces, some framed in orange—which I had been primed to link with high status, some with blue—which I had been taught to associate with low status. The task was simple: come to a decision, within the one and a half seconds each image was on the screen, as to their status level, and then press buttons on both the left-hand and right-hand widget simultaneously.

I wasn't asked to determine whether one image was high status and the next low, merely to decide they were *something*. The
rest would be up to the study's architects. They would, in the
days following my test, analyze my brain responses during my
time in the machine, and explore which sorts of images triggered activity in what parts of my brain. Had I been a genuine
part of the experiment, they would then have fed the data from
my brain imaging into the broader pool of information from
test participants, ultimately calculating how brains tend to respond to different sorts of status-related stimuli and how those
responses differ by race. Their working hypothesis, backed up
by the data they were receiving, was that when participants see
what they are conditioned to believe is a low-status black person, the ventral medial prefrontal cortex and the amygdala are
particularly active—the former a part of the brain known to
be involved in evaluative responses to social stimuli; the second
known to be involved in processing perceived threats.

Sure enough, when they analyzed the brain scans from
their subjects, they found that there was, indeed, more blood
flow to those parts of the brain when images of black, low-status
individuals were flashed on the screens. As soon as the subjects
saw a low-status black person, unconsciously their threat evaluation centers kicked into high gear.

"Once you layer on this cultural learning that a particular
group is threatening," Jeni Kubota explained to me, "you see it's
very difficult for people to overcome these associations. They
have been acquired over a lifetime."[2]

Forty minutes after I was placed into the MRI, the technician took me out again, removed all the paraphernalia, and set
me free. On the way out of the lab, I passed a large computer
screen, on which were three cross-sectional images of my brain
from the last, six-minute scan. I wasn't supposed to see my brain

pictures, and the rule-conscious technicians certainly weren't going to show me, but for the few seconds I could sneak in as I walked slowly out of the room and back to pick up my coins and jacket and all the other metal I had had to leave behind, I could glimpse myself at my most elemental.

It was an eerie feeling: there I was, a series of whorls and folds and delicately shaped tissue, an organic machine that had taken billions of years to evolve. There I was, all of my emotions, my hopes, my fears, my prejudices, my loves, my hates, my biases, all stored and interpreted by complex neural networks in different parts of the brain. There was me, so proud of my individuality, my ability to parse ideas for myself, reduced to a few pounds of brain tissue surrounded by a skull, reduced to a set of images on a computer screen. That was the "self," nothing like the person who stared back at me when I looked in a mirror, who had, an hour earlier, so wanted to "succeed" on the Implicit Association Test by banishing all sign of prejudice from my responses, but who had, instead, shown himself to be full of unwanted, and unconscious, biases.

How would that brain, that bundle of neural networks that made me me, respond to endless images intended to trigger fear? How would that brain make decisions when flooded by cortisol because of being constantly stressed by the fast pace of modern life and the omnipresence of doom-and-gloom reports on social media, on the radio, on television?

On November 8, 2016, Donald Trump was elected the forty-fifth president of the United States. He lost the popular vote but won the Electoral College contest. Nearly sixty million voters chose to cast their lot with a man who had run a campaign unprecedented for its divisive, fear-driven rhetoric.

Trump won in part because he promised to bring jobs back to postindustrial cities. But he also won by promising a relentless focus on law and order, by pledging to wall the United States off from Mexico, by taunting Muslims, by making a show of ridiculing African American protestors, by embracing wholesale torture.

In the days after his victory, cities across the country saw spikes in hate crimes: racist graffiti went up in public locales— with messages ranging from "Black Lives Don't Matter" to "This country is for whites only"—Latino school kids were baited by their white classmates; Muslim women had their headscarves ripped from their heads.

"Fear makes you mean and makes you hateful," Lenore Skenazy told me. "The minute you can decide some group of people is subhuman, that's when we become evil."

THERE ARE, I HAVE to believe, alternative ways of dealing with our traumas and our anxieties than shaping our lives, our politics, and our national identity entirely around regimens of fear. For down such a path lies only pain and cruelty. Once one starts to look around every corner and under every rug for threats, there is no way to security. When one fear is dealt with, another stands ready to emerge. When one sets of risks is assuaged, more will, inevitably, develop. We are a dynamic, creative, adventurous species—which means that risk is a part of our heritage. Neutralize all risk, and we walk away from a part of what makes us human, unique. Let fear dominate our thoughts, our discussions, our politics, and we end up immobilized, stagnant.

Skenazy had ultimately decided to reject a style of parenting that she viewed as deeply harmful both to her children and also to herself. She had looked at the statistics, recognized the unlikelihood of her children being harmed were she to let them roam the streets and subway system of their home city without omnipresent adult supervision, and allowed them do what generations of children before them had always done—explore their environs.

So, too, the Meitivs had decided that their children were mature enough to walk to a playground, in the affluent northern suburbs of Washington, DC, by themselves.

On a sweltering early summer morning in Tucson, Arizona, on a demonstration against the harsh anti-immigrant policies and policing strategies that the state had adopted over the previous years, humanitarian workers called for solidarity with the undocumented men, women, and children, who traipsed through the brutal desert to escape extreme poverty, gang violence, and drug and people trafficking. "Give us your tired, your poor, your huddled masses . . . yearning to be free. This offer not valid in Arizona," was the sardonic message inked onto the T-shirt of one of the marchers.

One of those out that morning was a grandmother named Maria Ochoa, a Tucson Samaritan who had made more than one hundred trips deep into the desert over the previous thirteen years to look for those in need of assistance—if she found someone immobilized by dehydration, she called 911 and waited until law enforcement and medical aid arrived on the scene—and to recover the bodies of those who had perished. "We have no idea how many people have died out there," she acknowledged. "People wander off the patrol paths, and they run across remains. We visit the area to acknowledge there was a death and usually have a small ceremony." Those low-key, private events served to memorialize the dead, to recognize that a human being, rather than an "alien" or an "illegal," had lost his or her life in particularly cruel circumstances. Other times, the Samaritans would find someone still alive, and since they were legally prohibited from helping them continue on their journey, they would give them water and wait with them until the Border Patrol came to provide them with medical help and also arrest them.

"I feel sorrow. Anger. And sometimes a little desperation," Ochoa continued. "This person is out here with nothing. Because they leave everything behind. Not knowing where they're going, where they'll end up. It's an indescribable feeling." She was haunted by the migrants' vulnerability, by the horrors that could, and too often did befall them on their journey north. "Seven or eight years back," she said softly, "a woman died in the northern part of the desert here. We went out to have a service for her, two weeks after they'd picked up her body. And the spot where she'd laid, the outline of her body was still there, because of her body fluids. It affected me greatly. It was something I had never seen. It was just a sadness that I couldn't get rid of for a while. Her husband left her there; she couldn't go on."[3]

Maria and the other protestors walking through the quiet early-morning streets of Tucson had seen the ongoing failure of their political leaders to craft viable immigration reform, one that would provide some solutions for the roughly twelve million residents living in America without legal papers, and they had decided they could no longer remain on the sidelines.

For John Fife, like Ochoa one of the founding members of the Tucson Samaritans, "The vast majority of organizers and organizations believed that immigration reform was achievable in Congress or by executive action. Now that that illusion is clearly an illusion, I think we're going to see the move to active nonviolent resistance. There's never been substantive social change without resistance movements. It's the poor, of color, who are being excluded from full participation in the economy and in the culture of the United States. There's the growing gap in economic equality, and the rich and those who are the fearful middle class being threatened by this inequality, they know deep down that it can't last; that the poor are always going to rise up and demand justice. And they're trying to hang on—the rich trying to maintain inequality, and the middle class trying to hang on despite the awareness that they're the most vulnerable in the future. You've got gated communities and the resegregation of urban areas. All feeds into the same basic phenomenon: growing economic inequality and racism—which makes people easy prey for fear and the rhetoric of fear." Fife quoted the Bible to explain why resistance to authority, to the blind trust that the powerful have always demanded of the weak, was so important. "We have historic texts that say you can't put your trust in horses and chariots—when the prophets were speaking to the monarchy in Israel, to the tradition we call Christianity now. The conclusion is inevitable," Fife continued. "History and the Creation have always taught that empire and militarization and conquest and the exploitation of the poor will not prevail. You must be a community of resistance to those values and that whole rhetoric."

IN AN AGE OF anxiety, it is too easy to assume that everyone has fallen into the fear trap. That the choice isn't whether to fear but simply what to fear. That was Trump's demagogic gamble—and in the short term it paid off for him hugely. It is also too easy to assume that the lowest common denominator form of political rhetoric will always work: that political speech that sows discord will drown out that which seeks unity; that race and religion baiting will beat the language of universalism; and that those who urge the harshest responses to crime will always crowd out the voices and emotions of those who seek common ground.

Yet even in a season of rage one encounters people who insist on bucking the trend. One encounters people who understand that the language of fear and hatred is, too often, simply a manifestation, in mutated form, of deeply unfair power relationships. "Those of us privileged to witness and survive such events and conditions," wrote Paul Farmer, "are under an imperative to unveil—and keep unveiling—these pathologies of power."[4]

During the awful weeks following the decision by Texas attorney Keith Bollinger and his colleagues to represent Ahmed Mohamed's family, dozens of people phoned in or emailed with hate messages. Yet, amidst all the din, some people found the need to phone the attorneys to offer their support, to tell them that the hate messengers didn't speak for everyone.

And when the Bureau of American Islamic Relations began sending armed men and women to intimidate worshippers at mosques in Texas, hundreds of people rallied in opposition to their actions. In Dallas, members of Black Lives Matter and New Black Panthers came out to defend the mosque. Elsewhere, interfaith coalitions formed to protest the vigilantes.

For Dionne Wilson, her moment of epiphany came several years after her police officer husband Dan was shot and killed, in a senseless, random act of horror by a drug addict in the small town of San Leandro in Northern California.

When the shooting occurred, in 2005, Wilson, a mother of two young children, was thirty-six years old. Suddenly widowed, she spun into despair, wanting nothing more than to see the man who had destroyed her life put on death row and then executed. For nearly five years, the rage, the fury, the sense of absolute, incandescent anger tore her up. "It was killing me, having that level of anger and hatred," she recalled, nearly a decade after the murder, sitting in a café in Berkeley, her brown hair covered by a beanie, her ears adorned with artisanal earrings. "It started spilling over into other parts of my life. I was drinking a lot, not giving my children the attention they needed; I was sick all the time, was exhausted. It's really hard to hate somebody that intensely for that long. It really was destroying my life. I did anything to make me feel better in that moment. There's no true healing in that; only Band-Aids to pacify the pain. If you stomp on a bonfire, the flame may go out, but the coals are still burning." Wracked by nightmares, she was perpetually terrified that Dan's killer would escape from prison and come after her and her children.[5]

And then, more than four years after her husband's murder, Wilson decided that she had had enough; that she needed to start talking with prisoners, that she wanted to learn about their lives and their struggles, about all the things that had led up to their crimes, and that, as a part of her own healing process, she wanted to discuss with them the pain and heartbreak their actions had caused others. She began visiting women prisoners in Chowchilla. Then, at the invitation of a group called the Inside Prison Project, she starting traveling to San Quentin prison, working with men who had been convicted of murder. "It's the best thing in my life," she explained, smiling shyly, as if sharing a deep secret. "It's been a really profound experience, and I'm very grateful. That's where my healing existed—in there, sitting with them." She found that many of the men had reinvented themselves while behind bars. "They had done their work; they were in a different place than they were when they committed their crime. I started to realize people are not the worst thing they have ever done."

In 2010, on the fifth anniversary of Dan's murder, Dionne Wilson sat down at her desk and wrote a long letter to his killer, telling him that she forgave him. It was, she felt, "one of the most cathartic moments" of her life.

For Wilson, who had every reason to remain embittered and vengeful—and whom no one in their right mind would have blamed for so doing—the meetings with prisoners slowly changed her perspective on life. "I was willing to have my eyes opened, and that's half the battle. Are you willing to learn from people you don't think you have anything to learn from?"

Now, five years on from that life-changing letter, and working with a criminal justice reform organization named Crime Survivors for Safety and Justice, Wilson was journeying around the country arguing for criminal justice reform, urging audiences to think about prisoners as individuals, as real people with real lives. She asked them to resist the "demonization of 'scary people.'" She urged them to recognize that in many instances prisoners "are the mistakes we've made." She called for a fundamental rethinking of a process by which "we try to punish our way out of a situation created by our traumas. That will never work, but this is how we deal with it."

WILSON HAD A SIXTY-YEAR-OLD friend, a man named Tom Ruddigaw. He was a one-time social worker in the tough New Jersey city of Camden, who had spent several years in the 1990s living in India, where he studied religious texts and spiritual practices like meditation. These days, he lives in Oakland, California, in a large house that he shares with several roommates. Inside the front door was a framed photo of Mahatma Gandhi. In the living room, over the fireplace, was another Gandhi image, this one in color, showing the Mahatma sitting at his spinning loom.

A decade earlier, Ruddigaw had also been living in the commuter town of San Leandro, the same town in which Dionne's husband had worked and died. Walking toward the transit station at about nine o'clock one night, he was accosted by four teenagers, one of whom got right up into his face and began explaining to him how they were going to beat him. "He grabbed me by the shoulder," Ruddigaw recalled, "and that's the last thing I remember."

Savagely punched with fists and stomped with boots, his brain injured, Ruddigaw spent days in a coma, hovering on the edge of death. But, he says, something happened deep inside his soul when he was lying unconscious in the hospital. "When I woke up, my roommate was by my bed, and the first thing I said was 'I have to forgive these guys.' I fell back asleep, and it was done. I woke up in total forgiveness."

The instigator of the attack, caught soon afterwards, was a seventeen-year-old whose parents were in prison and who had been raised by his grandmother until she died when he was twelve. Since then, he had made his own way, living on the streets, foraging with friends, fighting, selling drugs, robbing people.

Over the years that followed, while his attacker served time in prison, Ruddigaw set up a correspondence with him so as to try to understand what had motivated the random beating. He sent a letter explaining that he forgave his attacker. And he reacted with satisfaction when he later heard that that letter had convinced the young man to go into therapy, to study for his

GED, to get an associate's degree, and to work hard on making something out of his life. Because of his letter, Ruddigaw believed, crying gently as he retrieved this moment from his still-damaged brain's memory vaults, he had helped set a very hurt person "on the path of being healed."[6]

It was, for me, an extraordinary moment, watching Ruddigaw, so grievously harmed by the beating, as he talked so empathically about the man who had orchestrated the beating. "Tell me, when will we realize that we are each of us the same?" Ruddigaw had written in one of a number of rambling, spiritual songs that he had composed in the years following the assault, as he struggled with speech and memory problems, headaches, and dizziness. "When will we look in each others' eyes and see we all feel the same pain?"

There was something entirely humbling about this man's demeanor. In similar circumstances I hope I would have such magnanimity of spirit, though, if I am honest with myself, I don't know if I would. What I do know is that the world is a better, braver place because of people like Tom Ruddigaw.

As a culture, we win when we follow these roads less travelled. The crime victim with the gift of empathy for prisoners. The parent who refuses to be cowed by social pressures to keep her child always on a tight leash: Sasha Meitiv, for example, who refused to let fear, the "better safe than sorry" mentality, guide how he raised his children, and his wife, Danielle, who similarly refused to abide by the myth "that there is a predator around every corner. The idea of being controlled by fear is such anathema to me."[7] The borderlands dweller who treks out into the mountain wildernesses in the scorching desert heat to leave water for migrants, simply because they are fellow human beings in distress.

The concerned citizen with the intuitive understanding that scapegoating a schoolboy because of his religious beliefs is wrong.

These men and women illuminate their journeys with bright lights. They choose a humble path, recognizing that what they do not know is as powerful a force as what they do know; that fear and violence close down pathways rather than expanding one's options and experiences. Danielle Meitiv remembered hiking atop some cliffs, one summer many years earlier, with a friend in Maine. At a certain point, the ground leveled off just enough so that what had been a hidden drop off to the side suddenly became a visible abyss. The danger hadn't, in reality, changed, but the perception had suddenly shifted. Danielle's friend froze; she couldn't get her feet to move. "The danger was no more present there than the part of the walk where the drop was there but hidden from view," Danielle realized. "But she could see it, and it paralyzed her."

In finding a way to navigate out of that fear, that paralysis, we move toward a healthier way of living, a calmer, less vengeful notion of community.

"I just explored," explained Wilson, of her decision to ditch her furies. "I looked at societies and groups of people and individuals who healed from tragedy. I sought that out. A common theme kept emerging—the thing that stood out for me was forgiveness. By the time I was ready to do that, the pain was so intense that when I let go of it, it was the biggest relief I'd ever experienced in my life. I felt light and alive, and I was able to reconnect with people."

Wilson recognized that certain individuals or situations would still push her toward fear and panic. Her husband's murderer was a Hispanic man, and she generally now feared Hispanic men. She had, as a teenager, she said, been attacked by an Arab man and saw in herself an instinctive wariness toward

Arabs. But she had decided not to let her fears overwhelm her. When someone scared her, when her emotional walls started going up and her fight-flight-or-freeze responses kicked in, she forced herself to slow down. "Think about what you've been through in your life that makes that person scary to you. Is it media? Is it something someone told you? Bring awareness to it. Analyze it. Not 'Why is that person scary?' but 'Why are *you* viewing that person as scary?'"

Now in her late forties, Dionne Wilson had spent much of the previous decade thinking about how she, and the broader community of which she was a part, calculated risk and dealt with fear. She had concluded that, too often, we feared what we were taught to fear by a sensationalist media and an opportunistic political class, and bought into supposed solutions, oftentimes peddled by demagogues, which did more harm than good. Our anxieties and terrors were being nurtured by people and institutions who stood to make a buck out of those fears, or build a reputation, or mobilize a crowd around them.

In the campaign for the US presidency in 2016, those fears were nurtured as never before. The result was the election to the most powerful office on earth of a ruthless demagogue, a man who promised to register people because of their religion and to torture terrorism suspects "because they deserve it." "The fox eats all the hens, then takes a sledgehammer and smashes the hen house to bits," Wilson explained. "And then it says, with blood dripping from its teeth, 'How are we going to solve this problem?' It's crazy."

How we navigate this brutal reality in the years to come will be the dominant question of our age. How we work to make our dreams of a fairer, less divisive, less fear-driven world come true will be the defining challenge of our time.

Acknowledgments

O f the eight books that I have written over the past fifteen years, *Jumping at Shadows* took the most work to wrestle into shape. For to understand the way in which fear plays out both at the individual level and in a community, I had to immerse myself not just in what for me are the familiar worlds of politics, social justice activism, criminal justice, and policing strategies, but also, for months on end, in the *terra incognita* of psychology and neuroscience.

I make no claims to being a scientist, and yet this is a story the telling of which requires at least some familiarity with ideas about how the brain and body operate while under stress, with ideas about how we come to understand, to interpret, and to interact with our environment and with the people with whom we share our lives.

Over the course of the two-plus years during which I worked on this narrative, numerous scientists, both in the United States and overseas, generously agreed to talk me through their research, to help me navigate key concepts, and to brainstorm with me about how to understand recent cultural and political phenomena. Their names are too numerous to list here, although most of them do show up at one point or another in the pages of this book. That said, I do want to acknowledge some of them directly. At Caltech, in Pasadena, Damian Stanley was invaluable in talking me through the ways in which the brain is continually trying to process risk. At the University of Chicago, Jeni Kubota, Jasmin Cloutier, and their team of psychologists were generous to a fault. They let me participate in one of their brain imaging experiments, giving me an intimate, and somewhat disconcerting, view of what my brain, that few pounds of tissue that, at the most fundamental level, makes up *me*, actually looks like. And they patiently answered my questions over several days in September 2016. At the University of Notre Dame, Darcia Narvaez made herself available for a series of conversations on how humans' moral and empathic circuits are generated, and what can go wrong when children, over prolonged periods of time, are subjected to stress, to anxiety, and to fearful environments. At Indiana University, Bloomington, Stephen Porges's ideas were invaluable in helping me to understand some of the neural circuitry that integrates emotions and threat assessment.

In Israel, at Tel Aviv's Bar-Ilan University, the psychologist Yair Berson made it possible for me to understand some of the ways in which charismatic politicians, playing on a public's fears and anxieties, connect with large audiences. Crowds are, of course, made up of individuals, but group behavior cannot always be reduced to simply the sum of its parts. Berson showed me why.

In England, Daniel Bor, at Oxford University, very generously agreed to read over many of the more complex science passages, correcting my errors along the way.

To these, and many others, I owe my profoundest thanks. Your availability over the years when I was working on this book allowed me to feel I was a student once more. It is a feeling that, for a lifelong learner, is always wondrous. That said, I am all too aware that in *Jumping at Shadows* I am, at times, exploring worlds far removed from those I formally studied at university. While I have tried my best to follow the arguments that all of my new mentors have laid out in our conversations, if there are errors in this volume, the fault is mine alone.

IN ADDITION TO READING many psychology and neuroscience books and papers, I also read the works of, and talked with, sociologists, anthropologists, economists, consumer advocates, statisticians, epidemiologists, legal scholars, education theorists, and criminal justice experts. Again, the list is too long to mention in full here. But special thanks to Ralph Nader; to Paul Slovic; to Garen Wintemute, who has, over the years, patiently explained, and reexplained, to me the epidemiology of gun violence; to my friend Jessica Bartholow, at the Western Center on Law and Poverty; to Dionne Wilson, at Californians for Safety and Justice, who began this project as one of my sources and ended up a friend. Each of you helped me to frame central themes in the book.

Around the country, dozens, possibly hundreds, of men, women, and children spoke to me about different ways they had been caught in the matrices of fear. I owe particular debts of gratitude to the Meitiv family, in Maryland, for sharing their stories. To Lenore Skenazy, a tireless advocate for rolling back the fog of fear from how we parent and educate our children. To Floyd Dent, who survived a most vicious assault by police officers in Inkster, Michigan, and to his family, all of whom understood what I was hoping to say in this book and were, as a result, willing to share their stories with me. To the men and women in Tucson, Arizona—to Maria Ochoa, John Fife, Ed McCullough, Kathryn Ferguson, Tom Miller, and the many other border activists I met—who go out into the hot desert to try to save the lives of fellow human beings. You represent for me something immensely precious: the extraordinary importance of not staying silent in the face of moral wrong. To Ahmed Mohamed's family, for being willing to share the details of a painful and humiliating ordeal.

Over the course of the two years, many friends lent me spare rooms to sleep in, offered company and good conversation after a hard day's reporting, or simply were there, at the other end of the phone line, or in person, if I just needed to vent after encountering a particularly enraging or dispiriting set of events. Particular thanks to Chris Stamos, for your marvelous hospitality during my research trip to Tucson; to Alex Ralph and Lizzie Hatton, in Ann Arbor, Michigan, for a delightful dinner after I had spent a long few days reporting in Inkster; to Jason Ziedenberg, in Washington, DC, who is always available to *kvetch* about crime and punishment, about schools and zero tolerance, about the war on drugs, or any number of other topics; and to Mark Sorkin, who is both a wonderful editor and a great friend, for opening up his apartment to me when I was working in Chicago.

Numerous other friends were also involved in this project, through being always willing to talk through ideas or to help me frame the narrative. I doubt very much whether this book would have made it to fruition without the encouragement and advice of Sam Freedman, my mentor from Columbia University days, of Eyal Press, Adam Shatz, George Lerner, Glenn Backes,

Robert Rooks, Theo Emery, Maura McDermott, Kim Gilmore, Kitty Ussher, Kate Raworth and Roman Krznaric, Steve Magagnini, John Hill, Anci Titus, Ofelia Cuevas, Bruce Haynes, Simon Sadler, Joy and Jerry Singleton, Miriam Porter and Jack Reynen, Karma Waltonen, Morgan Simon, Lina Srivastava, Jesse Moss, Andrew Moss, Jessica Garrison, Michael Soller, Jon Wedderburn, and many, many others.

And to all of my colleagues in the University of California at Davis's University Writing Program, a huge thank you for creating such a stimulating environment in which to teach and to think.

I am, too, most grateful to my editors at the *Nation*, the *American Prospect,* the *Independent,* the *New Statesman, Ha'aretz, Sacramento Magazine,* and *Sacramento News & Review*, all of whom have, over the years, assigned me articles on themes relating to fear, to perceptions of risk, to imbalances of power within society, and, more recently, to demagogic political forces. Your support over the years, and your willingness to let me incorporate materials from these reporting ventures into my book, has been invaluable. Thanks too, of course, to Alessandra Bastagli, at Nation Books, for recognizing the importance of this project, and to my wonderful literary agent, Victoria Skurnick, for having confidence, from the get-go, in my ability to bring this narrative to completion.

Finally, no acknowledgments would be complete without, once again, giving my love and gratitude to my family: to my parents, Lenore and Jack; to my brother, Kolya, and my sister, Tanya; and, of course to my wife, Julie Sze—an extraordinary scholar, a loving wife, and a wonderful mother, who has tolerated my obsessions with risk and fear for far too long—and my two incredible children, Sofia and Leo. It's humbling to realize that both of you are now quite capable of holding your own during a conversation about fear, or risk, or any of the other topics tackled in this book.

To all of you, I love you very much.

Notes

NOTES TO INTRODUCTION

1. Harvard School of Public Health/Robert Wood Johnson Foundation Survey Project on Americans' Response to Biological Terrorism, International Communications Research, October 24–28, 2001.

2. Data quoted in FEMA Emergency Management Institute training manual, 2002.

3. FEMA Emergency Management Institute training manual, chap. 6, case study 6.1.

4. George Gray and David Ropeik, "Dealing with the Dangers of Fear: The Role of Risk Communication," *Health Affairs* 21, no. 6 (November 2002): 106–116, http://content.healthaffairs.org/content/21/6/106.full.

5. Christopher Cox, introductory comments on the Homeland Security Advisory System, Hearing Before the Select Committee on Homeland Security, House of Representatives, 108th Congress, Second Session, February 4, 2004, Serial No. 108-35.

6. Lori Robertson, "High Anxiety," *American Journalism Review* (April 2003), http://ajrarchive.org/Article.asp?id=2881.

7. Phone interview with Daniela Schiller, May 9, 2016.

8. For more information on the plasticity of the brain, and of the complex neural networks that generate fear and anxiety responses, see Joseph LeDoux, *Anxious: Using the Brain to Understand and Treat Fear and Anxiety* (New York: Viking, 2015).

9. Phone interview with Schiller, May 19, 2016.

10. Phone interview with Yair Berson, May 25, 2016.

11. Phone interview with Uri Hasson, November 3, 2016.

12. LeDoux, *Anxious*, 68–69.

13. Ibid., 92.

14. For more details on this, see Chris Mooney, "The Science of Why Cops Shoot Young Black Men," *Mother Jones*, December 1, 2014, http:// motherjones.com/print.265386.

15. Joshua Correll and Bernd Wittenbrink, "Across the Thin Blue Line: Police Officers and Racial Bias in the Decision to Shoot," *Journal of Personality and Social Psychology* 92, no. 6 (2007).

16. Donald Trump, *Think Like a Champion: An Informal Education in Business and Life* (New York: Vanguard, 2009).

NOTES TO CHAPTER ONE

1. Phone interview with Anthony Bond, March 30, 2016.

2. Texas newspapers reported extensively on this in 2011. See Kim Horner, "Irving ISD Trustees Halt Staff Diversity Training Sessions by Author of Controversial Race Study," *Dallas Morning News*, September 2011, http://www.dallasnews.com/news/education/2011/09/19/irving-isd -trustees-halt-staff-diversity-training-sessions-by-author-of-controversial -race-study.

3. Information on this suit from "Irving Clock Boy's Father Sues City, School District, Principal for 'Blatant Disregard' of Son's Civil Rights," *Dallas Morning News*, August 8, 2016.

4. Mark Keierleber, "'Clock Boy' Ahmed Mohamed Files Lawsuit Over Texas School Discrimination," *Huffington Post*, August 18, 2016, http:// www.huffingtonpost.com/entry/clock-boy-lawsuit_us_57b62d83e4b0b 51733a26c13 (originally published on The74Million.org).

5. Avi Selk, "Shariah Flap Pushing Irving Mayor into National Spotlight," *Dallas Morning News*, July 28, 2015, http://www.dallas news.com/news/irving/2015/07/28/shariah-flap-pushes-irving-mayor -into-national-spotlight.

6. "Letters Demand $15 Million, Say Irving Officials Worked to Smear Ahmed Mohamed After Clock Arrest," *Dallas Morning News*, November 23, 2015.

7. Ibid.

8. Email texts provided to the author by the Laney & Bollinger law firm.

9. "A Weekend of Angst Over Islam: Guns in Richardson, Marchers in Dallas, Quiet Conversation in Irving," *Dallas Morning News*, December 2015, http://thescoopblog.dallasnews.com/2015/12/a-weekend-of-angst-over-islam-guns-in-richardson-marchers-in-dallas-and-a-quiet-conversation-in-irving.html.

10. Jeff Bridgeman, "13 Star American Flag with Roman Numeral III," All Experts, http://en.allexperts.com/q/Flags-2191/2010/1/f/13-Star-American-Flag-1.htm.

11. Selk, "Shariah Flap."

12. Sarah Mervosh, "Armed Clash Over Black Mosque Triggers Anger in South Dallas," *Dallas Morning News*, April 2, 2016, http://thescoopblog.dallasnews.com/2016/04/tense-anti-mosque-protest-draws-armed-demonstrators-in-south-dallas.html.

13. "Tracy Mosque Firebomb Investigated as Possible Hate Crime," KCRA, December 27, 2015, http://www.kcra.com/news/tracy-mosque-firebomb-investigated-as-possible-hate-crime/37151640.

14. Information compiled by California State University San Bernardino college professor Brian Levin, as reported by NBC News, December 20, 2015.

15. Corky Siemaszko, "Hate Attacks on Muslims in U.S. Spike After Recent Acts of Terrorism," NBC News, December 20, 2015, http://www.nbcnews.com/news/us-news/hate-attacks-muslims-u-s-spike-after-recent-acts-terrorism-n482456.

16. Ben Norton, "Amid Escalating Anti-Muslim Violence, Suspect Arrested for Allegedly Setting Houston Mosque on Fire on Christmas," *Salon*, December 30, 2015, http://www.salon.com/2015/12/30/amid_escalating_anti_muslim_violence_suspect_arrested_for_allegedly_setting_houston_mosque_on_fire_on_christmas.

17. Willa Frej, "Muslim Taxi Driver Shot in Pittsburgh on Thanksgiving Day," *Huffington Post*, November 30, 2015, http://www.huffingtonpost.com/entry/muslim-taxi-driver-shot-thanksgiving_us_565c5f76e4b079b2818ad8ab.

18. Joseph Serna and Veronica Rocha, "State Worker Videotaped Throwing Coffee on Muslim Man Is Charged with Hate Crime," *Los Angeles Times*, December 17, 2015, http://www.latimes.com/local/lanow/la-me-ln-state-worker-muslim-coffee-hate-crime-20151217-story.html.

19. AnneClaire Stapleton and Brynn Gingras, "Family: Son Killed by Neighbor Who Called Him 'Dirty Arab,'" CNN, August 17, 2016, http://www.cnn.com/2016/08/16/us/tulsa-arab-american-shooting-trnd.

20. For a good overview, see Victoria Kim and Joseph Sterna, "For Sikhs, Often Mistaken as Muslims, It's 'a Hostile Time, a Scary Time,'" *Los Angeles Times*, December 29, 2015, http://www.latimes.com/local/california/la-me-sikhs-20151229-story.html.

21. Phone interview with Kelly Hollingsworth, January 8, 2016.

22. Phone interview with Bond.

23. Phone interview with Aldean Mohamed, March 30, 2016.

24. Tom McKay, "One Map Shows How Many People Police Have Killed in Each State So Far This Year," *Policy Mic*, July 13, 2015, http://mic.com/articles/122161/one-map-shows-all-the-people-police-have-killed-in-each-state-so-far-this-year.

25. Phone interview with James McLellan, January 6, 2016.

Notes to Chapter Two

1. Jan Morgan, "Why I Want My Range to Be a Muslim Free Zone," *JanMorganMedia.com*, September 28, 2014, http://janmorganmedia.com/2014/09/business-muslim-free-zone.

2. Philip Bump, "Donald Trump and the 'Terrorist Training Camps' Conspiracy Theory, Explained," *Washington Post*, September 18, 2015, https://www.washingtonpost.com/news/the-fix/wp/2015/09/18/donald-trump-and-the-terrorist-training-camps-conspiracy-theory-explained.

3. Phone interview with Jan Morgan, October 7, 2016.

4. Phone interview with Robert Muise, February 18, 2016.

5. Phone interview with Raja'ee Fatihah, April 8, 2016.

6. Phone interview with Adam Soltani, April 22, 2016.

7. Randy Krehbeil, "State Rep. John Bennett Wants Muslim Groups to Condemn Part of Quran," *Tulsa World*, January 9, 2015, http://www.tulsaworld.com/news/government/state-rep-john-bennett-wants-muslim-group-to-condemn-part/article_6d70ea56-9b56-57eb-a20f-5e3f3498111d.html.

8. Dylan Goforth, "Oklahoma Lawmaker John Bennett Doubles Down on Anti-Muslim Vitriol at Tea Party Event," *Tulsa World*, October 3, 2014, http://www.tulsaworld.com/news/government/oklahoma-lawmaker-john-bennett-doubles-down-on-anti-muslim-vitriol/article_13fdbb7c-eef9-5368-b4aa-12d56ea139d7.html.

9. Dean Obeidallah, "A New Low in Anti-Muslim American Bias,"

CNN, September 19, 2014, http://www.cnn.com/2014/09/19/opinion /obeidallah-anti-muslim-bias.

10. Marie Diamond, "GOP Legislator: Homosexuality Is 'More Dangerous' Than Terrorist Attacks Because We Have to Deal With It Every Day," *Think Progress*, September 9, 2011, https://thinkprogress.org/gop-legislator -homosexuality-is-more-dangerous-than-terrorist-attacks-because-we -have-to-deal-with-cc43b78a30c#.4p5cele8q.

11. Voicemails and emails provided to author by Oklahoma CAIR.

12. Lauren McGaughy, "Texas Agriculture Official Won't Apologize for Anti-Muslim Post," WBUR 90.9, August 18, 2015, http://www.wbur .org/hereandnow/2015/08/18/texas-anti-muslim-post.

13. Joel Ebert, "Tennessee Lawmaker Under Heat for Distributing anti-Muslim DVD," *Tennessean*, April 5, 2016, http://www.tennessean .com/story/news/politics/2016/04/05/representative-under-heat-passing -out-anti-muslim-dvd/82649822.

14. David Fahrenthold and Jose DelReal, "'Rabid' Dogs and Closing Mosques: Anti-Islam Rhetoric Grows in GOP," *Washington Post*, November 19, 2015, https://www.washingtonpost.com/politics /rabid-dogs-and-muslim-id-cards-anti-islam-rhetoric-grows-in-gop/2015 /11/19/1cdf9f04-8ee5-11e5-baf4-bdf37355da0c_story.html.

15. Phone interview with Daniela Schiller, May 9, 2016.

16. Ginger Gibson, "Exclusive: Most Americans See Muslims Like Any Other Group After California Shooting—Poll," Reuters, December 4, 2015, http://www.reuters.com/article/us-california-shooting -muslims-eclusive-idUSKBN0TO00320151205.

17. "Trump Supporters Think Obama Is a Muslim Born in Another Country," Public Policy Polling, September 1, 2015, http://www.publicpolicy polling.com/main/2015/08/trump-supporters-think-obama-is-a-muslim -born-in-another-country.html; and "Trump Still Leads Iowa; Clinton in Good Shape," Public Policy Polling, September 22, 2015, http://www .publicpolicypolling.com/main/2015/09/trump-still-leads-iowa-clinton -in-good-shape.html#more.

18. Max Fisher, "It's Not Just Trump: Islamophobia in America Is Spiraling Out of Control," *Vox*, December 7, 2015, http://www.vox.com /2015/12/1/9822452/muslim-islamophobia-trump.

19. Matthew MacWilliams, "The One Weird Trait That Predicts Whether You're a Trump Supporter," *Politico*, January 17, 2016, http:// www.politico.com/magazine/story/2016/01/donald-trump-2016 -authoritarian-213533.

NOTES TO CHAPTER THREE

1. Laurie Kellman, "Donald Trump Revises Position on Guns in Nightclubs," Associated Press, June 20, 2016, http://www.pbs.org/newshour /rundown/donald-trump-revises-position-on-guns-in-nightclubs.

2. In the first four years of the Obama presidency, according to CNS News, more than 65 million guns were purchased. Gregory Gwyn-Williams Jr., "65.4 Million Gun Purchases Since Obama Took Office, 91% More Than Bush's First-Term Total," CNS News, February 11, 2013, http://cnsnews.com/blog/gregory-gwyn-williams-jr/654-million-gun -purchases-obama-took-office-91-more-bushs-first-term. In 2016, the *New York Times* reported that in some months during this period more than 2 million guns had been sold. Gregory Aisch and Josh Keller, "What Happens After Call for New Gun Restrictions? Sales Go Up," *New York Times*, June 13, 2016, http://www.nytimes.com/interactive/2015/12/10/us /gun-sales-terrorism-obama-restrictions.html.

3. Lions of Trump, www.lionsoftrump.net.

4. This quote was reported by, among other outlets, the *Hill*. Jonathan Easley, "Colorado GOP Chairman Getting Death Threats," *Hill*, April 13, 2016, http://thehill.com/blogs/ballot-box/presidential -races/276134-colorado-gop-chairman-getting-death-threats.

5. In-person interview with Doug Elmets, August 25, 2016.

6. The estimated numbers of mass shootings vary depending on exactly what is considered a mass shooting. The number I chose to use was four or more people hurt in a single incident. On June 21, 2016, CNN reporter A. J. Willingham published a story, "A Visual Guide: Mass Shootings in America," showing the varying estimates depending on definitions of mass shooting (http://www.cnn.com/2016/06/13/health /mass-shootings-in-america-in-charts-and-graphs-trnd).

7. Garen J. Wintemute, "The Epidemiology of Firearm Violence in the Twenty-First Century United States," *Annual Review of Public Health* 36 (2015): 5–19.

8. Jan Morgan's Facebook page, https://www.facebook.com/Jan MorganMedia.

9. "End the Gun Violence," editorial, *New York Times*, December 5, 2015, http://www.nytimes.com/2015/12/05/opinion/end-the-gun-epidemic -in-america.html.

10. Nick Bryant, "US Set For Year of Fear," BBC, January 4, 2016, http://www.bbc.com/news/word-us-canada-35111615.

11. FEMA Emergency Management Training Manual, 2002, chap. 6, 13.

12. Jennifer Mascia, "More Than 500 People Were Shot in America During the Week After Orlando," *Trace*, June 20, 2016, https://www.thetrace .org/2016/06/everyday-gun-violence-orlando-pulse-nightclub-shooting.

13. Julia Jones and Eve Bower, "American Deaths in Terrorism vs. Gun Violence in One Graph," CNN, December 30, 2015, http://www.cnn .com/2015/10/02/us/oregon-shooting-terrorism-gun-violence.

14. Margot Sanger-Katz, "Gun Deaths Are Mostly Suicides," *New York Times*, October 8, 2015, http://www.nytimes.com/2015/10/09/upshot /gun-deaths-are-mostly-suicides.html.

15. Jones and Bower, "American Deaths in Terrorism."

16. Rupert Cornwell, "Guantanamo: Three Years On," *Independent* (London), January 9, 2005, http://www.independent.co.uk/news/world /americas/guantanamo-three-years-on-14252.html.

17. All of these techniques and more were detailed in the US Senate Intelligence Committee report issued in December 2014, http://www .feinstein.senate.gov/public/index.cfm/senate-intelligence-committee -study-on-cia-detention-and-interrogation-program.

18. "Arkansas Gun Violence," Fact Sheet, Center for American Progress, https://cdn.americanprogress.org/wp-content/uploads/2013/04 /ArkansasGunViolence1.pdf.

19. Kate Murphy and Jordan Rubio, "At Least 28,000 Children and Teens Were Killed by Guns Over an 11-Year-Period," News21, August 26, 2014, http://gunwars.news21.com/2014/at-least-28000-children-and -teens-were-killed-by-guns-over-an-11-year-period.

20. Ibid.

Notes to Chapter Four

1. "The Cost of Delaying Action to Stem Climate Change," Executive Office of the President of the United States, July 2014.

2. Phone interview with Yaacov Trope, May 13, 2016.

3. The *Lancet*'s article ran in February 2010. It was widely picked up and Wakefield's controversial theories discredited.

4. "Are You Dangerously Stuck in the Matrix?," AntiCorruption Society, May 16, 2014, https://anticorruptionsociety.com/2014/05 /16-are-you-dangerously-stuck-in-the-matrix.

5. In-person interview with Catherine Martin, June 7, 2016.

6. Phone interview with Amy Pisani, June 1, 2016.

7. Global Health Observatory (GHO) data published by the World Health Organization.

8. There are many references on the Internet to a cheerleader suffering dystonia after either an antiflu vaccine or an anti-HPV shot. Dystonia is a brain disorder that results in the patient having uncontrollable muscle spasms in one or many parts of the body; some patients find that they cannot walk forward without spasms but can walk backwards with no symptoms.

9. "General Statistics: Yearly Snapshot 2014," Insurance Institute for Highway Safety, Highway Loss Data Institute, http://www.iihs.org/iihs /topics/t/general-statistics/fatalityfacts/overview-of-fatality-facts.

10. "Total and Pedestrian Fatalities in U.S. Traffic Crashes from 2001 to 2014," Statista, http://www.statista.com/statistics/198475/total-and -pedestrian-fatalities-in-us-traffic-crashes.

11. Niall McCarthy, "The United States of Air Crashes," Statista, July 8, 2013, https://www.statista.com/chart/1251/the-united-states-of-air-crashes.

12. Matt Richtel, "It's No Accident: Advocates Want to Speak of Car 'Crashes' Instead," *New York Times*, May 23, 2016, http://www.nytimes .com/2016/05/23/science/its-no-accident-advocates-want-to-speak-of-car -crashes-instead.html.

13. Olga Khazan, "A Surprising Map of Countries That Have the Most Traffic Deaths," *Washington Post*, January 18, 2013, https://www.washing tonpost.com/news/worldviews/wp/2013/01/18/a-surprising-map-of -countries-that-have-the-most-traffic-deaths.

14. "Countries and Regions with the Highest Number of Fatal Civil Airliner Accidents from 1945 through November 1, 2016," Statista, http://www.statista.com/statistics/262867/fatal-civil-airliner-accidents -since-1945-by-country-and-region.

15. Rick Seaney, "Fear of Flying? Some Good Things to Know," ABC News, October 7, 2013, http://abcnews.go.com/Travel/fear-flying -good-things/story?id=20471481.

16. Fear Of: The Ultimate List of Phobias and Fears, http://www .fearof.net.

17. Gerd Gigerenzer, "Dread Risk, September 11, and Fatal Traffic Accidents," *Psychological Science* 15, no. 4 (2004): 286–287, https://www .mpib-berlin.mpg.de/volltexte/institut/dok/full/gg/GG_Dread_2004.

18. "Unintentional Drowning: Get the Facts," Centers for Disease Control and Prevention, http://www.cdc.gov/HomeandRecreational Safety/Water-Safety/waterinjuries-factsheet.html.

19. "Deaths and Mortality," Centers for Disease Control and Prevention, http://www.cdc.gov/nchs/fastats/deaths.htm.

20. Dana Blanton, "Fox News Poll: Many Say Gov't Hiding Info on Ebola, Most Support Flight Bans," Fox News, October 15, 2014, http://www.foxnews.com/politics/2014/10/15/fox-news-poll-many-say-govt-hiding-info-on-ebola-most-support-flight-bans.html.

21. Rachel Brody, "Americans Are Really Worried About Ebola," *US News & World Report*, October 21, 2014, http://www.usnews.com/news/blogs/data-mine/2014/10/21/gallup-americans-are-really-worried-about-ebola.

22. "Sharks: Half (51%) of Americans Are Absolutely Terrified of Them and Many (38%) Scared to Swim in the Ocean Because of Them," Ipsos, July 7, 2015, http://www.ipsos-na.com/news-polls/pressrelease.aspx?id=6911.

23. "Facts About Melanoma," American Melanoma Foundation, http://www.melanomafoundation.org/facts/statistics.htm.

24. Paul Slovic, Melissa L. Finucane, Ellen Peters, and Donald G. MacGregor, "Risk Analysis and Risk as Feelings: Some Thoughts about Affect, Reason, Risk, and Rationality," *Risk Analysis* 24, no. 2 (2004).

25. For a good overview of the James-Lange Theory and Damasio's Somatic Marker Hypothesis, see Barnaby Dunn, Tim Dalgleish, and Andrew Lawrence, "The Somatic Marker Hypothesis: A Critical Evaluation," *Neuroscience and Biobehavioral Reviews* 30 (2006): 239–271, http://www.brainmaster.com/software/pubs/brain/Dunn%20somatic_marker_hypothesis.pdf.

26. Phone interview with Stephen Porges, October 4, 2016.

27. Phone interview with Joseph LeDoux, circa January 2016.

28. I visited Damian Stanley at Cal Tech on June 13, 2016, and June 14, 2016.

29. Phone interview with Porges.

30. Details on this project were provided to me by Jeni Kubota during my visit to the University of Chicago in September 2016.

31. In-person interview with Jeni Kubota, September 15, 2016. I spent two days with Kubota and her colleagues.

32. This is a hypothesis that many stress specialists I talked with, while researching this book, said was plausible. However, I could not find any large-scale studies, over time, showing that cortisol levels were rising across the population over a prolonged period of time. In 2009, two researchers, Emma Adam of the School of Education and Social Policy, and

Meena Kumar of the Department of Epidemiology at University College London published a paper detailing a number of research projects in recent years that had shown that increased cortisol levels over time among specific populations did predispose them to higher incidences of certain diseases and behavioral patterns. Emma Adam and Meena Kumar, "Assessing Salivary Cortisol in Large-Scale Epidemiological Research," *Psychoneuroendocrinology* (2009).

33. Tori Rodriguez, "Descendants of Holocaust Survivors Have Altered Stress Hormones," *Scientific American*, March 1, 2015, http://www.scientificamerican.com/article/descendants-of-holocaust-survivors-have-altered-stress-hormones.

34. B. T. Heijmans et al., "Persistent Epigenetic Differences Associated with Prenatal Exposure to Famine in Humans," Proceedings of National Academy of Science 105, no. 44 (2009): 17046–17049.

35. Susanne Krauss-Etschman, Karolin F. Meyer, Stefan Dehmel, and Machteld N. Hylkema, "Inter- and Transgenerational Epigenetic Inheritance: Evidence in Asthma and COPD?" *Clinical Epigenetics* 7, no. 53 (2015), http://clinicalepigeneticsjournal.biomedcentral.com/articles/10.1186/s13148-015-0085-1.

36. Ewen Callaway, "Fearful Memories Haunt Mouse Descendants," *Nature*, December 1, 2013, http://www.nature.com/news/fearful-memories-haunt-mouse-descendants-1.14272; and Brian Dias and Kerry Ressler, "Parental Olfactory Experience Influences Behavior and Neural Structure in Subsequent Generations," *Nature Neuroscience* 17 (2014): 89–96, http://dx.doi.org/10.1038/nn.3594.

37. Phone interview with Darcia Narvaez, September 22, 2016.

38. This work was conducted by McGill University neurologist Michael Meaney.

39. The team was led by Michel Dugas, professor of psychology at the University of Quebec. The Intolerance of Uncertainty Measure was first developed in 1994. Dugas and his colleagues have written many papers on this. Among the most relevant here are: M. Dugas, N. Laugesen, and W. M. Bukowski, "Intolerance of Uncertainty, Fear of Anxiety, and Adolescent Worry," *Journal of Abnormal Child Psychology* 40, no. 6 (2012): 863–870; and M. Dugas, M. Fresston, and R. Ladouceur, "Intolerance of Uncertainty and Problem Orientation in Worry," *Cognitive Therapy and Research* 21 (1997), http://link.springer.com/article/10.1023/A:1021890322153.

40. Phone interview with Sally Winston, February 1, 2016.

41. Phone interview with Jeni Kubota, May 9, 2016.

42. Phone interview with Mahzarin Banaji, June 6, 2016.

43. In-person interview with Trisha Allen-Gibby, February 18, 2016.

44. In 2015, a group of Chinese researchers, funded by the National Science Foundation of China, wrote an overview paper on this phenomenon, based on dozens of papers from around the world exploring why some soldiers were more vulnerable than others to PTSD. Chen Xue, Yung Ge, Bohan Tang, Yuan Liu, Peng Kang, Meng Wang, and Lulu Zhang, "A Meta-Analysis of Risk Factors for Combat-Related PTSD Amongst Military Personnel and Veterans," *PLoS One* 10, no. 3 (2015), https://www.ncbi.nlm.nih.gov/pmc/articles/PMC4368749.

45. In-person interview with Sonia Bishop, June 22, 2016.

46. Phone interview with Mahzarin Banaji.

47. Mahzarin Banaji and Anthony Greenwald, *Blind Spot: The Hidden Biases of Good People* (New York: Delacorte, 2013), 106.

48. Experiment described to me by Mahzarin Banaji, June 6, 2016.

49. For more information on this, see Joshua Correll, Bernadette Park, Charles Judd, and Bernd Wittenbrink, "The Influence of Stereotypes on Decisions to Shoot," *European Journal of Social Psychology* 37 (2007): 1102–1117, http://faculty.chicagobooth.edu/bernd.wittenbrink/research /pdf/cpjw07.pdf.

50. Phone interview with Sheila Jasanoff, January 2, 2015.

51. Phone interview with Dale Hattis, November 18, 2014.

52. Phone interview with Alec Pollard, February 3, 2016.

53. Phone interview with David Ropeik, November 20, 2014.

54. David Ropeik, *How Risky Is It Really? Why Our Fears Don't Always Match the Facts* (New York: McGraw Hill, 2010), 98–99. Data on radon-induced lung cancer fatalities from EPA: http://www.epa.gov /radon/health-risk-radon.

55. Mary Douglas, *Purity and Danger: An Analysis of the Concepts of Pollution and Taboo* (New York: Routledge, 2002), 4.

Notes to Chapter Five

1. "How to Find the Best Anxiety Treatment Center," Calm Clinic, http://www.calmclinic.com/anxiety/treatment/anxiety-treatment-center.

2. Peter Wehrwein, "Astounding Increase in Antidepressant Use by Americans," *Harvard Health Publications*, October 20, 2011, http:// www.health.harvard.edu/blog/astounding-increase-in-antidepressant -use-by-americans-201110203624.

3. Brendan Smith, "Inappropriate Prescribing," *American Psychological Association* 43, no. 6 (June 2012): 36, http://www.apa.org/monitor/2012/06/prescribing.aspx.

4. "Facts and Statistics," Anxiety and Depression Association of America. http://www.adaa.org/about-adaa/press-room/facts-statistics.

5. Sally Curtin, Margaret Warner, and Holly Hedegaard, "Increase in Suicide in the United States, 1999–2014," Centers for Disease Control and Prevention, *NCHS Data Brief No 41*, April 2016, http://www.cdc.gov/nchs/products/databriefs/db241.htm.

6. "Anxiety Effects on Society Statistics," Anxietycentre.com, http://www.anxietycentre.com/anxiety-statistics-information.shtml.

7. *Quick Facts: Mental Illness and Addiction in Canada*, 3rd edition, Mood Disorders Society of Canada, November 2009, http://www.mood disorderscanada.ca/documents/Media%20Room/Quick%20Facts%203rd%20Edition%20Referenced%20Plain%20Text.pdf.

8. "Table 4: Top Five Prescription Medications Use, by Sex, Age Group, and Medication Class, Household Population aged 25 to 79, Canada, 2007 to 2011," Statistics Canada, http://www.statcan.gc.ca/pub/82-003-x/2014006/article/14032/tbl/tbl4-eng.htm.

9. "Antidepressant Prescribing," *Quality Watch*, The Health Foundation, Nuffield Trust, http://www.qualitywatch.org.uk/focus-on/antidepressant-prescribing.

10. Skye Gould and Lauren Friedman, "Something Startling Is Going On with Antidepressant Use Around the World," *Business Insider*, February 4, 2016, http://www.techinsider.io/countries-largest-antidepressant-drug-users-2016-2.

11. Catherine Shanahan, "Special Report: The Anti-Depressant Generation," *Irish Examiner*, March 19, 2015, http://www.irishexaminer.com/ireland/special-report-the-anti-depressant-generation-319128.html.

12. OECD, "Health at a Glance 2015, OECD Indicators," OECD Publishing, Paris, http://www.keepeek.com/Digital-Asset-Management/oecd/social-issues-migration-health/health-at-a-glance-2015_health_glance-2015-en#page6.

13. "International Suicide Statistics," Suicide.org, http://www.suicide.org/international-suicide-statistics.html.

14. Richard A. Friedman, "A Drug to Cure Fear," *New York Times*, January 24, 2016, http://www.nytimes.com/2016/01/24/opinion/sunday/a-drug-to-cure-fear.html.

15. Smith, "Inappropriate Prescribing."

16. http://www.angelnet.com/store/books/home-courses/home-cd
-dvd-course.

17. "2014 Crime in the United States," FBI, Uniform Crime Report, https://www.fbi.gov/about-us/cjis/ucr/crime-in-the-u.s/2014/crime
-in-the-u.s.-2014/tables/table-16.

18. "Crime in the United States 2011," FBI, Uniform Crime Report, https://www.fbi.gov/about-us/cjis/ucr/crime-in-the-u.s/2011/crime
-in-the-u.s.-2011/tables/table-1.

19. "Global Study on Homicide," United Nations Office on Drugs and
Crime (UNODC), http://www.unodc.org/gsh.

20. Fox Butterfield, "Historical Study of Homicides and Cities Sur-
prises the Experts," *New York Times*, October 23, 1994, http://www
.nytimes.com/1994/10/23/us/historical-study-of-homicide-and-cities
-surprises-the-experts.html.

21. NISMART report, issued by US DOJ, Office of Justice Programs,
Office of Juvenile Justice and Delinquency Prevention, October 2002.
Reports can be accessed at ojjdp.ncjrs.org.

22. "Sudden Unexpected Infant Death and Sudden Infant Death Syndrome," Data and Statistics, Centers for Disease Control and Prevention,
www.cdc.gov/sids/data.htm.

23. "Asthma Facts," Allergy and Asthma Foundation of America,
http://www.aafa.org/page/asthma-facts.aspx.

24. "In Home Danger: CPSC Warns of Children Drowning in Bathtubs, Bath Seats and Buckets More Than 400 Deaths Estimated Over
a Five-Year Period," United States Consumer Product Safety Commission, http://www.cpsc.gov/en/Newsroom/News-Releases/2012/In-Home
-Danger-CPSC-Warns-of-Children-Drowning-in-Bathtubs-Bath-Seats
-and-Buckets-More-than-400-deaths-estimated-over-a-five-year-period.

25. J. J. Sacks, L. Sinclair, G. C. Golab, and R. Lockwood, "Breeds
of Dogs Involved in Fatal Human Attacks in the United States Between
1979 and 1998," *Journal of the American Veterinary Medical Association* 216,
no. 6 (2000): 836–840, https://www.ncbi.nlm.nih.gov/pubmed/10997153.

26. Joe Spring, "The Deadliest Animals in the U.S.," *Outside*, July 5,
2012, http://www.outsideonline.com/1915661/deadliest-animals-us.

27. Karin Bilich, "Child Abduction Facts," *Parents*, http://www.parents
.com/kids/safety/stranger-safety/child-abduction-facts.

28. Peter L. Bernstein, *Against the Gods: The Remarkable Story of Risk*
(New York: John Wiley & Sons, 1998), 1.

29. Ibid., 3.

NOTES TO CHAPTER SIX

1. The information contained in this chapter is based on numerous in-person interviews I conducted in April 2015. Melendez was asked, via his attorney, to talk, but his attorney declined to have his client be interviewed for this book. It is also based on news coverage, court documents and transcripts, and the available video imagery of the beating.

2. "Police Killed More Than 100 Unarmed Black People in 2015," Mapping Police Violence, http://mappingpoliceviolence.org/unarmed.

3. On July 7, 2016, the *New York Times* published a long article by Timothy Williams, "Study Supports Suspicion That Police Are More Likely to Use Force on Blacks," summarizing these findings (http://www.nytimes.com/2016/07/08/us/study-supports-suspicion-that-police-use-of-force-is-more-likely-for-blacks.html). The report documented that in response to similar crimes, police were more than three times more likely to use force against black suspects than white suspects.

4. Phillip Goff, Matthew Jackson, Brooke DiLeone, Carmen Culotta, and Natalie DiTomasso, "The Essence of Innocence: Consequences of Dehumanizing Black Children," *Journal of Personality and Social Psychology* 106, no. 4 (2014): 526–545, http://www.apa.org/pubs/journals/releases/psp-a0035663.pdf.

5. Phone interview with Jasmin Cloutier, May 20, 2016.

6. Phone interview with Jeni Kubota, May 9, 2016. Research findings to be published in the *Journal of Social, Cognitive and Affective Neuroscience*.

7. Jim Kiertzner, interview with William Melendez, April 16, 2015, http://www.wxyz.com/news/inkster-officer-speaks-out-after-beating-caught-on-video.

8. Dylan Sevett, "Harvard Medical Scientists Say Police Killings Should Be Recorded as Public Epidemic," *US Uncut*, December 27, 2015, http://usuncut.com/black-lives-matter/harvard-medical-police-killings-public-epidemic.

9. Killed By Police, http://www.killedbypolice.net.

10. Mapping Police Violence, http://mappingpoliceviolence.org.

11. "Fatal Police Shootings," Inquest, http://www.inquest.org.uk/statistics/fatal-police-shootings.

12. Jamiles Lartey, "By the Numbers: US Police Kill More in Days Than Other Countries Do in Years," *Guardian* (London), June 9, 2015, https://www.theguardian.com/us-news/2015/jun/09/the-counted-police-killings-us-vs-other-countries.

13. Associated Press, "Brazil: Police Killed 11,000 People Over Five-Year Period, Report Says," *New York Times*, November 11, 2014, http://www .nytimes.com/2014/11/12/world/americas/brazil-police-killed-11000 -people-over-five-year-period-report-says.html.

14. Phone interview with Jim Allen, May 13, 2016.

15. Kiertzner, interview with Melendez.

16. Phone interview with Jennifer Lerner, August 30, 2016.

17. Jennifer Lerner, Roxana Gonzalez, Deborah Small, and Baruch Fischoff, "Effects of Fear and Anger on Perceived Risks of Terrorism: A National Field Experiment," *Psychological Science* 14, no. 2 (March 2003).

18. Ibid.

19. Jennifer Truman and Michael Planty, *Criminal Victimization, 2011*, US Department of Justice, Office of Justice Programs, Bureau of Justice Statistics, October 2012, NCJ239437, http://www.bjs.gov/content/pub /pdf/cv11.pdf.

20. Goff, Jackson, DiLeone, Culotta, and DiTomasso, "The Essence of Innocence."

21. Adam Weinstein, "The Trayvon Martin Killing, Explained," *Mother Jones*, March 18, 2012, http://www.motherjones.com/politics/2012/03 /what-happened-trayvon-martin-explained.

NOTES TO CHAPTER SEVEN

1. The longest of my articles was published in the UK's *Independent* newspaper, on December 11, 1999, titled "The Serious Torture Squad."

2. Mohamedou Ould Slahi, *Guantánamo Diary*, edited by Larry Siems (New York: Little, Brown, 2015), 18. The diary was written in the early years of the war on terror. The US government fought for nearly a decade to keep it away from the public. When it was finally published it was subject to extensive censorship. On many pages entire passages have, at the government's insistence, been blacked out.

3. Ibid., 19.

4. Ariel Dorfman, *Other September, Many Americas: Selected Provocations, 1980–2004* (New York: Seven Stories, 2004).

5. Jeff Strickland, "The Whole State Is on Fire: Criminal Justice and the End of Reconstruction in Upcountry South Carolina," *Crime, History, Societies* 13, no. 2 (2009): 89–117, https://chs.revues.org/1115.

6. "Statistical Report," South Carolina Department of Corrections, http://www.doc.sc.gov/pubweb/research/statistics.jsp.

7. Details on the Debra Harrell case garnered from news reports, from phone interview with Harrell's attorney, Robert Phillips, October 9, 2014, and email correspondence with Phillips.

8. Data on local crime rates and property values came from a variety of local sources, including: https://www.neighborhoodscout.com/sc/north-augusta/crime/ and http://www.areavibes.com/north+augusta-sc/crime/.

9. This case, in June 2014, received widespread media coverage. One particularly interesting overview was by Conor Friedersdorf, "Working Mom Arrested for Letting Her 9-Year Old Play Alone at Park," *Atlantic*, July 15, 2014, http://www.theatlantic.com/national/archive/2014/07/arrested-for-letting-a-9-year-old-play-at-the-park-alone/374436.

10. Sarah Jarvis, "Mom Who Left Kids in Car Sentenced to 18 Years Probation," *USA Today*, May 15, 2015, http://www.usatoday.com/story/news/nation/2015/05/15/shanesha-taylor-kids-in-car/27375405.

11. Phone interview with Lisa Deckert, April 14, 2015.

12. Mark O'Mara, "Does Leaving Kids Along Make Parents 'Criminals'?" CNN, August 7, 2014, http://www.cnn.com/2014/07/31/opinion/omara-parents-children-unattended.

13. "Say What Now? Single Mom Arrested for 'Abandoning' Her Kids at the Food Court While Interviewing for a Job 30 Ft. Away," Lovebscott.com, July 18, 2015, http://www.lovebscott.com/news/say-what-now-single-mom-arrested-for-abandoning-her-kids-at-the-food-court-while-interviewing-for-a-job-30-ft-away.

14. The letter was mailed to the Meitivs on February 20, 2015, signed by W. Don Thorne, assessment worker, and Rachel Kavanagh, assessment supervisor.

15. I learned details about these events during both phone conversations throughout the spring and summer of 2015 and an in-person visit with the Meitivs on October 10, 2015.

16. This is a September 13, 2015, Facebook posting from "Mary Pat."

17. Association for Safe International Road Travel, http://asirt.org/initiatives/informing-road-users/road-safety-facts/road-crash-statistics.

18. "Crime Statistics," Maryland Governor's Office of Crime Control & Prevention, http://www.goccp.maryland.gov/msac/crime-statistics.php.

19. Justin George, "Homicides Decline in 2014, But Year Also Saw Unsolved Slaying of Children," *Baltimore Sun*, January 1, 2015, http://www.baltimoresun.com/news/maryland/crime/blog/bs-md-ci-year-end-homicide-20141231-story.html.

20. "The Most Dangerous States to Drive In," *24/7WallSt*, May 24, 2012, http://247wallst.com/special-report/2012/05/24/the-most-dangerous-states-to-drive-in/3.

21. I interviewed Lenore Skenazy at her vacation home in the Catskill Mountains on May 24, 2015.

22. Corey Robin, *Fear: The History of a Political Idea* (New York: Oxford University Press, 2004), 33.

23. Marjorie Connelly, "Poll Finds Racial Divide in Viewing Response to Ferguson Unrest," *New York Times*, August 21, 2014, http://www.nytimes.com/2014/08/22/us/politics/racial-divide-seen-in-response-to-ferguson-unrest-poll-finds.html.

24. "Black, White, and Blue: Americans' Attitudes on Race and Police," Roper Center for Public Opinion Research, Cornell University, https://ropercenter.cornell.edu/black-white-blue-americans-attitudes-race-police.

25. Eric Geller, "White People and Black People See Anti-Police Protest Completely Differently," *Daily Dot*, May 4, 2015, http://www.dailydot.com/layer8/baltimore-police-brutality-protests-poll-racial-divide.

26. Katie Sola, "The 25 Countries with the Most Billionaires," *Forbes*, March 8, 2016, http://www.forbes.com/sites/katiesola/2016/03/08/the-25-countries-with-the-most-billionaires/#29293f771f6c.

27. Talk Poverty, https://talkpoverty.org/basics.

28. "State Health Facts, Poverty Rate by Race/Ethnicity, Timeframe 2015," The Henry J. Kaiser Family Foundation, http://kff.org/other/state-indicator/poverty-rate-by-raceethnicity.

29. Phone interview with Darcia Narvaez, October 6, 2016.

30. In-person interview with Jeni Kubota, September 15, 2016.

31. "Human Shark Bait: Shark Attack Facts," National Geographic, http://natgeotv.com/ca/human-shark-bait/facts.

32. *Bulletin of the Atomic Scientists*, http://thebulletin.org/timeline.

33. Candice Leigh Helfand, "Expert: 'Biggest Nuclear Threat to the American People Might Well Be' Russia," CBS, October 4, 2013, http://washington.cbslocal.com/2013/10/04/expert-biggest-nuclear-threat-to-the-american-people-might-well-be-russia.

34. Sheri Ledbetter, "America's Top Fears 2015," Wilkinson College of Arts, Humanities and Social Sciences, Chapman University, October 13, 2015, https://blogs.chapman.edu/wilkinson/2015/10/13/americas-top-fears-2015.

35. Phone interview with Baruch Fischoff, December 22, 2014.

36. Phone interview with Ralph Nader, December 5, 2014.

37. Jeremy Gray, "After Years of Increase, Alabama's Suicide Rate Well Above National Average," *Al.com*, September 28, 2015, http://www.al.com/news/index.ssf/2015/09/suicide_on_the_rise_in_alabama.html.

38. US Environmental Protection Agency, "Health Risk of Radon," https://www.epa.gov/radon/health-risk-radon.

NOTES TO CHAPTER EIGHT

1. Darcia Narvaez, *Neurobiology and the Development of Human Morality: Evolution, Culture, and Wisdom* (New York: Norton, 2014), 161.

2. Rick Montgomery, "Lockdown 101: School Staff Join in Active Shooter Training," *Portland Press Herald*, March 15, 2015, http://www.pressherald.com/2015/03/15/lockdown-101-school-staff-join-in-active-shooter-training.

3. Andy Proffet, "Shelbyville Ranked Among Indiana's Safest Cities," *Shelbyville* [Indiana] *News*, August 1, 2015, http://www.shelbynews.com/news/article_e472c082-387d-11e5-930c-c358d06ea3ba.html.

4. "Shelbyville, Indiana Crime Statistics," Find The Data, http://city-crime-statistics.findthedata.com/l/90071/Shelbyville.

5. Andy Proffet, "Investigation Notes Details of Fatal Shooting," *Shelbyville News*, January 31, 2016, http://www.shelbynews.com/news/article_84d42bd1-b7d6-560a-8e15-5dafdd797ef5.html.

6. Jeff Rossen, "Southwestern High School Tests State-of-the-Art Security Measures," WTHR Channel 13, September 8, 2015, http://www.wthr.com/story/29980040/shelbyville-high-school-tests-state-of-the-art-security-measures.

7. "Average Teacher Salary in Shelbyville Central Schools," http://www.teachersalaryinfo.com/indiana/teacher-salary-in-shelbyville-central-schools.

8. Rossen, "Southwestern High School Tests State-of-the-Art Security Measures."

9. Email to Abramsky from Paula Maurer, February 4, 2016.

10. Data on Stockton and other school districts was compiled by researchers from the San Francisco–based Center on Juvenile and Criminal Justice. This research formed the basis of a lawsuit filed against the Stockton school district by the ACLU; see https://www.aclunc.org/sites/default/files/20160628-writ.pdf.

11. Phone interview with Kenneth Trump, September 23, 2015.

12. Phone interview with Ed Burke, January 11, 2016.

13. Phone interview with Derek Peterson, January 14, 2016.

14. There are a variety of estimates, ranging from a low of less than three hundred to a high of nearer one thousand. The online journal *Slate* produced a chart estimating fewer than three hundred killings. Chris Kirk, "Since 1980, 297 People Have Been Killed in School Shootings," *Slate*, December 19, 2012, http://www.slate.com/articles/news_and _politics/map_of_the_week/2012/12/sandy_hook_a_chart_of_all_196 _fatal_school_shootings_since_1980_map.html. There is also data from the National Center on Education Statistics' report "Indicators of School Crimes and Safety: 2014," http://nces.ed.gov/programs/crimeindicators /crimeindicators2014/key.asp.

15. "Updated Information on K-12 and University School Shooting Deaths: The Number of Deaths Has Been Declining Over Time," Crime Prevention Research Center, June 13, 2014, http://crimeresearch .org/2014/06/updated-information-on-k-12-school-shootings-deaths-the -number-of-deaths-has-been-declining-over-time.

16. "Estimating Seasonal Influenza-Associated Deaths in the United States," Centers for Disease Control and Prevention, http://www.cdc.gov /flu/about/disease/us_flu-related_deaths.htm.

17. "CDC Reports About 90 Percent of Children Who Died from Flu This Season Not Vaccinated," March 22, 2013, Centers for Disease Control and Prevention, http://www.cdc.gov/flu/spotlights/children-flu -deaths.htm.

18. *Top 20 Pneumonia Facts—2015*, American Thoracic Society, https:// www.thoracic.org/patients/patient-resources/resources/top-pneumonia -facts.pdf.

19. In-person interview with Sonia Bishop, June 22, 2016.

20. TB Facts, http://tbfacts.org.

21. Haeyoun Park and Matthew Bloch, "How the Epidemic of Drug Overdose Deaths Ripples Across America," *New York Times*, January 7, 2016, http://www.nytimes.com/interactive/2016/01/07/us/drug-overdose -deaths-in-the-us.html. This set of interactive maps charts how, county by county, the overdose epidemic in the United States grew in the early years of the twenty-first century.

22. Data from a series of World Health Organization reports and tables. These include: *Burden of Disease from Household Air Pollution for*

2012, World Health Organization, http://www.who.int/phe/health_topics
/outdoorair/databases/FINAL_HAP_AAP_BoD_24March2014.pdf,
and "World Health Statistics 2016: Mortality Due to Air Pollution,"
World Health Organization, http://www.who.int/gho/publications/world
_health_statistics/2016/whs2016_AnnexA_MortalityAirPollution.pdf.
Some estimates are slightly lower than WHO's but still show same general trends: Lauren B. Kleimola, Archana B. Patel, Jitesh A. Borkar, and
Patricia L. Hibberd, "Consequences of Household Air Pollution on Child
Survival: Evidence from Demographic and Health Surveys in 47 Countries," *International Journal of Occupational and Environmental Health* 21,
no. 4 (2015): 294–302, http://www.tandfonline.com/doi/pdf/10.1179/20493
96715Y.0000000007.

23. World Health Organization Global Health Observatory Data.

24. Paul Farmer, *Pathologies of Power: Health, Human Rights,
and the New War on the Poor* (Berkeley: University of California Press,
2003), 6.

25. This number is quoted by the Swedish sociologist Göran Therborn,
in his book *The Killing Fields of Inequality* (New York: Wiley, 2013).

26. Quoted in Therborn's *The Killing Fields of Inequality*. He attributes
this data to Michael Marmot's book *Status Syndrome* (London: Bloomsbury, 2004), 196.

27. J. Olshansky et al., "Differences in the Life Expectancy Due to
Race and Educational Differences Are Widening, and May Catch Up,"
Health Affairs 31, no. 8 (2012): 1803–1810.

28. Farmer, *Pathologies of Power,* 25.

29. Phone interview with Ralph Nader, December 5, 2014.

30. This estimate was provided by the Food and Drug Administration (Matthew Herper, "David Graham on the Vioxx Verdict," *Forbes*,
August 19, 2005, http://www.forbes.com/2005/08/19/merck-vioxx-graham
_cx_mh_0819graham.html). Other estimates range far higher, with some
claiming that as many as five hundred thousand might have died.

31. In-person interview with anonymous investor, February 17, 2016.

32. Bureau of Justice Statistics survey, accurate as of December 31, 2012.

33. Human Rights Watch report on sex offender laws, from 2007.

34. In-person interview with former Salt Lake City mayor and civil
rights attorney Rocky Anderson, February 17, 2016.

35. Sarah Gonzalez, "How School Zero Tolerance Rules Turn Bad
Behavior into a Crime," State Impact project of National Public Radio,

February 25, 2013, https://stateimpact.npr.org/florida/maps/map-florida
-students-arrested-for-bad-behavior-not-criminal-behavior.

36. Libby Nelson, Dara Lind, "The School to Prison Pipeline, Explained," Justice Policy Institute, February 24, 2015, http://www.justice
policy.org/news/8775.

37. Halimah Abdullah, "Minority Kids Disproportionately Impacted
by Zero-Tolerance Laws," CNN, January 30, 2014, http://www.cnn
.com/2014/01/24/politics/zero-tolerance.

38. Ibid.

39. "5-Year-Old Girl Suspended for Bringing Bubble Gun to School,"
Fox News, May 18, 2016, http://www.foxnews.com/us/2016/05/18/5-year
-old-girl-suspended-for-bringing-bubble-gun-to-school.html.

40. Danny Cevallos, "Boy Suspended for Bringing Own Hand to
School," CNN, May 28, 2014, http://www.cnn.com/2014/04/09/opinion
/cevallos-kid-points-finger-gun.

41. "Boy Faces Suspension for Bringing Butter Knife to School,"
KETV7 ABC News, September 28, 2005, http://www.ketv.com
/Boy-Faces-Suspension-For-Bringing-Butter-Knife-To-School/10087994.

42. "Zero Tolerance," University of Virginia, Curry School of Education, http://curry.virginia.edu/research/projects/violence-in-schools
/zero-tolerance, and "Boy Suspended Over Utensil Gets Reprieve,"
Today News, October 14, 2009, http://www.today.com/id/33289924/ns
/today-today_news/t/boy-suspended-over-utensil-gets-reprieve.

43. Jack Cafferty, "10-Year-Old Arrested for Using Knife in School
Lunchroom?" Cafferty File, CNN, December 18, 2007, http://caffertyfile.
blogs.cnn.com/2007/12/18/10-year-old-arrested-for-using-knife-in-school
-lunchroom.

44. "'Pop Tart' Suspension Should be Upheld, School Official Says," CBS News, July 1, 2014, http://www.cbsnews.com/news
/examiner-recommends-school-board-uphold-pop-tart-suspension.

NOTES TO CHAPTER NINE

1. In late 2015, ThinkProgress.org broke down the candidates' positions on this issue: Emily Atkin, "A Complete Guide to How the GOP
Candidates Reacted to Syrian Refugees After the Paris Attacks," Think
Progress, November 17, 2015, https://thinkprogress.org/a-complete-guide
-to-how-the-gop-candidates-reacted-to-syrian-refugees-after-the-paris
-attacks-d7907203bdc4#.jicltxmt3.

2. The report, released in September 2016, was issued by the Cal State San Bernardino Center on Hate & Extremism.

3. Sasha Abramsky, "After Pushing the Tea Party Agenda, Maine Governor Paul LePage Faces a Fierce Backlash," *Nation*, July 18–25, 2011, http://www.thenation.com/article/after-pushing-tea-party-agenda-maine -governor-paul-lepage-faces-fierce-backlash; Randy Billings, "LePage in Spotlight for Saying Drug Dealers Impregnate 'White Girls,'" *Portland Press Herald*, January 7, 2016, http://www.pressherald.com/2016/01/07 /lepage-accused-of-making-racist-comment-at-bridgton-meeting; Tal Kopan, "Maine Gov. Paul LePage: Bring Back the Guillotine for Drug Traffickers," CNN, January 27, 2016, http://www.cnn.com/2016/01/26 /politics/paul-lepage-maine-guillotine.

4. Amanda Terkel, "Paul LePage Warns of Dirty Asylum Seekers Bringing the 'Ziki Fly,'" *Huffington Post*, February 27, 2016, http://www .huffingtonpost.com/entry/paul-lepage-ziki-fly_us_56c4eaf1e4b0b40245c 8e429.

5. Maureen Craig and Jennifer Richeson, "On the Precipice of a 'Majority-Minority' America: Perceived Status Threat From the Racial Demographic Shift Affects Whites Americans' Political Ideology," *Psychological Science* 25, no. 6 (2014): 1189–1197, http://groups.psych.northwestern.edu /spcl/documents/Craig_RichesonPS_updatedversion.pdf.

6. In 2014, the International Organization for Migration estimated that between 2000 and 2014 at least six thousand migrants had died crossing the southern border into the United States. *Fatal Journeys: Tracking Lives Lost During Migration*, International Organization for Migration, 2014, http://www.iom.int/files/live/sites/iom/files/pbn/docs/Fatal-Journeys -Tracking-Lives-Lost-during-Migration-2014.pdf.

7. I went out on patrol with Ferguson and two other Samaritans on June 21, 2015.

8. In-person interview with James Lyall in Tucson, Arizona, June 23, 2015.

9. Details of this report were published by the *Arizona Republic* in June 2013. Brenna Goth and Bob Ortega, "Report: 1 in 8 Migrants Who Died Were Younger Than 19," *Arizona Republic*, June 5, 2013, http://archive .azcentral.com/news/arizona/articles/20130605arizona-border-deaths -report-migrants.html.

10. I attended Operation Streamline, June 23, 2015, and interviewed Judge Velasco in person afterwards.

11. Jared Yates Sexton, "American Horror Story," *New Republic*, June 15, 2016, https://newrepublic.com/article/134329/american-horror-story.

Notes to Chapter Ten

1. Corey Robin, *Fear: The History of a Political Idea* (New York: Oxford University Press, 2004), 162.

2. In-person interview with Jeni Kubota, September 15, 2016.

3. In-person interview with Maria Ochoa, June 20, 2015.

4. Paul Farmer, *Pathologies of Power: Health, Human Rights, and the New War on the Poor* (Berkeley: University of California Press, 2003), 22.

5. The information on Dionne Wilson comes from in-person interviews with Dionne Wilson, December 14, 2014, and January 18, 2015.

6. Information for the Tom Ruddigaw section is from in-person interview with Tom Ruddigaw, January 22, 2015.

7. In-person interviews with Sasha and Danielle Meitiv, October 10, 2015.

Index

photo © Lala Meredith Vula

Sasha Abramsky is a widely published journalist and book author. His work has appeared in the *Nation*, the *Atlantic*, the *New Yorker* online, *Rolling Stone*, and many other publications in the United States and the United Kingdom. His 2013 book *The American Way of Poverty* was listed as a *New York Times* Notable Book of the Year. And his 2015 volume *The House of Twenty Thousand Books* was selected by Kirkus as among the best nonfiction books of the year. Abramsky lives in Sacramento, California, with his wife and their two children.

 NATION
BOOKS

The Nation Institute

Founded in 2000, **Nation Books** has become a leading voice in American independent publishing. The imprint's mission is to tell stories that inform and empower just as they inspire or entertain readers. We publish award-winning and bestselling journalists, thought leaders, whistleblowers, and truthtellers, and we are also committed to seeking out a new generation of emerging writers, particularly voices from underrepresented communities and writers from diverse backgrounds. As a publisher with a focused list, we work closely with all our authors to ensure that their books have broad and lasting impact. With each of our books we aim to constructively affect and amplify cultural and political discourse and to engender positive social change.

Nation Books is a project of The Nation Institute, a nonprofit media center established to extend the reach of democratic ideals and strengthen the independent press. The Nation Institute is home to a dynamic range of programs: the award-winning Investigative Fund, which supports groundbreaking investigative journalism; the widely read and syndicated website TomDispatch; journalism fellowships that support and cultivate over twenty-five emerging and high-profile reporters each year; and the Victor S. Navasky Internship Program.

For more information on Nation Books and The Nation Institute, please visit:

www.nationbooks.org
www.nationinstitute.org
www.facebook.com/nationbooks.ny
Twitter: @nationbooks